D1631974

PHL

54060000145549

The Rape of Egypt

PETER FRANCE

The Rape of Egypt

How the Europeans Stripped
Egypt of its Heritage

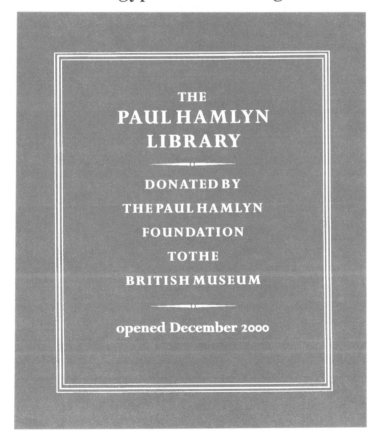

THE
**PAUL HAMLYN
LIBRARY**

DONATED BY

THE PAUL HAMLYN

FOUNDATION

TO THE

BRITISH MUSEUM

opened December 2000

BARRIE & JENKINS
LONDON

932 FRA

THE BRITISH MUSEUM WITHDRAWN
THE PAUL HAMLYN LIBRARY

First published in Great Britain in 1991 by
Barrie & Jenkins Ltd
20 Vauxhall Bridge Road, London SW1V 2SA

Copyright © Peter France 1991

All rights reserved. No part of this publication may be
reproduced, stored in a retrieval system, or transmitted
in any form or by any means, electronic, mechanical,
photocopying, recording or otherwise, without prior
permission in writing from the publisher.

Peter France has asserted his right to be identified as
the author of this work.

A catalogue record for this book is available from
the British Library

ISBN 0 7126 2102 4

Typeset in Imprint by SX Composing Ltd
Printed and bound in Great Britain by
Mackays of Chatham

Contents

List of Illustrations

Plates 1, 2, 7, 8, ,9, 10, 13, 16, 20, 21, 24, 26, 27, 28 and 29 are reproduced by permission of the Mansell Collection. Plate 11 is reproduced by permission of the Bridgeman Art Library and the British Museum.

Introduction

An Antique Land

COUNT ALESSANDRO DI CAGLIOSTRO was sentenced to death by the Holy Office in Rome on 21 March 1791. The sentence was commuted to one of 'perpetual imprisonment in a fortress where the culprit is to be guarded without any hope of pardon whatever'. And yet the Count was hardly a threat to the stability of the Universal Church; he was simply an itinerant quack, living in an age when competition in his chosen profession was fierce.

Having been expelled in his youth from a monastery where he was training for the priesthood, the Count launched himself on a dissolute life. He married a beautiful and unprincipled woman, Lorenza Feliciani, with whom he travelled the world selling love potions and elixirs of youth and beauty. For a time the Count turned a dishonest penny in an alchemical laboratory in Whitcomb Street, London. A number of legal actions followed however, and he moved to Salzburg. Here the Cardinal Prince of Rohan proved agreeably credulous, and introduced the wonder-working couple to the highest circles in Europe. The Count and his wife were fêted in the courts of Louis XVI and of Catherine the Great; and their popularity soon extended to all levels of society, so that whenever they appeared in public military guards had to be called out to keep order. When the Inquisition finally pronounced its judgement, Lorenza Feliciani was sent to a convent, and the Count to the fortress of San Leo, where he died in 1795.

1

Count Cagliostro's life reads like a Gothic tale, and indeed it inspired novels by Dumas and Schiller, as well as satires by Goethe and Catherine the Great. If Cagliostro is remembered at all today it is in the amiably dotty pages of the literature of the occult. But he deserves a place in history as a witness to something far more significant than his own career: the hold over the imagination of his age of the land he claimed as the source of his supernatural powers. That land was Egypt.

Although born simply Giuseppe Balsamo to a poor family in Palermo, as he explained to his audiences, the Count had been carried off to Egypt as a child. Here he had been to a cave beneath the Great Pyramid, where a spirit called the Great Copht had appeared and initiated him into the timeless mysteries of the Nile. The young boy was told that the Great Truth – of which the Pharaohs had been appointed guardians – was to be maintained through the performance of a series of arcane rituals known as the 'Egyptian Rite'. Giuseppe was charged with the duty of re-introducing these rituals to the world by making them the basis of international Freemasonry. Years later he founded the Mère Loge d'Adoption de la Haute Maçonnerie Egyptienne in Paris, and built a sacred Temple of Isis, over which he would preside as the reincarnation of the Great Copht. It was in this role that the Count brought down on himself the judgement of Rome, for the Church was not kindly disposed either to Freemasonry or to the Egypt of the occult.

The notion that Egypt possessed some kind of ancient wisdom had been current ever since Roman times, and among the early Christian Fathers. It was revived during the Age of Reason, when the authority of the Church was being challenged by the revelations of science and was in retreat. People were drawn to the physics of Newton and to the philosophy of Locke, and moved away from what Voltaire called the 'prone submission to the heavenly will' enjoined from the pulpit. They listened rather to the teachings of liberty and moderation – which they interpreted as the liberty to be moderate about their religion. This was only a short step from replacing religious faith with ethical idealism.

Many, however, found that ethical principles without mystical or supernatural support did not satisfy the imagination. Cults that preached a search for ethical perfection through secret truths revealed to initiates by the performance of esoteric rituals began to flourish. The Rosicrucians and the Masons prospered, both claiming an Egyptian origin to their secrets.

In the 1730s, the novel *Sethos*, which chronicled the trials and rituals necessary for the attainment of wisdom, began a period of literary Egyptomania; Egyptian-style buildings began to decorate the European landscape. Obelisks and pyramids were popular on the great estates; Castle Howard had four large pyramids; the park at Stowe had a pair of pyramid-roofed Boycott Pavilions, as well as an 'Egyptian Pyramid' sixty feet high designed by Sir John Vanbrugh; the gateway of Sherborne Castle in Dorset bore Egyptian figures holding votive tablets; the steeple of St Luke's Church, Finsbury, was in the shape of an Egyptian obelisk; and the billiard-room at Cairness House, Aberdeenshire, was plastered with Egyptian motifs.

Books on astrology, cosmology, alchemy, and magic were popular. Many of these claimed as their source the Hermetic writings of Hermes Trismegistos, a name that stands for a whole literature of magic and alchemy, and which the Greeks had equated with the Egyptian god Thoth. Although scholars regularly disputed the ascription of the writings and the identity of the author, Egypt was sufficiently remote, ancient, and enigmatic to be cited confidently by those wishing to evoke the mysterious and to authenticate the inscrutable.

So it was that in 1791 – the year Count Cagliostro was condemned – Tamino and Pamina first walked the boards of the Theater auf der Wieden in Vienna to hear the high priest Sarastro call on the Egyptian gods Isis and Osiris to admit them to the wisdom of the ages.

18th-century Egypt was not only the antique land where occultists located the crucibles of their forbidden arts, or the source of inspiration for landscape gardeners seeking exotica for their clients. She was also the arena in which hard-headed men of science did battle with the Church. The antiquity of Egypt was disputed with as much fervour as the miracles in the Bible. According to Dr John Lightfoot, Vice-Chancellor of Cambridge University, and celebrated in the 17th century as a distinguished biblical and rabbinical scholar, the universe itself was of no great age since 'heaven and earth, centre and circumference, were

created together in the same instant, and clouds full of water';
and 'this event took place and man was created by the Trinity on
the twenty-third of October, 4004 BC, at nine o'clock in the
morning.' The dates were supported by James Ussher, Archbishop of Armagh, and were printed in the margins of the
Authorised Version of the Bible from 1701, where they were
accorded the same infallibility as the text itself. So it was
accepted, on the authority of the Bible, that Egypt could hardly
have nourished an ancient civilisation in biblical times because
the world had not been in existence long enough. Rather, Egypt
was the primitive land to which the patriarchs fled in time of
famine; a place of superstition and barbarism, only redeemed by
the message of the Gospel.

This view of history had been challenged: in his *History of the
World* (1603-16), Sir Walter Raleigh had pointed out the fact that
in the time of Abraham 'Egypt had many magnificent cities . . .
and those not built with bricks but of hewn stone . . . which
magnificence needed a parent of more antiquity than those other
men have supposed.' And the patron saint of scepticism, Voltaire, went to the Old Testament for evidence and recalled the
story of the gifts that Abraham received from the pharaoh in return for his wife's favours: sheep and oxen and he-asses and men
servants and maid servants and she-asses and camels. Surely this
indicated that Egypt was at the time a very rich, powerful and
therefore very ancient civilisation.

During the 18th century theologians and philosophers were
able to engage in long armchair debates about the antiquity of
Egypt because so few people had at that time actually visited the
place. Much of what was widely known about Egypt was untrue,
and the truth about Egypt was unknown. Herodotus had probably been there in the middle of the 5th century BC, having written about the Nile and its animals, the gods and the kings, and
describing the practice of embalming in detail. He was the first
to suggest that the Greeks had learned their religious rituals and
myths of the gods from the Egyptians. His fellow Sicilian, Diodorus – who gave his name to a library of books which, he
claimed, had involved many dangerous journeys, including
those to Egypt in 60-57 BC – was a great purveyor of unexamined
tales. In ancient times, Diodorus believed, Egypt was the most
densely populated area of the known world, and had contributed

much to the culture of Athens.

Early in the 18th century a few travellers had ventured into the more accessible regions of the Nile delta and brought back tales and curiosities from Alexandria or Cairo. In 1723 Thomas Sergeant, collector of antiquities, brought to the Society of Antiquaries in London 'a parcel of Egyptian Gods lately come from Grand Cairo'. It consisted of 'a brass Osiris, a brass Harpocrates, a terminus, a naked brass figure distorted of better taste, Isis and bambino, a little Egyptian priest, a cat, a stone beetle with wings and hieroglyphics in a curious paste of blew colour'.

Between 1720 and 1733, the Rev. Thomas Shaw – precursor of a host of English divines, who had made a particular study of the Bible and of botany – travelled around Alexandria and Giza. He examined the Sphinx and the pyramids, concluding that the latter were temples and not tombs. He published his findings in 1738, observing that 'no diversion can be attended with greater pleasure than travelling upon the Nile.'

The Rev. Richard Pococke ventured further in 1737, sailing up the Nile as far as Philae and returning to publish two folio volumes of *A Description of the East* in 1743-5. Travelling separately at the same time was Frederick Ludwig Norden, a Danish naval captain who published a collection of drawings and engravings. Norden was so impressed by what he saw in Egypt that he declared the classicists' view that Greece and Rome had cradled European civilisation was wrong. Siding with Herodotus and Diodorus, he wrote, 'Let them talk no more of Rome, let Greece be silent.'

The classical scholars were not to be intimidated by a Danish sea captain. The debate on biblical chronology and cultural supremacy was fierce in a vacuum of almost total ignorance. On 30 November 1775 the Society of Antiquaries heard a paper by Dr John Woodward, FRS, FRCP, which set about with vigour those who alleged that the people of Israel or the Greeks could have learned anything from Egypt. How could Egyptian culture possibly be of such high antiquity when all her architecture consisted of pyramids – simple heaps of stones placed one on top of the other? The temples, which travellers had waxed lyrical about, were barbarous and ill-contrived, their decorated figures stiff and ill-proportioned. As for the claim that the decorations celebrated victories in war, what possible victories could the

Egyptians have had to celebrate? Had not Cambyses conquered the entire country and taken Pelusium with ease simply by leading cats and dogs in front of the army of Egypt, causing the soldiers to surrender rather than risk hurting their sacred animals? As for the notion that Egypt might harbour some immortal wisdom, Dr Woodward pointed out that the Egyptians had the custom of taking the brains and the bowels out of corpses before preserving them for the future use of the wandering souls. What possible use could the body be if it had neither brains nor bowels?

As the Age of Enlightenment drew to a close, the land of Egypt seemed to be all things to all men: to the subculture of the occult it was the repository of the ancient mysteries: to the humanist it offered evidence that might destroy the biblical view of history and the chronology of the Church; to the Church it was a barbarous land made holy by the visions of Moses and the presence of Jesus; to the artist it challenged received ideas of beauty and proportion, and to the historian it threatened the cultural supremacy of ancient Greece and Rome. Speculation, however, only can thrive where there is no certain knowledge. In the spring of 1798 an assembly of savants was gathering from all over France to the port of Toulon for an invasion that finally dislodged Egypt from the world of 'A Thousand and One Nights' to find its true place in the history of mankind.

Chapter One

General Bonaparte, Academician

THE FRENCH FLEET THAT ASSEMBLED in the port of Toulon during the early spring months of 1798 was an invasion force marshalled to strike a blow at England. Its supreme commander, General Napoleon Bonaparte, age twenty-eight, had accepted the position with the intention of taking the army across the Channel and defeating the English on their own soil. However, there were delays in the organisation of the ships; the government appeal for a loan of eight million francs to finance the invasion had failed; and the return of fighting men to France from campaigns in Italy and Germany was putting a new burden on the Republic. The Armada was called off.

Hatred of the English, who alone stood in the way of French expansion in Europe, was a popular sentiment at the time. When General Bonaparte proposed attacking them through an invasion of Egypt, which would threaten British India, the Directorate was happy to agree. They had their own reasons for being glad to see Bonaparte setting out for foreign parts; they were only too delighted to see him on his way anywhere. He had become the focus of a patriotic fervour which the Directors felt belonged more rightly to themselves.

Egypt was not only comfortably distant from Paris, but also a convenient target for a French invasion at the time: the French conquest of northern and central Italy meant there were ships on hand for the Mediterranean fleet, Venice alone furnishing nine sail of the line and twelve frigates. With the transports, stores, and sailors from Genoa, Civitta Vecchia, and Ancona, an invasion fleet against Egypt could be assembled without crippling the exchequer. The plan was approved.

Bonaparte saw Egypt as easy pickings. The country was in theory an outpost of the Ottoman Empire, which by the end of the 18th century was too weak and disorganised to defend itself. For more than five-and-a-half centuries Egypt had been ruled by the Mamelukes, a military force of Georgian and Circassian stock who paid only a small and irregular tribute to the Porte, the Ottoman court at Constantinople. The Mamelukes had only cavalry to defend themselves against the artillery of the French, and Alexandria, the port of disembarkation, was unprotected and open to attack. Once Egypt was conquered, the French army could strike against the Ottoman Empire, and perhaps even British India. They could march north and east in the footsteps of Bonaparte's hero Alexander the Great, and might well repeat his triumphs.

In the event, the main consequences of the invasion did indeed flow from Bonaparte's imitation of his hero but not as conquering general. Alexander, a pupil of Aristotle, had been in the habit of taking with him on his journeys a company of scholars – geographers, astronomers, geologists, meteorologists, and artists – so that each military expedition was also an exploration. In a similar way, General Bonaparte decided to bring with him on his invasion of Egypt a company of savants who could investigate the cultural and natural resources of the land. While the military expedition ended in defeat, the work of the savants laid the foundation for the revelations of the Nile Valley that followed. General Bonaparte may have achieved little in Egypt; Academician Bonaparte deserves to be remembered.

On his return from Italy in 1797 Bonaparte had been elected to the Academy of Sciences, a division of the Institut de France. This honour might have been due less to his intellectual distinction than to his enrichment of the museums of France with the treasures of Rome and Florence. He was proud of his election and developed the habit of signing his letters and decrees 'Member of the Institute' before 'General-in-Chief'. He also regularly attended Academy meetings, wearing the splendid Academician's uniform that had been designed by Jacques Louis David.

Academician Bonaparte had a special interest in Egypt. In the spring of 1798 he addressed the Academy on the importance of the Nile Valley to international scholarship, and issued orders that the savants who accompanied his invasion force would settle once and for all the question of Egypt's contribution to the civilisation of the ancient world.

Accordingly, the Commission on the Sciences and the Arts was assembled. Their practical and immediate task was to provide the most accurate scientific data possible to help conduct the war, and subsequently to set up a permanent French colony when victory had been achieved. The scheme was simple: France would benefit from the import of Egyptian agricultural produce, grown with the very latest scientific advice, and from the export of her manufactured goods. Egypt would gain by having a settled and civilised government, as well as an assured overseas market. In this way the Egyptians would slowly be civilised by close contact with the most refined culture of modern Europe. In return, European scholarship would be advanced by research into the true history of the Egypt of the pharaohs, and the real significance of her ancient monuments.

The Commission consisted of twenty-one mathematicians, three astronomers, seventeen civil engineers, fifteen ordnance survey officers, ten engineering draughtsmen, and three gunpowder experts. The functions of these technicians in a modern invading and colonising force seems obvious; less utilitarian were the sculptor, musicians, and men of letters who were also enrolled. They took with them a library of around five hundred volumes, including the entire *Encyclopédie*, the transactions of the Académie des Sciences, the works of Voltaire, the Koran, the Hindu Vedic scriptures, as well as a collection of travellers' tales, manuals of military history, and technical works on engineering and surgery.

Most of the members of the Commission were young, some only in their early twenties. The most venerable and illustrious was the mathematician Gaspard Monge, and he was only fifty-two, although his wife had opposed his setting off at such an advanced age, calling him an 'old lunatic'. Bonaparte fired them all with his enthusiasm, and as they set out Monge set the tone for the Commission in a letter to the General-in-Chief:

9

So here am I transformed into an Argonaut. It is one of the miracles of our new Jason who is not ploughing the seas for the conquest of a Fleece, of which the material cannot greatly increase in value, but is carrying the torch of reason into a country where its light has not penetrated for a very long period, is extending the domain of philosophy, and is carrying into more distant fields the national glory.

Once on board *L'Orient*, a ship of the line with 120 guns, Bonaparte spent most of the voyage to Egypt in his cabin, which had been specially selected by Admiral Bruyes as suitable for a commander-in-chief who anticipated being seasick for the entire voyage. Bonaparte had ordered Monge to locate and place on board Arabic and Greek printing presses so he could start the propaganda war before the actual fighting began. In planning the establishment of a French colony in Egypt, Bonaparte realised that colonial powers can only be secure with, if not the consent, at least the acquiescence of those they govern. He therefore had to persuade the Egyptian people that a change of masters should be welcomed. The first step was to convince them that the French came not to enslave but to liberate. As the fleet moved out from Malta, Bonaparte at last felt well enough to dictate his proclamation to the Egyptians:

> What wisdom, what talents, what virtues distinguish the Mamelukes that they alone should have a soft and pleasant life? Is there good land? It belongs to the Mamelukes. Is there a fine slave, a fine horse, a fine house? They all belong to the Mamelukes. If Egypt be their private estate, let them show the lease that God has granted.

While the cry against the injustice of entrenched privilege had been wonderfully effective in Revolutionary France, the reference to God was risky in Egypt because the Egyptians, as Moslems, were unlikely to welcome a force of infidels, however well-intentioned. So the proclamation went on:

> People of Egypt, you will be told that I have come to destroy your religion; do not believe it! Reply that I respect God, his prophet Mohammed and the Koran more than the

Mamelukes! . . . Is it not we that destroyed the Knights of Malta because, in their madness, they believed that God wanted them to go to war against the Mussulmans?

Bonaparte's resolve to project himself as sympathetic with the followers of the Prophet was to be severely tested in Cairo, but on board his flagship he only reminded his troops that if they were to be accepted as liberators of the Egyptian people, they should check any impulse to act as conquerors:

> The people with whom we are going to live are Mohammedans; their first article of faith is this: 'There is no other God but God and Mohammed is his prophet'. Do not contradict them; behave with them as we have behaved with Jews and Italians; show respect for their muftis and their imams as you have done for rabbis and for bishops . . . The Roman legions protected all religions.

The proclamation expressed a fine sentiment, and there is no reason to suppose it cynical. Bonaparte saw his mission as a civilising one, and the first essential of civilisation, in the tradition he tried to emulate, was religious toleration. He went on to forbid his troops absolutely from indulging in plunder: '. . . pillage enriches only a small number; it dishonours us and destroys our resources; and it makes enemies of the people whom it is in our interests to have as friends.' He declared pillaging to be a capital offence.

It was no idle threat. When the city of Alexandria, which Bonaparte half hoped might throw open its gates to welcome the French liberating army, turned out to be raggedly defended, its fortified walls crowded with women and children shouting defiance, the troops had to be sent in. After a few hours of street-fighting, Bonaparte was able to set up headquarters in the centre of town, where he received the surrender of the garrison leaders. The French troops had been fired on by civilians, but when a French soldier was brought before him and accused of taking a dagger from a peaceable Arab, the fact was verified and Bonaparte ordered the man shot on the spot.

Cairo was next. The troops were divided into two columns, one to march around the coast to Rosetta, accompanied by a small flotilla of boats carrying provisions, and the other to march directly inland to a rendezvous on the Nile, where the combined army would march on the city.

The campaign of 25 July 1798 is one of the most stirring in military history. The French troops, crippled by dysentery, marched across the desert, harassed by bedouin tribesmen as well as Murad-Bey and the Mameluke cavalry, and on to victory at the Battle of the Pyramids, their leader rallying them with the celebrated reminder that forty centuries were looking down upon them.

Bonaparte's proclamations printed on board *L'Orient* had been circulated widely before the army reached Cairo, and carried to the city by Egyptian sailors, who had been told to spread the news that the French came as 'true Mussulmans' to liberate their brothers from the Mameluke. The proclamations had no effect. The population was terrified, and when news reached them of the defeat of the Mameluke army they panicked. Merchants heaped their goods on to the backs of donkeys and headed for the outskirts of the city, where they were attacked and robbed by other fleeing citizens as the mob fired and looted the palaces. After two days, during which the French army watched the fires from across the river, the hysteria subsided and Bonaparte entered a subdued city to face a curious, apprehensive, but no longer hostile, population.

The victorious General-in-Chief took over the palace in the centre of town that had belonged to Qassim-Bey, one of the wealthiest of the Mamelukes, and set about winning over the leaders of the people. He established a council of Egyptian elders to advise him, appearing before them in Egyptian costume. He invited them to banquets, where he ate with his fingers and sat crosslegged on the floor. He is said to have told them that 'When I am in France I am a Christian; when in Egypt, a Mohammedan.' Finally, Bonaparte took the name of Grand Sultan, or Sultan Kebir, and ordered that the feasts celebrating the life of the Prophet should be celebrated by the French troops as well. More significantly, he issued an order on 2 August 1798 for the selection of a building suitable to house the Institute of Egypt. It was to be modelled on the Institut de France, to which the most distinguished scientists and artists might be elected to advance knowledge of both Egypt's present condition and of her history of arts and sciences.

A collection of palaces was chosen in the suburb of Nasrieh that suitably reflected the high aspirations of the Institute. Here were to be housed the observatory, the chemical laboratory, the engineering workshops, as well as the many collections of specimens that were anticipated. The palace of Qassim-Bey had a lofty meeting-hall in which the savants could assemble and address each other, as well as shady gardens in which they could stroll about and exchange ideas. The objectives of the Institute were officially defined:

- The progress and propagation of knowledge in Egypt.

- The research, study, and publication of the natural, industrial, and historical data of Egypt.

- Advice on the different questions on which it shall be consulted by the government.

The Institute was divided into four sections – mathematics, physics, political economy and literature and art – and each section was to have twelve members. At the first meeting of the Institute on 23 August 1798, Bonaparte was elected Vice-President. He insisted that within the precincts of the Institute he should be addressed simply as 'Citizen Bonaparte' until some contribution to the Institute's knowledge brought him further distinction.

Bonaparte saw the Institute as an embodiment of the finest principles of revolutionary idealism. All knowledge was attainable by the free spirit of scientific enquiry, and since knowledge ennobled mankind, even an army of occupation still struggling with an unsubdued enemy should not neglect its pursuit. And so, while the French army was advancing up the Nile Valley, clashing with the Mameluke hordes, their scholarly compatriots were assembling in the cool palace of Qassim-Bey to hear papers on 'The Optical Phenomenon known as the Mirage', and 'Some observations of the Wing of an Ostrich'.

The push into the valley of the Nile was not simply an exploration, although the discoveries made and recorded were its most lasting memorial. Murad-Bey, leader of the Mamelukes, had settled with about 2,000 men near the oasis of Faiyum, and had been joined by 5,000 irregular Arab cavalry. He was also able to count on support from the bedouin for forays against the French, and was in contact with rebels in Cairo and Alexandria. Bonaparte decided that he had to be defeated or driven up the valley if the plan for a peaceful colony was to have any chance of success, and sent a force of 5,000 under the command of General Desaix to deal with the leader of the Mamelukes.

With the French force, or more often some little way behind it, was the Baron Dominique Vivant Denon, representative of the Institute of Egypt. The Baron had asked to accompany Bonaparte to Egypt because, at the age of fifty-one, he had become more interested in the history of mankind than in its future. Denon – artist, playwright, archaeologist, and diplomat – had been a friend of Voltaire's and a favourite at the court of Louis XV. In Italy when the Revolution broke out, instead of counting himself lucky to have escaped, Denon returned to France to save his property while most of the aristocracy were heading in the opposite direction. His possessions had been confiscated and redistributed. By the time he arrived home he was reduced to working for the artist Jacques Louis David, being given the humiliating task of copying fashion designs. Denon, however, had both old friends and an engaging personality that allowed him to make new ones, Robespierre being among these. Most of Denon's property soon was recovered and returned to him, and he began to be invited to the soirées at the salon of Josephine de Beauharnais, where he met Bonaparte. Humiliation behind him, Denon was re-established as a nationally famous artist and elected to the Academy.

Denon was received enthusiastically in the salons of Paris largely because of his *Oeuvres priapiques*, a series of phallically inspired sketches that were circulated among his friends and published in 1793. His inspiration in Egypt was to be the desert and the ancient monuments on which he looked with an eye unprejudiced by a commitment to classicism. During the 18th century, the most influential work on Egyptian antiquities in France was Monfauçon's *L'Antiquité expliquée et représentée en figures* (1719-24). While beautifully produced and written, Montfauçon judged Egyptian art by the fashion of the time, pronouncing it horrible, bizarre and in bad taste. Denon was accepted as a man of sensibility and authority; his response to the art and architecture of the Nile Valley was to shape that of his generation.

Although an arbiter of taste, Denon was no shrinking aesthete. When he volunteered to accompany General Desaix into the desert, he knew that the journey was to be into a strange land where survival was uncertain. Nobody on the expedition had yet experienced the conditions Desaix and his men were to face: heat, sandstorms, hostility from unknown peoples to the south, uncertainty of supplies and regular harassment from an enemy whose strength was growing, and who knew the land. Denon wrote: 'I was accustomed to bivouacking and was not afraid of an army biscuit.' The expedition set out on 25 August 1798: 3,000 infantry in heavy serge uniforms with scarlet and yellow facings, 200 horses, and eight pieces of artillery, making up a column over two miles long, trudging across the sands. At its head was a diminutive figure who seemed to swell at the approach of the enemy: General Desaix, a vigorous thirty-year-old professional soldier; bringing up the rear, sometimes so engrossed in his sketches that he lost sight of the column, was the aristocrat and artist Denon.

Murad-Bey rallied his forces for a token charge at the oasis of Faiyum, but then realised that this was the proven tactic for heavy losses against the French square. His forces were more mobile than the French with their supplies and artillery. Accordingly he retreated up the valley and camped by the riverside until the French were almost upon him, before moving south into the unknown land, occasionally swinging back to attack the French column from the rear and cut its supply lines.

The campaign continued through the heat of the late summer. Desaix was impatient to catch up with the enemy and force him into a pitched battle; Denon was content to marvel at the wonders being revealed as they marched from temple to monument to ancient city, while he sketched furiously to preserve the sights for himself and for posterity.

Despite their professions, and although they were a generation apart, Desaix and Denon had much in common. Denon would become so gripped by the beauty of what he saw around him that he was indifferent to the heat, the passage of time, or his own personal safety. Often, left behind by the column, his absence would be noticed only when camp was made at the end of the day, and an escort had to be sent galloping back to rescue him from the bedouin. At these times Denon hardly noticed what he ate or wore. On a campaign, Desaix was equally distracted by the task in hand. Bonaparte wrote of his favourite general that in battle he was 'always badly dressed, sometimes even ragged, and despising comfort and convenience . . . wrapped up in a cloak, Desaix threw himself under a gun and slept as contentedly as if he were in a palace.'

But Egypt had a quite different impact on the two men. In the vast immensity of the desert, where the eye is oppressed by limitless space, where, as Denon wrote, 'the silence of non-existence reigns in solitude over immensity', Desaix became depressed. One evening, as they talked in their camp on the edge of the desert, he confided in Denon that he thought Egypt a forgotten land, an incomplete land. Providence, he said, having provided lavishly for the needs of the rest of the world, must have run out by the time it got around to Egypt, and had left the land unfinished. Denon's reply, surprisingly modern, blamed man rather than Providence. 'Is it not rather', he countered, 'the decrepitude of that part of the world most anciently inhabited? May it not have been the abuses of human industry that have reduced it to this state?'

The monuments continued to astonish Denon. At Hermopolis, in Middle Egypt, he visited the famous portico and declared it to be a building that had waited 4,000 years to impress him with its perfection. 'The Greeks', he wrote, in defiance of classical scholarship, 'never performed anything of a grander character'. He was dragged away from the site by Desaix before he had a chance to complete his sketches, and fretted for three weeks because the exigencies of the military campaign failed to match the locations of the ancient monuments. Then, however, Murad-Bey moved further south again, and in pursuit the French came upon Dendera, which set the seal on Denon's conviction that it was Egypt – not Greece – that had given birth to the most sublime arts of mankind.

During the Age of Reason, it was deemed necessary for aesthetic as well as scientific judgements to be founded upon reason, true beauty being an expression of proportion and reason. Denon's enthusiasm for what he saw was no exception. The architecture of the temple at Dendera he found to be 'clearly directed by a powerful reason', the decoration of its walls 'always founded upon reason, always agreeing with each other . . . a taste founded upon truth and a concatenation of profound reasonings'. Here was classical purity without excess or romanticism: 'no negligence, no effusion of distinguished genius; unity and harmony reigned throughout'.

Here lay the key to the question of the antiquity of Egypt that had divided scholars for centuries. Denon was able to argue against the biblical chronology of the Church by pointing out that the art of Dendera was ancient without being primitive. This meant that Egypt was indeed the cradle of civilisation:

> . . . how many ages must have been occupied in leading a creative nation to these results, to this degree of perfection and sublimity in the arts! How many other ages to bring about the utter oblivion of such a multitude of things and to reconduct man . . . to the state of nature in which we found him!

At Dendera Denon sketched in a frenzy. At any moment news might reach them that Murad-Bey was within reach, and they might have to pack up and leave the most sublime spot in Egypt, perhaps forever. 'I had not eyes nor hands enough,' he wrote, 'my head was too small to see, draw, and classify everything that struck me.' He ran out of pencils and melted down bullets to draw with until supplies should catch up with the troops.

At Dendera, where Hathor, suckler of the king, the golden one, had been worshipped since earliest recorded times, something of the numinous seemed still to hang over the great lonely building at the edge of the desert. One of the officers confessed to Denon, 'Ever since I came to Egypt I have felt cheated in every way and been constantly depressed and ill. Tentara has cured me. What I saw today has paid me back for all my misery. I don't care what happens to me during the rest of this expedition. I shall always be happy to have been in it.'

As they pushed on from Dendera, moving south and upstream in pursuit of the Mamelukes, an incident occurred that seemed to demonstrate that the officer was not alone in his response to the beauties of Egypt. It was 9 o'clock in the morning when they rounded a bend in the river and saw spread out before them the ruins of the cities of Luxor and Karnak; the full panorama of ancient Thebes. In a spontaneous response to this magnificent sight, the entire division halted. 'Without an order being given,' wrote an officer, 'the men formed their ranks and presented arms to the accompaniment of the drums and the bands.' A touch of Gallic romanticism, perhaps, but there are independent accounts that tell of the troops halting in wonder and clapping their hands. Denon was in no doubt about the men's enthusiasm for the beauties of the ancient buildings. They would cluster around him to keep the sun off his back as he drew, and he wrote of 'the electrifying emotion of an army of soldiers whose refined sensibility made me rejoice in being their companion and proud of being a Frenchman'.

News reached General Desaix that Murad-Bey was encamped at Esna, about thirty-one miles south, and the last village of any size in Egypt at the time. Again Denon was torn away from his sketching to set off in pursuit of the enemy. They arrived only hours after the Mamelukes had left, burning their tents and heavy baggage to lighten their flight. However, there were artistic delights at Esna to compensate for the military frustrations. Denon pronounced the ruins of the temple to be 'the most perfect remains of ancient architecture', and found here further evidence of the pre-eminence of the Egyptians. The decorations of the temple were illustrations of the natural products of Egypt: the lotus, the vine, the palm, the reed, and so on, showing that the Egyptians had borrowed from none in reaching the perfection of their art: they had copied nature. 'The Greeks', wrote Denon, 'have only added fables to the robberies they have committed upon them.'

There remained the problem of how a culture that had reached such perfection in ancient times could have declined into its present condition at the end of the 18th century. Denon had found an answer, and it was one that was deeply satisfying to an idealist of the Enlightenment: Egypt had been dragged down by the same influence that had held back the progress of Europe for centuries, the same tyranny from which France had just liberated herself: the priests. Just as the Church had clothed its mysteries in a dead language to maintain its hold on the minds of common men, so the priests of ancient Egypt had hidden their arcane secrets in the impenetrable symbols of the hieroglyphics that covered the walls of the temples. Denon saw a clear parallel between the Jesuits of his own time and the priests of ancient Egypt: 'humble and hypocritical despots . . . possessing all the sciences and wrapping them in emblem and mystery that they might place a barrier between themselves and the people. The king was served by priests, advised by priests, fed by priests, sermonised by priests.' Even the magnificence of Thebes provoked his social conscience, and he scribbled irritably, 'Temples! Still temples! Always temples! . . . No walls, no quays, no bridges, no baths; not an edifice for public use nor convenience!'

Back at the Institute, the frontiers of learning were expanding cautiously. Every five days the scholars assembled in the hall of the palace of Qassim-Bey to discuss the latest discoveries and plans. The chemist Bertollet read papers on the formation of ammonia and on the Egyptian methods for producing indigo; Dutetre outlined a proposal for a school of fine arts for the Egyptians; Monge discoursed on capillary attraction; Fourier and Corrancez on higher mathematics. Foreshadowing the activity that was to bring Egyptologists and less respectable visitors to the Nile Valley for the next century was a paper by the geologist Dolomieu containing proposals for the 'selection, conservation and transportation of ancient monuments' from Egypt to France. There is no evidence in the proceedings that the proposals caused any rumblings of conscience; they were merely following the precedents set in Italy, whose national treasures had been 'liberated' from Italian museums to find a secure home in the Louvre. It seemed only reasonable that the nation called on by destiny to reveal the true significance of Egypt should have her museums enriched by its monuments.

As a first step to trans-shipment to France, a collection was established at the Institute. Dolomieu was placed in charge and given assistants for 'the careful collection of all the ancient monuments they may be able to procure, distinguishing those which local interest renders worthy of attention but which could not be removed without drawbacks'. We shall hear more of these. The earliest specimens at the Institute came from the Delta area, but Desaix, even in full pursuit of the Mamelukes, did not forget his duty to contribute. He sent back two statues for the collection, one of Apollo and one of Antinoe, but the fellah charged with their transportation found Apollo too heavy, and flung him overboard into the Nile.

For Bonaparte the Institute was more than just a centre of learning or for acquiring Egyptian antiquities. He saw it as a means of winning the respect and trust of the country's leaders, in which he had not been making much progress. He was aware, perhaps unusually so, of the need to govern a country through those he found to be traditionally in charge. As a system for maintaining a colonial power in office this method of indirect rule has much to recommend it, but it depends on a sensitive awareness of the culture and the traditional leadership which it seeks to manipulate. Bonaparte lacked this. He knew he had to be seen to support the authority of the muftis, imams, and sheiks and he decided one way to do this would be to allow them to continue to bear arms, a right that had been denied the rest of the population. Bonaparte also evaluated correctly the matter of their self-esteem in ordering that they be offered respect in public, even by the French troops. But when he went on to insist they wear a tricolour sash as a badge of rank so that his troops would recognise them, he was treating them like French provincial officials and the honour was declined. While his orientalists were able to advise Bonaparte on current theories relating to Egyptian antiquities, they knew little of the Egyptian culture of his day. Bonaparte was sailing in uncharted waters in seeking to win the confidence of a people whose way of life was so alien.

One priority, however, was shared between the Egyptians and the citizens of the Enlightenment: a respect for education. Cairo was the seat of the internationally renowned mosque of El-Azhar, which was both a sacred temple and a Moslem university. In the time of the Khedives, 12,000 students had attended regularly from all parts of the world, studying a wide range of sacred and secular subjects. Bonaparte found that the 'Sorbonne of El-Azhar' had shrunk to around 1,200 students, who spent their whole time on the Koran and Islamic dogma. But the trappings of scholarship were still in evidence: the committed students, the library, the courses of lectures, and the bearded professors who Bonaparte invited as a gesture of hospitality between scholars to visit the Institute. The chronicler El Djabarti wrote:

When a Moslem wished to visit the establishment, he was

not prevented from doing so but, on the contrary, was made very welcome . . . I myself repeatedly had occasion to visit the library. I saw there, among other things, a large volume on the history of our Prophet (May God bless him!); his holy features were shown in it as faithfully as the artists' knowledge permitted . . . There were also many Moslem books in French translation . . . Some of the French were studying Arabic and learning verses from the Koran by heart.

So impressed were the teachers of El-Azhar that they spread the news among the leaders of Cairo that the French interest in Islam was genuine. They began attending theological discussions at the Institute at the invitation of Bonaparte, who played the role of committed seeker after truth, and disinterested searcher. When it became clear to Bonaparte that he was making more progress in winning the respect of these men by chairing religious discussions than by dressing up and eating sheep's eyes, he decided to press his advantage. Was it not probable, he asked, that the successes that had attended his expeditions were a sign of Divine favour? He managed to quote passages from the Koran, furnished by his scholars, which could be interpreted as prophesies of the French invasion, and asked whether he could have been so victorious against the Mameluke hordes without the assistance of the Prophet. If the French were in Egypt with the blessing of the Prophet, and in accordance with what he foretold, would the religious leaders then not issue a *fetwa*, an interpretation of the Koran, directing their people to take the oath of allegiance to the French, so they could become peaceful citizens of the mother country overseas?

The imams and muftis conferred briefly, replying that the signs were indeed favourable, and that the hand of the Prophet might well be distinguished in Bonaparte's victories. It only remained for Bonaparte to show his gratitude by publicly embracing Islam; they would then be honoured to direct the faithful to swear their allegiance. It would of course be appropriate if not only the General-in-Chief, but the entire French army should respond in this pious way as well.

Bonaparte had few scruples about religion and was fond of quoting Henry IV: 'Paris is well worth a Mass.' Similarly, he was ready to commit himself to any faith that would make him master of Egypt. 'Is it conceivable', he was to write, 'that the eastern empire and perhaps the subjection of all Asia would not have been worth pantaloons and a turban'. Embracing Islam, however, involved more than a change of costume. There was one essential introductory ritual that Bonaparte felt he could not call on his troops to make; they would give up their lives for him, but not their foreskins.

Bonaparte tried to explain this to the muftis. Ready as he was to submit to the true faith, it might take some time for his troops to become fully seized of the great blessings of Islam that made the rite of circumcision such a joyful surrender. The mufti went away to reflect on the matter. Four of them, the most senior, returned with a *fetwa* that seemed to clear the way to a settlement: as a special recognition of the limitations of their cultural inheritance, the French in Egypt would be allowed to enter Islam uncircumcised. The decree was read out in all mosques.

There was, however, a further obstacle: the army might be allowed to enter the fold of Islam as entire men, but they would have to renounce the drinking of alcohol forever. The General felt he had about the same chance of separating his troops from their tipple as from their foreskins, and put the problem to the muftis. More discussions followed. The proposition then was floated that the French might be admitted as true, but ineradicably bad Moslems, culturally deprived of the capacity for moral conduct; but this failed to win support. Eventually a solution was found: the French troops could be left to their sins so long as they agree to pay to charity one-fifth of their income instead of the customary tenth.

There was a pause in the discussions while Bonaparte considered this. But not very seriously; both sides of course, were posturing. Bonaparte knew that the support of the religious leaders would win him the submission of the people. He was quite ready to emulate Alexander the Great, who was said to have worshipped the son of Jupiter at the tomb of Amon Ra. He had no qualms about the spiritual allegiance of his troops, who, as he pointed out, did not attend church in Italy, and showed no interest in doing so in Egypt. He was proud to write of the army under his command that 'every external trace of Christianity, indeed every religious habit had disappeared from its ranks'. Even accepting the concessions made, however, a general conversion to Islam would involve submission to an authority that lay outside the army, and so had to be rejected.

As for the religious leaders of El-Azhar, they had few illusions about Bonaparte's motivation: his military genius won their respect; as a civil ruler he had to be manipulated; and his ineradicable perfidy was never in doubt. The two sides drew apart.

Bonaparte was forced to change his policy from one of appeasement to one of terror. There were rebel movements in Cairo to be put down, and the executions that he ordered became so frequent that governor Dugua wrote to him, 'shootings are becoming so persistent in the citadel that I propose to substitute a headsman. That will save our cartridges and make less noise.' Bonaparte approved. When the venereal diseases spread by prostitutes in the city threatened to decimate the French troops, he agreed to tackle the problem in accordance with local custom, and had the girls sewn up in sacks and thrown into the Nile.

While nothing the French inflicted on the local population could approach the barbarities of the Mamelukes, the Egyptians still refused to accept the French as preferable overlords. The Mamelukes were understood: they oppressed the common people in order to enhance their own security and well-being. This was natural, honest, and to be expected. The French, on the other hand, seemed to be duplicitous: they expressed a concern for the Egyptian peasantry, which was out of place in a victorious army; they talked about equality and fraternity; and insisted on paying for goods and services that they could have taken by force. Clearly they were not to be trusted.

Even if the Institute had failed to act as a bridge between cultures, it pressed on with its work, pushing back the frontiers of knowledge and maintaining civilised standards. When Bonaparte led an expedition into Syria against the Mamelukes, a number of senior scholars accompanied the troops. Monge and Bertollet, in deference to their age, were allowed to travel in the General's carriage. They made observations on the natural history of the desert, and collected insects, lizards, snakes, and smaller quadrupeds for the Institute; the orientalist Jaubert was inspired to write a paper on 'The Nomenclature of the Arab Tribes Camped Between Egypt and Palestine'. At the same meeting they heard a

paper from Bertollet on 'The endiometric action of alkaline sul-
phides and of phosphorus', and an 'Imitation in verse of an idyll
of Gessner'. Geoffroy de Saint-Hilaire presented a detailed
study of the fishes of the Nile, painted by his colleague Redoute;
Fourier introduced the world prèmiere of a new algebraic
theorem, and the astronomer Nouet commented on the different
methods for the measuring of time. However the Institute meeting that most influenced the growth of Egyptology took place on
19 July 1799, when a letter was read from Citizen Lancret, member of the Institute, reporting 'the discovery, at Rosetta, of some
inscriptions that may offer much interest'.

In 1799 Captain Bouchard, Officer of the Engineers, had been
digging the foundations of a defensive position called Fort St
Julien on the west bank of the Nile, when he noticed a large
chunk of black basalt with inscriptions on its face lying in the
mud. When the rock was cleaned, it could be seen that the inscriptions were in three separate bands, the lowest in Greek, the
second in unknown characters, and the third in hieroglyphics. If
the inscriptions turned out to be translations into different languages of the same text, the stone might provide a key to the
decipherment of hieroglyphics. The philologists of the Institute
identified the middle band of writing as 'cursive characters of the
ancient Egyptian language', and recognised Egyptian words in
the Greek band. The first step had been taken towards the greatest advance of knowledge in the history of Egyptology.

A month after the reading of the letter, Bonaparte boarded a
small boat on the Nile a little after midnight and sailed to Alexandria, there to trans-ship for France. He had received news that
the French army in Italy was in retreat, Malta was blockaded,
and the political situation in Paris, under the shaky control of the
Directorate, was degenerating.

The dream of an empire in Egypt was almost over. It lingered
on while General Kleber attempted to follow the detailed instructions he had been left: to complete the colonisation of
Egypt during what was promised to be a brief absence of his
leader. 'I will arrive in Paris,' wrote Bonaparte, 'I will chase out
this gang of lawyers who mock us and who are incapable of
governing the Republic, and I will consolidate this magnificent
colony.' He promised to send out reinforcements as soon as he
arrived in France, but was soon caught up by other ambitions.

The reinforcements never arrived. Egypt was forgotten.

Kleber soon found himself under attack by the Turks and the British. He managed to negotiate a peace with honour allowing the French to leave Egypt carrying their arms, but the British government was not so easily placated and repudiated the agreement. Another eighteen months of desultory fighting had to pass until a combined force of British and Turkish troops forced the French to agree to harsher terms in the spring of 1801.

The most important provision of the Treaty of Capitulation for the history of Egyptology was Article XVI, which stated that all of the collections of the Institute became forfeit to the British. The members of the Institute tried to escape with their collections to France, but were turned back by British ships. The collections of the Institute, they said, were incomprehensible to the world without the knowledge of those who had made them. It was a crime to separate the scientists from their raw materials, and one the world would not forgive. 'Sooner than permit this iniquitous and vandal spoliation', they declared, 'we shall burn our riches ourselves. It is celebrity you are aiming for. Very well, you can count on the long memory of history: you also will have burned a library in Alexandria.'

General Menou – Kleber by then had been assassinated – could not understand what the fuss was about: 'I have just been informed', he wrote to General Hutchinson, 'that several of our collection-makers wish to follow their seeds, minerals, birds, butterflies or reptiles wherever you choose to ship their crates. I do not know if they wish to have themselves stuffed for the purpose, but I can assure you that, if the idea should appeal to them, I shall not prevent them.' Eventually a compromise was arrived at and the French were allowed to keep most of the collection and to ship it back to France. The Rosetta Stone – whose significance had been accepted even though its writings remained undeciphered – was kept by General Hutchinson and sent as a gift to George III, who passed it on uncomprehendingly to the British Museum. Its French connection, however, was not severed: the scholars had their own copy in Paris.

The French had failed to establish an empire in Egypt; the threat to the British in India was short-lived. The adventure ended with no military advantage secured, although the power of the Mamelukes had been shattered. Something momentous, however, had been achieved: for the first time Egypt was open to the investigations of historians and archaeologists. The Institute furnished them with a prodigious guide-book; if the French were unable to conquer Egypt, they did succeed quite magnificently in describing it in the monumental *Description de l'Egypte*, which was published in Paris between 1809-28 in thirteen volumes of superb plates, and a further ten of text.

While Bonaparte had laid the foundations for the science of Egyptology, he also had indulged in a practice that dogged its development. On leaving Egypt he carried away with him as presents for Josephine seven small antiquities, which she installed at Malmaison. One of them, a Middle Kingdom statue of a seated Egyptian, was put up for a sale a century later and bought by Lord Amherst of Hackney; in 1921 the American press baron William Randolph Hearst bought it from the Amherst sale and it ended up in the Brooklyn Museum. The plundering of the treasures of Egypt had begun in earnest.

Chapter Two

A Field for Plunder

BEFORE THE EXPLORATION OF THE NILE VALLEY could
be pursued, the country had to be pacified. When the
French left, the authority of the Mamelukes had been dislodged but not destroyed, and the Turkish government stepped
in to finish the job. They sent messages of reassurance to Britain,
and more traditional instructions to the high admiral Husain
Pasha. The latter invited the leading Mameluke-Beys to an
entertainment on board his flagship, and proceeded to blow
them out of the water as they crossed Abugir Bay in open boats.

General Hutchinson, the officer commanding British troops,
stepped in to prevent the systematic slaughter of survivors, even
demanding the release of prisoners. Clearly matters could not be
satisfactorily settled while the British were still around; in
March 1803 they left. The sole official British representative was
the consul, Colonel Misset, left behind in Alexandria with
patronising instructions:

> . . . to convey to the British Government authentic informa-
> tion of the events which should take place in Upper and
> Lower Egypt during those contests for dominion which it
> was foreseen must ensue between the Mamelukes and the
> Turks, when either party should no longer be overawed by
> the presence of our army; and when they should lose their
> recollection of the wholesome counsel of the British Com-
> mander, given as it had been to them from the most upright

and disinterested views; and supported by a calm, conciliatory and dignified conduct.

With the wholesome counsellor safely on his way back to London, it remained only for the Turkish governor, Muhammad Khosrev, to rally his troops and march south along the valley to a final confrontation with the Mameluke force. His troops, which consisted mainly of Albanian mercenaries whose pay was in arrears, refused to march anywhere. When the governor responded to their demands by firing on them from the citadel, they stormed the place and drove him out.

His replacement fared even worse. Tahir Pasha, having assumed command of a force of loyal Turkish troops, lasted only twenty-three days before they too ran out of patience with the delay in settling their arrears and assassinated him. The final destruction of the Mamelukes had to be shelved while those who had been sent to accomplish it settled their differences.

There followed a period of civil war during which the Albanians fought the Turks (1806-9), and the Mamelukes made occasional raids on both. It was a time of confusion, brought to an end, as so often happens, by a strong man who came to power by manipulating the warring factions and playing them off against each other.

Muhammad Ali, the son of an Albanian peasant farmer, came to Egypt as the leader of an Albanian mercenary force. He supported both Turks and Mamelukes in the civil war, and eventually established himself as an independent authority in Cairo, with a force of 10,000 Albanians. He protested that he was concerned only with the maintenance of law and order in the capital. In 1805 Ali felt secure enough to take the next step: with the support of the Egyptian sheiks, he imprisoned the Turkish governor and sent a friendly message to Constantinople saying that he was taking charge, only as a temporary measure, to keep order. The following year, the Sublime Porte, the Turkish government – which had centuries of experience in the limitations of governing at a distance, and had cultivated the ability to accept those things it could not change – appointed Muhammad Ali as Pasha of Egypt.

The Mamelukes were driven up the Nile into southern Egypt, and so were not available to lend a hand when the British expeditionary force landed in 1807 to restore them to power. This intervention sprang less from British confidence in the Mamelukes' administrative abilities than from a wish to strike a blow against the Turks, who had sided with Napoleon in Europe. Muhammad Ali, who was on a campaign against the beys at the time, sent messages promising to comply with all their demands if they would join him in expelling the invaders. The combined forces destroyed the British at Alexandria; they then forced the survivors to march to Cairo carrying the heads of their dead comrades, which were impaled on spikes around Esbekiah Square.

The Mamelukes were divided between the allies of Muhammad Ali, who were against the British, and those who looked to the British to be restored to their former power in Egypt. There were still occasional skirmishes around Cairo, and Muhammad Ali decided on a change of tactics. He invited the Mameluke-Beys in Cairo to an entertainment in honour of his son, who was to be invested with the command of the army. After taking coffee in the citadel, the Mamelukes were led in procession down the steep and narrow road leading to the great gate, a guard-of-honour to the front, and one to the rear. As soon as the Albanian troops, who preceded the beys, were through the gate, it was shut on the Mamelukes. The Albanians climbed the walls and began to fire on them. Those who tried to retreat were shot by the guards behind; all 470 Mamelukes were killed, with the exception, legend has it, of one bey, who rode his horse straight at the ramparts and leapt over. The horse was killed by the fall, and the rider survived.

Muhammad Ali was now in complete control of the country. He had defeated the British, won the support of Egyptians, taken authority from the Turks, and destroyed the Mamelukes. He had absolute power. Edward Lane, an English visitor, wrote that: 'He may cause any one of his subjects to be put to death without the formality of a trial, or without assigning any cause; a single horizontal motion of his hand is sufficient to imply the sentence of decapitation.'

Once established in power, Muhammad Ali set out to turn Egypt into a modern nation. He could afford to take on the rôle of benevolent despot. As he told a European visitor of his early struggles, 'I do not love that period of my life, and what would the world profit by the recital of that interminable tissue of combat and misery, cunning and bloodshed, to which circumstances imperatively compelled me? . . . My history shall not commence till the period when, free from all restraint, I could arouse this land . . . from the sleep of ages.'

In attempting to make Egypt fit for the contemporary world, Muhammad Ali looked to the West for help. He was fond of comparing himself to Napoleon, and often drew attention to the fact that the two great leaders had been born in the same year. Napoleon had tried to modernise Egypt, and Muhammad Ali committed himself to continuing the work. Western experts were called in to help with the organisation of the country's economy; Western traders were welcomed. Finally, to protect the interests of foreigners in Egypt, Muhammad Ali encouraged the setting up of consulates. It was through such steps that the Anglo-French struggle was carried from the battle-fields of Europe to the Nile Valley, where it was waged with the same antipathy, but rather more guile and less bloodshed.

During the long ascendancy of Muhammad Ali there had been little consular activity in Egypt, mainly because there were no settled authorities with which to be diplomatic. The great powers, however, had maintained representatives who had busied themselves with other matters, for example Colonel Misset, who had been left behind in 1803 as disinterested observer for the British, and the French consul Bernardino Drovetti. The busier of the two, Drovetti set the fashion for extraconsular activities by becoming the most organised and energetic collector of antiquities of his time.

Piedmontese by birth, Drovetti was tough, intelligent, and resourceful. He had studied law before joining the French army, and served as a colonel with Bonaparte in Egypt. On his return to Europe in 1801 at the age of twenty-five, he was appointed military judge in Turin. The following year he returned to Egypt as vice-consul in Alexandria. When the Turks recognised Napoleon as emperor of France, the British retaliated by cultivating the Mamelukes in Alexandria. Drovetti moved to Cairo to work for the support of the opposition, which soon proved to be Muhammad Ali. He had backed the winner, and when Muhammad Ali took control of the country, Drovetti was established as ally and friend.

The practical effect of this was that for a time Drovetti controlled excavations in the Nile Valley. Previous excavations had been conducted haphazardly, but now Muhammad Ali ruled that only those with his express permission, in the form of a firman or letter of authority, should be given safe conduct and allowed to dig. Drovetti was responsible for submitting the applications for the firmans to the Pasha, and so could obstruct any rivals. He amassed a large personal collection during his career in Egypt, which he delighted in showing to visitors, declaring that one day it would enrich the museums of Paris.

Colonel Misset, who was in bad health for the whole of his service in Egypt and paralysed for the latter part, was no serious rival to Drovetti. On Misset's resignation in 1815, however, a man arrived in Egypt to replace him who had been commissioned to recover antiquities for the British Museum. The race for the treasures of the Nile had begun.

Henry Salt was a product of the age of patronage. Because his rise to power was brought about by manipulating aristocrats and officials in a manner no longer openly admitted as normative, he has not been well thought of by modern historians of Egypt.

Salt was the youngest of eight children of a Lichfield doctor, whose practice had enabled him, in the words of Salt's biographer, 'to accumulate a handsome competency'. Part of this was spent on supporting young Henry as an unsuccessful portrait painter in London. His fortunes began to change when one day he spotted Lord Valencia, son and heir to the Earl of Mountnorris, strolling around Fuseli's gallery in Pall Mall accompanied by his tutor, the Rev. Thomas Butt. The Rev. Butt happened to be Henry's uncle, so the young man saw an opportunity for acquaintance with the aristocracy and immediately introduced himself. He was accepted into the outer reaches of the family circle.

In 1802 Lord Valencia announced that he was planning a trip to India. Henry Salt immediately wrote to him asking to be taken along as secretary/draftsman. His Lordship replied that he really had no need of either, but, in consideration of the young man's melancholy situation and desire to quit the pursuit in which he was then engaged, he might as well come along. They were away for four years. During the voyage they spent some time in Abyssinia; when they returned, and Lord Valencia recommended that Britain open trade negotiations with Abyssinia, Henry Salt was sent there bearing gifts from the king of Great Britain to the emperor. His credentials as a British representative to the Middle East were established.

After Salt returned to London, he spent some years writing up his travels and dining out on his experiences, but England did not suit him, and he was constantly ill. When he heard that Colonel Misset, consul-general in Egypt, had resigned through ill-health, he saw his chance and went after the job. His strategy consisted in dashing around London, and asking influential acquaintances to write on his behalf to the Foreign Secretary, Lord Castlereagh. Two of his backers were Lord Valencia and Sir Joseph Banks, then president of the Royal Society. Salt's lobbying was successful, and when he was appointed he showed his gratitude by promising both gentlemen that he would collect antiquities for them. Lord Valencia wanted to embellish the family seat at Arley Hall, and Sir Joseph Banks was sure that anything Salt could pick up in the Nile Valley would be welcomed by the British Museum, of which he was a trustee. William Hamilton, an Under-Secretary at the Foreign Office, from whose patronage Salt had also benefited, urged him to hunt for another Rosetta Stone, and added encouragingly: 'Whatever the expense of the undertaking, it would be most cheerfully supported by an enlightened nation, eager to anticipate its rivals in the prosecution of the best interests of science and literature.'

The position secured, it remained only for Salt to find a wife to share his burdens and diplomatic status. He focused on a Birmingham heiress who had prospects of a considerable fortune, courting her in person and verse, in spite of her father's reservations. But Salt was forced to set sail for Egypt alone; neither father nor daughter felt that a young lady of quality, with all the refinements that Birmingham could offer, should be exposed to the privations of Cairo.

The batchelor's quarters that Salt set up in Cairo in 1816 would have been tolerable even to a Birmingham heiress. He engaged the necessary staff to maintain his social position, and he had a secretary 'whom I provide with everything'. Since his rent was fifty pounds a year, Salt wrote complainingly to London that the maintenance of the minimum essentials for consular respectability was costing him the whole of his salary. He needed a supplementary income, and his efforts to attain it opened a new chapter in the story of Egyptology.

Tomb robbery in Egypt has an ancient and dishonourable history. Because it was the practice to bury kings and noblemen with their costliest possessions, the first of the living to profit from the dead were the workmen who entombed them. Many of the ancient papyri record legal proceedings against the violators of tombs. An official investigation of 1130 BC states:

> These are the tombs and sepulchres in which rested the blessed ones of old, the women and the people of the land on the west of the city: it was found that the thieves had broken into all of them, that they had pulled out from their coffins and sarcophagi their occupants, thrown out upon the desert, and that they had stolen their articles of furniture which had been given them together with the gold, the silver, and the ornaments which were in their coffins.

During the 17th and 18th centuries, gentlemen of leisure were in the habit of wandering in foreign lands, collecting oddments with which to fill their cabinets of curiosities at home, exciting the wonder of their friends. This did not seriously diminish the vast store of treasures in the Nile Valley, but the appetite grew during the 18th century, and by the time Salt had set himself up in Cairo there was a flourishing trade in antiquities and forgeries.

A French sculptor, Jean Jacques Rifaud, who arrived in Egypt in 1805 and spent more than forty years there, wrote that the Arabs were long puzzled by the high value set by foreigners on useless old bits of stone and statues. They worked out their own explanations: some said the excavators were pagans who worshipped the ancient gods because they had been seen caressing the statues; and, because they would occasionally moisten the stone with their tongues to identify its composition, they were said to be bestowing secret kisses on their idols. Others, puzzled by the trouble and expense to which Europeans would put themselves to recover fragments, explained that the ancient marbles contained gold, and that the excavators had discovered the secret of extracting it.

Salt discovered on his arrival that antiques were becoming difficult to purchase because demand had temporarily exceeded supply. Drovetti, meanwhile, was on a tour of Upper Egypt, buying everything he could find for his own collection, which Salt had examined and pronounced worth about 4,000 pounds. There was at the time no agreed market value for Egyptian antiquities, and this was to give rise to appalling complications later in Salt's career; but he knew from his very first weeks in Egypt that money was to be made from excavation, and he needed money. He wrote to his aristocratic patron, who had succeeded to the title of Earl of Mountnorris:

> I have taken every possible means to collect, and am glad to say that I have been very successful; so that I shall, in spring, have to send you a cargo of such things as you have not before seen. I must however inform you that I am so bit with the prospect of what may still be done in Upper Egypt, as to feel unable to abstain from forming a collection myself; you may however depend on coming in for a good share, and although my collection may prevent yours from being unique, yet you may rely on the refusal of it, should I ever part with it, and upon my leaving it to you, should I die. In the first instance I have been compelled to launch into considerable expense to establish a name . . .

The establishment of a name involved dislodging Drovetti from his monopoly over the trading in antiquities. Drovetti had established agents at all the principal sites along the Nile Valley, with instructions to discourage all digging that did not have the permission of the French consul. He laid claim to exclusive rights over all the sites which he had visited. Fortunately for Salt, Drovetti had been ordered to transfer to Alexandria shortly before his arrival. This left Salt free to exploit an acquaintance with Muhammad Ali dating back to an earlier visit to Egypt in the company of Lord Valencia. He soon reported that they were getting on famously, that the French influence was at a low ebb, and that, because the Pasha 'will scarcely attend to any other remonstrances but those which I represent . . . the merchants, in all emergencies, apply for my good offices in their favour'; and foreigners who had no consul in Egypt continually applied to him 'to be permitted to rank themselves under our banners'. The

outcome was that the two consuls agreed to divide the spoils between them, Drovetti having the east and Salt the west bank of
the Nile. The explorer Richard Burton was to write: 'Nile-land
was then, as now, a field for plunder; fortunes were made by digging, not for gold, but antiques; and the archaeological field became a battle plain for two armies of Dragomen and Fellah-
navvies. One was headed by the redoubtable Salt; the other
owned the command of Drovetti . . .'

Although Salt was a decade behind Drovetti in entering the
market for antiquities, he was soon to catch up. This was largely
through the efforts of an acquaintance/employee/colleague – the
exact description is unclear, but was to be highly significant – to
whom Salt had given a commission when he had fallen on hard
times, and who became one of the most celebrated figures in the
history of Egyptology: the 'pantomine giant', the 'circus strongman', the 'Patagonian Samson' – Giovanni Battista Belzoni.

Belzoni was born in Padua in 1778, the son of a barber, and
spent his youth in England working in fairs and theatres as an
actor, magician, and strongman. He appeared at Sadler's Wells
in 1803 with Grimaldi, the famous clown, in the rôle of the Giant
killed by Jack and also gave demonstrations of feats of strength.
Less strenuously, and of greater importance in his future career,
Belzoni presented 'aqua-dramas' in theatres near the Thames, in
which model ships did battle with each other in tanks of real
water while coloured fountains played.

In the spring of 1815 Belzoni was staying in Malta with his
wife Sarah and an Irish lad, James Curtin, when he met an agent
of Muhammad Ali called, improbably, Captain Ishmael Gibral-
tar, who was on the lookout for Western technicians to help in
the great plan to modernise Egypt. For millenia the country's
greatest problem had been irrigation, and it suddenly occurred
to Belzoni that he was the man with the solution. Using his background in theatrical hydraulics, Belzoni felt certain he could
design a water-wheel that could be reproduced on a grand scale,
extending the cultivable area of the Nile Valley. He so impressed
the Pasha's agent, that by the following August he was set up in a
Cairo house, in receipt of an allowance from Muhammad Ali of
100 Spanish dollars a month (about twenty-five pounds) and left
to work on his invention.

It was not until the spring of 1816 that Muhammad Ali

attended a demonstration of Belzoni's wheel. Driven by an ox, it worked well, and the Pasha judged that it was four times as good as the old ones. He then asked to see what would happen if the wheel was driven by men. A dozen Arabs, followed by James Curtin, jumped into the drum. As the wheel began to turn, they all jumped out, the weight of the water spinning the drum backwards and throwing Curtin out. He broke a leg. It was a bad omen; the trial had failed.

Belzoni was desperate: his salary was five months in arrears and unlikely to be paid; he had a wife and a boy with a broken leg to look after, and no possible way to earn money. 'So much for the Pasha's encouragement of European artists,' wrote a friend of Belzoni. 'They are enticed into this service by his emissaries in the Mediterranean, but are soon left to bewail their credulity.'

The friend was the Swiss explorer John Lewis Burckhardt, who, having studied Arabic at Cambridge, had travelled widely in the East, dressing as an Arab and using the name Sheih Ibra him. Three years before meeting Belzoni he had been on a visit to Upper Egypt. Spending a few days at Thebes, he had seen an enormous fallen statue lying in the sands in a ruined temple. It had been described by Salt's patron William Hamilton as 'certainly the most beautiful and perfect piece of Egyptian sculpture that can be seen throughout the whole country'. The local peasants told Burckhardt that the French had tried to take it away but could not manage to move it; the head weighed around seven tons and lay in soft sand.

Burckhardt determined to remove the head, and suggested to Salt that together they should meet the expenses of removal and present the piece to the British Museum. For this task Belzoni was the obvious agent.

Belzoni never lacked self-confidence. When he heard of the project to move the statue's head, he decided he was the man for the job: he had immense physical strength, and thought of himself as an engineer, a man who was at home with mechanical contrivances. He needed only money for transport, labour, and equipment. The new consul Henry Salt was clearly the man to approach since he had influence, could raise credit, and was trying to establish himself in the antiquities field.

Salt readily agreed to the project and issued instructions to

Belzoni to get started. Belzoni was to prepare the necessary equipment in Bulaq, then proceed to Asyut where he would deliver a letter of authorisation to Muhammad Ali's son, Ibrahim Pasha, who would furnish him with the necessary labour and boats. Next Belzoni was to proceed to Thebes where he was to 'spare no expense or trouble' in transporting the head to the banks of the Nile, if necessary waiting for the river to rise before attempting to get it into a boat. He was given detailed instructions on how to identify the head, and a warning against mixing it up with another, far inferior, which lay near the site. Finally he was told, 'Mr Belzoni will have the goodness to keep a separate account of the expenses incurred in this undertaking, which, as well as his other expenses, will gladly be reimbursed; as, from the knowledge of Mr Belzoni's character, it is confidently believed they will be as reasonable as circumstances will allow.'

At the time Belzoni seemed happy and grateful enough. He was also given a further 1,000 piastres (about twenty-five pounds) by Salt to buy any other antiquities he should find. He assumed that, as he was engaged by the British consul, these were to be officially acquired and shipped to the British Museum. Somehow the plundering of ancient sites had the colour of respectability when carried on in the interest of a nation rather than for the profit of an individual.

Belzoni went to Bulaq and loaded up the necessary equipment: fourteen squared baulks of timber, four rollers made from the trunks of palm trees and some lengths of palm tree rope. Then he set sail with his wife and James up the Nile in the cheapest boat he could find. He had a Copt interpreter who was fond of the bottle, an armed guard, and a crew of five. He was about to confront for the first time the hazards – natural and manmade – of the antiques business along the Nile Valley.

After five days they reached Manfalut, where they met Ibrahim Pasha on his way down the Nile to Cairo. With him was Drovetti, who had been visiting his agents in Upper Egypt and negotiating the purchase of antiquities to swell his collection. Both men were affable, though Drovetti cannot have been pleased to see his competitor's agent on his way to recover such a prize, and he told Belzoni he had no chance of hiring labour in Thebes. Open opposition, however, was rare between representatives of the two great nations, and there were other means of ensuring the failure of the competition. As a gesture of goodwill Drovetti even presented Belzoni with the granite cover of a sarcophagus that was lying in one of the tombs. He himself had tried, and failed, to get it out. Ibrahim Pasha told Belzoni to present his letter of authority to the Daftardar-Bey who had been left in charge at Asyut, and waved farewell.

The next day Belzoni arrived in Asyut to find the Daftardar-Bey absent. He went to see Dr Scotto, the Genoese physician who attended Ibrahim and who had been recommended to him by Salt as a helpful contact. Dr Scotto was obstructive: others had tried and failed, he said it would be impossible to hire labour; there were no adequate boats; and the statue was no more than a worthless chunk of granite. When Belzoni showed no signs of wilting, the doctor hinted darkly at other dangers: 'At last,' wrote Belzoni, 'he plainly recommended to me not to meddle in this business, for I should meet with many disagreeable things and have many obstacles to encounter.' The good doctor was, of course, in the antiques trade for himself.

When the Daftardar-Bey returned, he issued orders to the governor responsible for the supply of labour to Belzoni. The little boat went on its way and arrived at Luxor exactly three weeks and a day after leaving Cairo.

The party was amazed by the vast expanse of ruins that made Thebes the most extensive outdoor museum in the world; the great temple complexes of Luxor and Karnak that had astonished the French troops, and which even then were beginning to be staked out for excavation by Drovetti's agents. Belzoni records that he had time only to give them a passing glance before he hastened over to the west bank in search of the head.

There it lay in the Ramesseum, the mortuary temple of Ramesses II 'with its face upwards, and apparently smiling at me, at the thought of being taken to England'. The head was in fact from a seated statue of Ramesses II, but the Romans had mistaken it for the legendary hero Memnon, and so it was called then, as now, the Young Memnon.

Belzoni was impressed by the head's beauty but not overawed by its size, and immediately ordered the equipment brought from Cairo to be landed, settling Sarah in a stone hut inside the Ramesseum as a temporary lodging until the work was complete. The carpenter made a platform from the baulk timbers, called a cart, on which the head should ride to the river. Belzoni inspected the route; it was clear that the land between the Ramesseum and the river lay so low that it would be under water when the floods came. Not deep enough to float a boat, but deep enough to prevent his cart from passing. The floods were due in a month, so he had four weeks to get the statue to the river bank, or wait until the following summer. It seemed ample time.

Belzoni went to see the governor with his order for labour and was welcomed. His published account was based on his journals:

> He received me with that invariable politeness which is peculiar to the Turks, even when they do not mean in the slightest degree to comply with your wishes ... The smooth-faced protestations of friendship and partiality for a person whom they never saw before is so common amongst them that at last it becomes a matter of course, and no reliance is placed upon it except by those who are unacquainted with the customs of the country.

Among whom, in July 1816, Belzoni must have been numbered. His resilience might well have been dented by being told that the workers were all busy in the fields until the floods; that their work was for Ibrahim Pasha and could not be interrupted; that the fast of Ramadan was approaching when no one would work; and, finally, that the removal of the head was impossible without the help of Mahomet himself.

The governor, however, declared that he would go to an infinitude of trouble for his new friend to help overcome these immense difficulties, and promised that he would send men the following morning. When they failed to arrive, Belzoni set out to see the governor, equipped this time with presents of gunpowder and coffee. He left with an order to the local Caimakan to supply him with the men he needed. Belzoni's troubles were still not over however because the Caimakan was an agent for a dealer in Cairo, and naturally took it as part of good commercial practice to frustrate all rival collectors. No labour arrived until Belzoni himself went and bribed the men with high wages of 'thirty paras a day, which is fourpence halfpenny English money'. A small group arrived.

The head was levered on to the cart, which had the rollers

positioned underneath so that as it was dragged forward a roller would be released at the back and carried round and placed under the front – a simple technique that was common in ancient times and is still used today. The head lumbered forward across the sands, and Belzoni sent a triumphal message to Cairo to say it was on its way.

They were working in the fiercest of the Egyptian summer heat. After two days Belzoni collapsed and the work halted. He could not eat, but forced himself back to work, directing a group of workers who were forming the road in front of the cart, breaking down obstacles which lay in its path, changing over the groups of men who dragged the cart forward and those who walked beside it with levers to prevent the head from rolling off. After a week they were halfway to the river. But they had reached a dangerously low place, and Belzoni wrote:

> On the 5th we entered the land I was so anxious to pass over
> for fear the water should reach it and arrest our course; and
> I was happy to think that the next day would bring us out of
> danger. Accordingly, I went to the place early in the morning, and to my great surprise, found no-one there except the
> guards and the carpenter who informed me that the Caimakan had given orders to the Fellahs not to work for the
> Christian dogs any longer.

It was a plot. In a few days' time the depression in which the head sat would be covered by the rising Nile, and would have to be abandoned, becoming available for sale to the next enterprising European who should fancy it. The Caimakan had gone to Luxor to await developments. Belzoni records that he sought the man out trying 'to bring him into good humour by smooth words and promises', but failed. It was dawning on him that 'in a country where respect is paid only to the strongest, advantage will always be taken of the weak'. He goes on to record that the man then drew his sword, at which Belzoni picked him up, gave him a good shaking, and left him, taking away his sword and a brace of pistols.

The only possible solution was to win over the governor. Belzoni immediately went to see him and, handing over the pistols as a token of friendship, received the necessary orders for his labour. A week later the head arrived on the bank of the river.

There was one other matter to be settled – the removal of the sarcophagus cover that Drovetti had given him – Belzoni sent out a call for guides to find the tomb in which it lay. He was led to a small cavity in the rocks on the mountainside, and, having taken off most of his clothes, went in through a narrow passage with two Arabs and his interpreter. After crawling for a great distance they came to an open space, off which were several tunnels too small for Belzoni to pass through. He waited with one of the Arabs while his intepreter went on with the other, who insisted that the sarcophagus was close, although it was by then obvious it could not have been brought in by the way they had come. After a while Belzoni heard a crash followed by the sound of his interpreter's voice crying, 'O mon Dieu! Mon dieu! Je suis perdu!', followed by complete silence.

They waited. Belzoni asked the Arab if he knew the cave beyond the darkness, and was told the man had never been in the place before. The best thing seemed to be to return the way they had come and look for help, but on crawling back down through what Belzoni thought was the way in, they came to a dead-end. The candles were getting low, they were surrounded by skulls and human bones, and all the tunnels looked the same. They tried one tunnel after the other, but kept coming back to the same open space.

Finally Belzoni and the Arab found a tunnel that seemed to continue unimpeded for a long distance. On hearing a sound like the roaring of the sea at a great distance, they pressed on identifying the noise as human voices. Bursting out into the sunlight, the first man they saw was the interpreter, who explained that as they had neared the cave where the sarcophagus lay, the Arab with him had fallen into a pit. The Arab had cried out and then seen a light close at hand, and forced his way into the open air. The other Arabs, fearing for the safety of the man who had fallen, quickly cleared the space through which he had passed. Belzoni then realised they had blocked it up in the first place, and taken him through a long rear entrance to the cave so he would be unable to remove the sarcophagus lid until they had been rewarded for 'discovering' the larger entrance. Belzoni set the men to work enlarging the entrance, and retired to his stone hut in the Ramesseum to recover.

Three days later Belzoni returned to find that the governor had visited the site and ordered all his workmen to be bound and flung into jail. Drovetti's agents had been to visit him with presents from Alexandria, and after receiving them the governor had remembered that the sarcophagus lid was unavailable to Belzoni because he had sold it to the French consul.

Belzoni seems to have been unconcerned about his labour, saying only that he would write to Cairo about the sarcophagus, and ordered a boat from Salt to transport the head. He instructed a mud wall to be built around the Young Memnon, and set off up the Nile in search of other portable treasures. After all, Salt was paying for the hire of the boat, and it seemed sensible to keep it in use.

At Esna – the ancient town called Latopolis by the Greeks – Belzoni met Khalil-Bey, brother-in-law of Muhammad Ali, who had just been appointed governor of the Upper Provinces between Esna and Aswan. After reclining a while on a fine carpet and smoking a few pipes and drinking coffee, Belzoni was given a letter of recommendation to a Nubian prince, Hussain Kashif, and sent on his way. Belzoni had time to look over the temple at Esna, which is about 650 feet from the river and in the centre of town. He found it covered in rubbish, and noted that 'it is a great pity that such beautiful edifices should be inhabited by dirty Arabs and their cattle'. He then sailed on to Edfu.

Here, on a site near the river, raised up above the surrounding valley, is the temple of the Ptolemaic period, the most completely preserved in Egypt. Belzoni found it covered in huts and stables, and noticing vast heaps of ruins in the sands around the temple, guessed they might contain valuable antiquities. He went on his way, however, merely clearing away the sands from several sphinxes with 'a lion's body and female head, as large as life'.

At Aswan, where the first cataract interrupts the Nile, it was necessary to hire another boat for the journey on to the island of Philae and as far as the second cataract. This involved serious haggling with the Aga of Aswan, in which Sarah helped by presenting the Aga's two wives with beds and a mirror, and smoking a pipe of tobacco with them. This helped to reduce the boat hire from 120 dollars to 20 for the round-trip.

Belzoni's aim in pressing on to the second cataract was to

reach Abu Simbel where, he had heard from Burckhardt, an enormous temple lay buried beneath the sand. It seemed possible that a buried temple might remain unplundered, and a large one would contain rich pickings. The temple of Ramesses II at Abu Simbel was only partly visible above a mountain of sand, four enormous statues cut out of a wall of rock. If the temple itself matched the statues in size, it would be the greatest in Egypt, and never seen previously by modern man.

When Belzoni landed at Abu Simbel village, he found he had to deal with Dawud Kashif, son of Hussain Kashif, to whom he had a letter of introduction. When asked why he had come to such a remote place, Belzoni replied that he was 'in search of ancient stones'. Dawud laughed; it was a story he had heard before. A man had recently come from Cairo in search of treasure, he said, and had returned with a heap of gold in his boat; surely this was the real reason for the visit? Belzoni's reply was a touch ingenuous: 'I answered, the stones I wished to take away were broken pieces belonging to the old Pharaoh people; and that by these pieces we were in hopes of learning whether our ancestors came from that country which was the reason of my coming in search of ancient stones.' Dawud seemed to accept this as a respectably ingenious evasion of the truth, and went on to ask how Belzoni proposed to persuade the people to work for him since the temples were guarded by the devil. Belzoni's reply that they would be paid in cash only provoked Dawud to ask what could anybody possibly do with cash in Abu Simbel? As an introduction to the people of Abu Simbel of the benefits of a cash economy, Belzoni pointed out that all they need do was send the cash to Aswan, and they could buy the grain they needed for the winter. Dawud responded that if he were foolish enough to send cash to the merchants of Aswan, they would of course keep it and 'forget' to send him the grain. Belzoni was fingering a piastre coin during the discussion, and he handed it to one of the curious crescent of onlookers, saying that he could exchange it for enough grain to last a man for three days. As the man held up the tiny piece of metal the crowd hooted with laughter at the idea that anyone would exchange anything of value for it. Belzoni suggested the man try asking any of the crew on the foreigners' boat. When the man returned with three days' supply of grain, the people were impressed. Of course Belzoni had forewarned the crew.

Belzoni's demonstration had put him ahead of Drovetti, who a few months before had left 300 piastres at Abu Simbel to pay for the temple face to be uncovered, only to be handed back his money on his return trip and told the workers could find no use for it.

The work began slowly, forty men laboriously raking back the sand and erecting palisades of brushwood to prevent more pouring in from above; it was, as Belzoni wrote, rather like trying to make a hole in water. After a week they had uncovered at a depth of twenty feet the figure of the hawk-headed Re-Harakhty in the centre of the façade. Belzoni poured some water close to the wall over the place where he thought the door must be, which compacted the sand just enough to allow him to bore a deep hole to find the opening. He decided, however, that it would take more time to complete the work than he had available. He also had another problem: 'the want of that very article which, a few days before, was so despised and unknown; and now I absolutely could not proceed without it. It was money, which even here had shown its usual power among mankind of exciting avarice and of which those wild people soon became very fond.'

Belzoni decided to postpone the work, and in return for a few presents, having extracted from Dawud a promise not to allow anybody else near the work, he marked the level on the temple face to which they had cleared, and set sail down river. At Philae Belzoni went in search of anything he could load up to take with him to Cairo. There was an obelisk, twenty-two feet long and two feet wide at the base that was close enough to the water to be removable. It required a bigger boat, however, so Belzoni 'took possession' of it 'in the name of his Britannic Majesty's consul-general in Cairo', and gave the Aga four dollars to post a guard on it until he should return. The Aga not unreasonably asked what he was to be paid for giving his permission to remove the obelisk. Belzoni hesitated: 'Although I was authorised by the firman of the Bashaw to take what stones or statues I pleased, yet these fellows think they have a right to demand something, and if they cannot openly refuse, yet they have it in their power to throw such obstacles in the way as to entirely defeat your undertaking.' So he promised that the Aga would receive 300 piastres once the obelisk had been shipped successfully.

There was also on the island a beautiful series of carved blocks representing the god Osiris receiving gifts from priests and female figures. The blocks were three-and-a-half feet long and three feet wide, but were too bulky for easy transportation because they were too thick. Belzoni left money and orders with the Aga to have them cut down to a manageable thickness and shipped to Luxor by the next boat.

There were problems getting away from Aswan, the Aga having ordered that all boats be hidden so as to extract as much money as possible for the hire of his own. Eventually Belzoni and his party arrived at Luxor to find money from Salt, but no news of a boat for the head of Young Memnon. Fortunately, a large boat had just arrived from Cairo, carrying two of Drovetti's agents en route for Aswan: Jean Jacques Rifaud, a sculptor from Marseilles and enthusiastic collector, and Frédéric Caillaud, mineralogist and jeweller from Nantes. They were well placed to undermine Belzoni's confidence in his own artistic judgement and lost no time doing so. The two inspected the Young Memnon without enthusiasm, and taunted Belzoni for having wasted his money and energy on a useless piece of granite: the only reason the French had left it behind, they said, was because it was not worth carrying away. Less subtly, they assembled the local Arabs and announced that anyone who sold antiques to the English or to their agents would be beaten, by order of the local katcheff. To press the point further, their dragoman took Belzoni to one side and confided to him that if he did not stop his excavations, his throat would quite certainly be cut.

Belzoni was able to turn this dispiriting visit to his advantage by negotiating with the owners of the boat to return to Luxor from Aswan to collect the head, and to bring back the stone slabs that he had left in the care of the Aga. Because of the great weight of the head, and no doubt because of the absence of competition, the owners drove a hard bargain, insisting on a payment of 3,000 piastres (about seventy-five pounds) – for the charter, half to be paid in advance. Belzoni paid. He then returned to Karnak, where he had left twenty men busily turning over the compacted soil that had not recently been dug. They unearthed eighteen lion-headed statues of the goddess Sekhmet, six of which were perfect. Among them was a white statue of Jupiter Ammon. Belzoni transported the best of these to Luxor, planning to load them on to the boat with the stone slabs from Aswan.

There were no stone slabs on board when the boat tied up at Luxor; only dates. The owners had been convinced by Drovetti's agents of the riskiness of doing business with the British, and offered Belzoni his money back. The Nile was already sinking; no other boat was available. If Belzoni missed his opportunity Young Memnon would stay on the bank of the river until the following year. He decided to appeal to Khalil-Bey and ask that the boat owners be forced to honour their agreement; he had no great hopes of success since Khalil had already told him that no boat would withstand the great weight of the head. The day was saved by two small bottles of anchovies and two bottles of olives, without which the fine statue would not be in the British Museum today.

These objects had arrived at Luxor as presents for Khalil-Bey just as Belzoni was preparing to visit to ask for justice. The messenger who brought them confided in Belzoni that they had put the Bey into a terrible rage, who had received them as a present from Drovetti. The Bey had been so insulted to receive such an insignificant gift – worthy only to be passed on to another foreigner – that his dander was up against all things French. Belzoni was determined, as he wrote, to 'strike while his mind was hot', and set off immediately with the two boat owners to ask for fulfillment of his contract. He found the Bey still agreeably francophobic, and was given the judgement he sought.

One-hundred-and-thirty labourers were employed in loading the head. The deck of the boat was eighteen feet below the bank, and Belzoni formed a sloping bridge from the bank to the centre of the boat with four palm-tree poles to slide the seven tons of granite. The head was strapped to its cart of timber baulks, and restrained by ropes belayed around posts driven into the bank. A cushion of mats and straw was heaped at the foot of the bridge ready to receive the weight. A sack of sand was slung across the bridge to break the fall of the head should the ropes, or the labourers, give way.

As the great block inched its way down the ramp the owners moaned quietly, resigned to the loss of their boat, and onlookers debated whether the head would smash through the boat's timbers and sink, or settle safely on board before carrying the boat to the bottom of the river. Belzoni knew that if the head were to be lost here it could never be recovered. But the head slid smoothly down and settled on the deck; the boat rocked and remained afloat, and the owners rushed up to Belzoni and shook his hand. When they set out for Cairo three days later they carried the finest cargo of archaeological treasures to sail down the Nile in modern times.

Belzoni received 100 pounds for his efforts: Salt and Burckhardt each gave him twenty-five pounds for Young Memnon; Salt added fifty pounds of his own money, and feeling, perhaps, that this was a little inadequate, allowed Belzoni to keep two of the lion-headed statues. The rest were housed in the consulate, and Belzoni was instructed to take the head down to Alexandria to await shipment to England. He writes that he was surprised at the distinction made between the antiquities, since he believed himself engaged to collect for the British Museum. Salt, however, seemed to be thinking of them as his disposable property. Interestingly, Burckhardt took the same view. Having inspected the collection, he wrote to Salt at the time that 'Mr Belzoni has succeeded beyond the most sanguine hopes you could entertain, and has certainly done his best to execute the commission in full. He has brought, besides the head, seven statues which will be a most valuable ornament to your future gallery.'

As for the ultimate destination or ownership of the treasures, Belzoni seemed only concerned with returning to Abu Simbel and completing the excavation of the great temple before anyone could break in. He did, however, make one condition of his future relationship with Salt that was more significant than Salt understood: if he succeeded at Abu Simbel he would be given an official letter of introduction to the Society of Antiquaries in London. In return for his discoveries, Belzoni was seeking recognition as a gentleman and a scholar in the model of his friend Burckhardt – rather than the prospect of hard cash that was to draw so many gentlemen and scholars after him to the Nile Valley.

On the return trip to Abu Simbel Belzoni had for company Salt's private secretary, a young man called Henry Beechey, and a Greek interpreter employed at the consulate, Yanni Athanasi. No doubt Salt felt that someone he could trust should keep an eye on Belzoni, who had an unsettling tendency to demonstrate his initiative in grandiose and expensive projects. Beechey seems to have been sent as a moderating influence on Belzoni, and a reliable source of information for Salt. He also controlled the purse strings. Belzoni was happy enough to have him along.

The party was making slow progress against a strong southerly wind when they heard that two of Drovetti's agents were making a forced march to Karnak to get there ahead of them. Belzoni knew that the area he had excavated contained other treasures, and that he would lose them if he were not there to defend them. He set out with Yanni on donkey, horse, and camel across the desert, travelling 280 miles in five-and-a-half days. He was too late. The Daftardar-Bey had already ordered the area to be dug over on the pretext that he was thinking of forming a collection for himself. When Drovetti's agents arrived, they took over the work. They even engaged all the available labour at Karnak so Belzoni could do nothing but go in search of the boat that was labouring upstream with Beechey and the money. Belzoni decided to leave the French at Karnak and to concentrate on digging among the tombs on the west side of the river.

The east bank of the river, with its temple complexes of Luxor and Karnak, is known as 'Thebes of the living', and the west bank is known as 'Thebes of the dead'. On the west bank are the remains of temples stretching over five miles. They are mostly royal mortuary temples of the New Kingdom, maintaining the cults of the kings buried in tombs cut into the cliffs further to the west. William Hamilton had found ten accessible tombs here at the beginning of the century, and thought there must be many others buried under the sands and stones.

Belzoni began his search in a remote western part of the Valley of the Kings, beyond the tomb of Amenophis III, which the French had discovered. For a man of Belzoni's bulk, working in narrow underground tunnels packed with crumbling mummies had a particular horror, which he vividly conveys in his memoirs:

A vast quantity of dust rises, so fine that it enters into the throat and nostrils and chokes the nose and mouth to such a degree that it requires great power of lungs to resist it and the strong effluvia of the mummies . . . The blackness of the wall, the faint light given by the candles or torches for want of air, the different objects that surrounded me, seeming to converse with each other, and the Arabs, with the candles or torches in their hands, naked and covered with dust, themselves resembling living mummies absolutely formed a scene that cannot be described.

On one occasion at Qurna he arrived exhausted at the end of a long narrow passage to find a space in which he could pause:

I sought a resting place, and found one, and contrived to sit; but when my weight bore on the body of an Egyptian, it crushed it like a band box. I naturally had recourse to my hands to sustain my weight, but they found no better support; so that I sunk together among the broken mummies, with a crash of bones, rags and wooden cases, which raised such a dust as kept me motionless for a quarter of an hour, waiting till it subsided again. I could not remove from the place, however, without increasing it and every step I took I crushed a mummy in some part or other. Once I was conducted from such a place to another resembling it, through a passage of about twenty feet in length, and no wider than a body could be forced through. It was choked with mummies, and I could not pass without putting my face in contact with some decayed Egyptian; but as the passage inclined downwards, my own weight helped me on; however, I could not avoid being covered with bones, legs, arms and heads rolling from above.

By the end of April Belzoni had a pile of treasures at Luxor large enough to make up a second cargo. He had added to Drovetti's gift of the sarcophagus lid a large red granite head and arm from an enormous statue of Thothmes III at Karnak, four more lion-headed statues of Sekhmet, and a solid stone pedestal from the temple of Montu at Karnak, carved with the linked figures of Hathor, Montu, and Thothmes III.

Then an unwelcome visitor arrived. The Daftardar-Bey had heard from Drovetti's agents about Belzoni's progress, and felt obliged to demonstrate that their protection money was not being wasted by having the sheik who had supplied labour to Belzoni beaten unconscious. When Belzoni threatened to write

to Cairo to tell the Pasha how his son-in-law was responding to
the firman issued by his own hand, the Daftardar seemed to re-
lent, and issued what he claimed was an authority for Belzoni to
employ labour at Qurna. The people were assembled to hear the
orders of the Daftardar read out publicly. To his astonishment,
Belzoni heard a proclamation forbidding them to work for, or
supply antiques to, the English, and commanding them to co-
operate only with Drovetti or his agents.

It seemed time to call on help from Cairo. Beechey wrote immediately to Salt telling him what had happened, and demanded
reparations for the insult to British subjects travelling under the
protection of a firman issued at the request of the British consul.
Salt's reply is highly significant. He reported that he had seen
the Pasha, who would write to Daftardar-Bey, and make sure
that he never behaved in this way again; but he went on:

> I wish you, however, clearly to understand that I do not
> agree with you in considering this to be a national insult, or
> as having anything to do with my Consular character. You
> must be aware that neither yourself nor Mr Belzoni are at
> present engaged in my official employ; you are simply in the
> same situation as two travellers forming a collection; and
> are therefore only entitled to such reparation as any English
> gentleman would have a right to expect. It is absolutely
> necessary that this should be explicitly understood, for, as
> you know, I have no authority from government for
> employing any person in such pursuits, and that I am bear-
> ing the whole expense and collecting for myself, you can
> only be considered as acting in a private capacity.

It is possible that Beechey kept this part of the letter quiet
because Belzoni seemed most highly motivated when he thought
of himself as the official representative of the greatest nation on
earth, charged with the duty of collecting for its national repository – the British Museum. It is unlikely that the consular
secretary permitted himself to be on intimate terms with an un-
educated ex-circus performer, and indeed confided in Salt's
biographer that 'Belzoni was of so suspicious and dissatisfied a
disposition that it was in some respects difficult to keep on any
terms with him.' Beechey and Belzoni both knew they enjoyed

the protection of the British consul's name, that permission to travel and to excavate had been given because of Beechey's official status, and perhaps neither took very seriously the claim that they were exploring the temples and tombs of the Nile Valley simply to gratify the whim of Mr Henry Salt.

There was no point staying at Luxor confronted by an actively opposed Daftardar, and Belzoni decided to head up river, while waiting for a reply from Cairo, to collect the carved stone slabs he had left at Philae Island under the care of the Aga. He found them where he had stacked them – but they had all been defaced and broken. Someone had scrawled in charcoal the words *'operation manqué'*. Drovetti's agents, having prevented the transportation of the slabs as arranged, had made sure they would not be worth transporting in future.

There were, however, compensations on the island. A letter arrived from Salt that contained money and an agreement that Belzoni should use it to try and open the great temple at Abu Simbel. At the same time, a boat arrived carrying the Hon. Charles Leonard Irby and James Mangles, both captains in the Royal Navy. They were delighted to join Belzoni, who readily agreed, insisting only on pausing at Philae to celebrate the 4th of June, King George III's birthday. His Majesty would have approved of the proceedings. An old flag was found and planted on the highest point on the island. Precisely at midday the four men assembled and fired off a twenty-one-gun salute. The ceremony was repeated that night, to the terror and amazement of the Arabs, who could not understand why so much gun-powder should be used without killing anyone.

At Abu Simbel there were the usual problems over the hire of labour. Two Kashif brothers were in command, Dawud and Khalil. Belzoni sparked off a bout of sibling rivalry by handing his presents to Dawud. Khalil went into a sulk and hid in his hut, only agreeing to come to supper when he had been offered the gift of a gun plus powder and ball. The labourers were eventually organised, but worked so slowly that Belzoni decided to try using them on piece work. He said he would pay 300 piastres to have the door cleared, and 100 men set to work, driven on by Dawud and Khalil. As the job was estimated to take three days, Belzoni made a part payment when the work began, and completed the payment on the third day, when the workers remembered that Ramadan was about to begin, and no work was permitted. The job was unfinished; the money was irrecoverable.

The infidel Christians, however, were not bound by Ramadan. The two naval captains rose before dawn next day and with Belzoni, Beechey, Yanni the Greek interpreter, and the janissary climbed the hill to the temple face. They put in two-and-a-half hours digging before the sun grew too hot. In the evening they started again. For a fortnight the small party worked steadily at the sands, sometimes helped by the crews of the boats or joined by parties of local villagers.

When the top corner of a doorway appeared, Belzoni had palm trunks driven into the sand around it and poured water and mud down to prevent the fine sand from filtering through. They then continued to dig inside this fence, and by dusk of the following day had uncovered the opening. It was too dark to see inside, and the air escaping through the hole was foul, so Belzoni decided to wait until the following morning before entering the temple.

Just before dawn the party climbed the slope and began work to enlarge the hole. The crew stayed in bed. As daylight began to creep up the eastern sky, there was a commotion on the boat, and the captain rushed up the slope shouting that they must set sail immediately – if the foreigners did not get on board they would be left behind. Belzoni and his party were too engrossed in their work to take any notice, and and the crew knelt in a group and began to howl and throw sand over their heads. They had been ordered by Dawud and Khalil to distract the foreigners should they succeed in uncovering the door. The digging party ignored them, and one by one squeezed through the opening.

They found themselves in an enormous hall over fifty feet long and wide and thirty feet high. On each side were four squared pillars carved into the form of Osiris and the walls were richly decorated with hieroglyphics and battle-scenes. At the end of the hall a small chamber opened into the antechamber of the sanctuary in which the rays of the rising sun lit the seated figures of the gods.

The visitors were stunned by the buried grandeur they had uncovered. Belzoni, however, was not engaged to make discoveries but to remove valuable antiquities; in this Abu Simbel was a disappointment. He records that he found only 'two lions with hawks' heads, the body as large as life; a small sitting figure, and some copper work belonging to the doors'. Both Mangles and Belzoni made sketches, but the heat inside the temple was too great and they accordingly 'left this operation to succeeding travellers, who may set about it with more convenience than we could, as the place will become cooler'. As their provisions were low – they had eaten nothing for six days but grain boiled in water without salt – they decided to load the statues and head back to Luxor.

Belzoni decided that the most likely place to pick up a cargo was in the region of Thebes. On his arrival there he was frustrated to discover that the French had taken over the whole area on the east bank and were busily digging over the temples in both Luxor and Karnak. No labour was available, so Belzoni went over to the west bank and again began to search for undiscovered tombs in the Valley of the Kings. He claims that by this time he had an eye for signs that suggested a buried tomb, and certainly either skill or luck must have been operating from the beginning, because within three days he had discovered as many tombs. While beautifully decorated they yielded little in the way of spoils, apart from an earthenware jar and, in the tomb of Ramesses I, a life-sized wooden statue of the Pharaoh with a damaged nose. On unwrapping one of the mummies in search of undiscovered trifles Belzoni noticed that new wraps had been placed over the old, proving that the ancient Egyptians cared for their dead for many years; but there were no jewels, and few papyri.

About fifty feet from the tomb of Ramesses I was a slight depression at the foot of a steep hill, down which torrents of water poured when the rains came to Thebes. Belzoni decided to dig at this spot, despite the men pointing out that nobody would build a tomb at the foot of a torrent. Within two days they had uncovered a small entrance at a depth of eighteen feet. Belzoni squeezed through, and found himself in a corridor thirty-six feet long and eight feet high, that had beautiful paintings and carved hieroglyphics on the walls and ceiling. At the end of the corridor a flight of stairs led to another corridor, also finely decorated. Belzoni knew he was in the tomb of a great king. The second corridor, however, was interrupted by a great pit, thirty feet deep and fourteen feet wide, that stretched from wall to wall. On the other side of the pit he could see what looked like a wall of solid rock. It was in fact built of plaster and stone, and had been decorated like the surrounding rock to deceive earlier tomb robbers, but had failed to do so, as most false walls did. Across the pit Belzoni could see a hole broken through the wall and noticed that the palm ropes that had been used by the robbers to let themselves down and out of the pit had been left in place. They crumbled to dust as he touched them.

The next day they bridged the pit with a couple of beams, and Belzoni was able to enlarge the hole in the wall and climb through. He discovered a series of rooms more superbly decorated than any tomb so far unearthed in the Valley of the Kings. It was the sepulchre of Sethos I, father of Ramesses II, who had built the great hypostyle hall at Karnak, and the temples at Abydos and Qurna. Nothing could surpass the beauty and the preservation of the place. At its heart he found an awesomely lovely object, which, he wrote:

> ... merits the most particular attention, not having its equal in the world, and being such as we had no idea could exist. It is a sarcophagus of the finest oriental alabaster, nine feet five inches long and three feet seven inches wide. Its thickness is only two inches and it is transparent when a light is placed on the inside of it. It is minutely sculptured within and without with several hundred figures which do not exceed two inches in height ... I cannot give an adequate idea of this beautiful and valuable piece of antiquity, and can only say that nothing had been brought into Europe from Egypt that can be compared with it.

Before Belzoni was to succeed in bringing the sarcophagus to its final resting place in central London, it was to become the focus of all that is distasteful about the early days of Egyptology.

Before Belzoni's party had time to record details of all they had found, they had their first distinguished visitor to the site. Arabs from the mountains rushed into the camp saying they had seen a great company of Turkish horsemen galloping towards the valley. Belzoni was alarmed because the Turks tended to avoid the place. Half-an-hour later he heard gunfire echoing between the hills, and decided the place was to be stormed, just as a troop of armed cavalry rode into view.

The troops were escorting Hamid Aga, the commander of the eastern side of Thebes, who had heard of the new discovery and had come to view the treasures. He greeted Belzoni very cordially, and accepted the offer of a tour of the tomb with enthusiasm. Torches were mustered, and Belzoni led his guest along the beautifully decorated passages and through rooms rich with carvings and glowing colours. The Aga seemed distracted and unimpressed. His men followed, searching every hole and corner. Eventually they reached the centre and the still, white beauty of the sarcophagus. The Aga sat down in front of it, sent his men away, and asked Belzoni in great confidence if he could see 'the treasure'. When Belzoni replied that he had seen them all, the Aga answered that he had been told they had discovered a large golden cock, filled with diamonds and pearls, and he demanded to see it. The golden cock was part of Arabian folklore, and was as likely to turn up in an undiscovered tomb as a crock of gold at the foot of a rainbow. When the Aga finally was convinced that Belzoni had not found the cock, he swept out in frustration. Trying to improve his humour, Belzoni followed and asked the Aga what he thought of all the beautiful paintings, to which the Aga replied that it would be a good place for a harem, as the women would have something to look at all day. And he left.

The next visitors to arrive were more aesthetically finely tuned. Henry Salt arrived with three large boats containing everything an aspiring diplomat could wish: the Earl and Countess of Belmont, his cousin Juliana, the two sons, Lord Corry and the Hon. Henry Corry, and the Earl's brother, Captain Armar Lowry Corry, RN. The party's souls were in the care of the Earl's private chaplain, the Rev. Mr Lowry, and their bodies in that of his physician Dr Robert Richardson. They all paraded around the tomb and made agreeably astonished comments. Belzoni seems to have been well pleased with the visit, recording that Salt was so enraptured with the sarcophagus that he spent the next four months digging in the area with no results or, to use Belzoni's light irony, 'what he has found he will of course describe himself with more minuteness than I could do.' There is no hint in Belzoni's record of any friction between them.

Salt noted, however, that shortly after the departure of the Earl's party, Belzoni began to address him 'in a rather ambiguous style on the subject of payment'. It seems likely that Salt, wishing to impress, had been careful to define his relationship with Belzoni as that of master and servant. He would certainly not wish it to be thought that Belzoni was a colleague. No doubt Belzoni became aware of this and was offended. He asked Salt to clarify their relationship, and especially to come to an agreement on how much he was to be paid. Salt replied that he had thought of paying Belzoni an allowance of 300 to 500 piastres a month, independent of his expenses, but Belzoni's successes had so far exceeded expectations that second thoughts were clearly called for. What those thoughts were likely to result in, Salt felt unable to forecast, as he had laid out large sums and received nothing in return – but he would give the matter subsequent attention. Not unsurprisingly, Belzoni did not find this satisfactory, and returned to the subject the following day, when Salt promised him 1,000 piastres (about twenty-five pounds) a month, backdated to the time Belzoni had left Alexandria, and 'that I would besides cede to him any articles I might be able to spare which might prove advantageous to him . . . and that he might be assured I would give him other satisfactory proofs of my regard'. It was an arrangement that might have suited an aspiring consular clerk. Salt's claim that Belzoni seemed satisfied is probably due less to dishonesty than to insensitivity. Belzoni's satisfaction was to be short-lived.

A few days later Beechey arrived with another party of English travellers, and Salt, while showing them over the tomb, casually referred to the number of years Belzoni had been 'in his employ'. Belzoni exploded with resentment, telling the astonished group he had never been employed by Salt; that he worked for the British nation; that he was a man of independent means and would give his services to the nation without charge.

What Belzoni resented was Salt's consistent claim to the glory of the discoveries simply because he had funded them. But Belzoni had made the discoveries, and his name should be honoured with them. He refused the status of paid and unremembered employee. Salt, on the other hand, was encouraged by the English party to believe he was acting perfectly reasonably, even generously. After all, Belzoni was merely risking his neck; Salt was venturing his capital.

Since there was no bond of sympathy between Salt and Belzoni – each considering his behaviour perfectly reasonable while the other found it intolerable – it seemed a good idea to formalise the relationship. Accordingly the two men signed an agreement on 20 April 1818 that seemed to clarify matters:

> Whereas it appears that some erroneous ideas had been entertained by Sig. Giovanni Baptista Belzoni, with respect to the objects collected under the auspices and at the expense of Henry Salt Esq., in Upper Egypt as being intended for the British Museum; and whereas it has since been satisfactorily explained to Sig. Belzoni that such ideas were altogether founded on a mistake . . .

The preamble of the agreement made it clear that each party was acting on his own; the provisions went on to specify that Salt would pay the sum of 500 pounds to Belzoni within the following twelve months; that Salt would give Belzoni a lion-headed statue in the consulate yard; that Salt conceded to Belzoni the sarcophagus cover given to him by Drovetti, and such other objects as he may be able to spare; and that the alabaster sarcophagus should be offered to the British Museum within three years of the date of the agreement at a fair valuation: 'Sig Belzoni shall be considered as entitled to one half of the surplus of whatever price may be paid for the said sarcophagus exceeding the sum of two thousand pounds sterling.' In return Belzoni undertook to go to Thebes and collect the two sarcophagi remaining there 'under the auspices of' and 'at the expense of' Henry Salt, but not in his employ.

The money was still being provided by Salt, and by this time he was making inroads into a legacy of 5,000 pounds that had come to him on his father's death the previous year. Although he insisted on the right to dispose of the antiquities, having paid for their recovery and transport, Salt had no doubts as to their final destination. With the exception of the pieces he sent to sweeten his patrons, the Henry Salt collection was destined for the British Museum. He had no doubt that he would be adequately recognised and amply rewarded by that great national institution.

Chapter Three

'For Publick Use to all Posterity'

WHEN THE PRINCE AND PRINCESS OF WALES visited the Manor House, Chelsea, in June 1748, they were shown round by the owner, an eccentric and infirm elderly gentleman confined to a three-wheeled bathchair. Dutifully they admired a roomful of dried plant specimens, and wandered uncomprehendingly past lines of cabinets crammed with precious stones, strange fishes, stuffed birds, gold and silver medals, and unidentifiable objects of curiosity. The catalogue to this immense collection ran to forty volumes in folio; there was also a library of rare books extending to over 42,000 volumes. Prince Frederick 'expressed the great pleasure it gave him to see so magnificent a collection in England', adding that 'it must conduce to the benefit of learning . . . to have it established for public use to the latest posterity.'

The owner of the collection, Sir Hans Sloane, agreed. He had already made his will, expressing the wish that his collections,

> . . . tending many ways to the manifestation of the glory of God, the confutation of Atheism and its consequences, the use and improvement of physic, and other arts and sciences, and benefit of mankind may remain together . . . and that chiefly in and about the city of London . . . they may by the great confluence of people be of most use . . . and be seen by all persons desirous of seeing and viewing the same . . .

Sir Hans had led a full life as doctor to Royalty and the affluent classes in London. He was the first man to be granted a hereditary title for his services to medicine, and, living to the age of ninety-three, had been granted both the time and the money to indulge his great passion – collecting.

Sir Hans' will provided that after his death his collection should remain intact and be offered to the King for a token sum of 20,000 pounds. Should His Majesty decline, the offer would be passed on to Parliament. George II, the last British monarch to lead his troops into battle, was, like his father, not fond of 'boetry and bainting', and decided he could find better uses for his money; but Parliament, despite opposition from the Prime Minister, accepted its duty to form a national collection. The British Museum was born.

It was intended from the first to be an institution with the highest prestige: its official trustees, stipulated by Act of Parliament on 7 June 1753, included the Archbishop of Canterbury; the Lord Chancellor and the Speaker of the House of Commons as Principal Trustees; aided by the First Lord of the Treasury (the Prime Minister); the Lord Privy Seal; the First Lord of the Admiralty; the Lord Chamberlain, the Bishop of London; the Chancellor of the Exchequer; the Lord Chief Justice of England; the Master of the Rolls; the Attorney General, and the president of the Royal Society. In other words, the nation's museum was entrusted to the same administration as the nation itself. Later, the presidents of the Royal Academy of Arts and the Society of Antiquaries were added.

When Mrs Delaney, niece of Lord Lansdowne, who liked to keep in touch with events, heard of Sir Hans' will she first said how disappointed she was to miss the fun of an auction, but then added, 'I hope the King will . . . build a museum such as a King should have.' Four architects rapidly produced four designs – one Rococo and three Palladian – but from the start the distinguished trustees were circumspect in the use of public funds, and decided it would be cheaper to convert an existing building. Since by law the Museum had to be 'one General Repository', to remain 'for publick Use to all Posterity', they were looking for something capacious and lasting. They turned down the offer of Buckingham House, ancestor of Buckingham Palace, for 50,000 pounds as being too expensive and bought instead Montagu

House in Bloomsbury from the Earl of Halifax for a modest 10,250 pounds.

To Montagu House, now the British Museum, were brought the first Egyptian antiquities to be purchased on behalf of the nation and placed on show. They were small objects – figures of gods in bronze, stone, terracotta, and glazed composition; amulets, a few scarabs – such as might have been found in the bazaars of Cairo and Alexandria and ending up in the cabinets of Sir Hans Sloane.

In 1756, the British Museum acquired its first mummy and coffin, the bequest of Colonel William Lethieullier. The trustees were pleased to accept a further donation of exhibits, which included a second mummy and coffin together with a 'pelican of the wilderness'.

The items were all placed on exhibition in the elegant upper rooms of the Museum. When the antiquities taken from Bonaparte's savants arrived in 1802, however, including stone objects weighing several tons, it was obvious the floor would not support them and they were housed in temporary sheds in the garden. When the trustees decided to purchase the Townley Marbles – Greek and Roman antiquities that had been on view at a private gallery in Mayfair – they were inspired to construct a new wing on the north-west corner of Montagu House. The Townley Gallery, opened on 3 June 1808, became the home of groups of classically naked figures – and also some of the larger pieces of the Egyptian collection.

It was to enhance the Egyptian collection that Sir Joseph Banks, president of the Royal Society and ex-officio trustee of the British Museum, had urged Henry Salt to extend himself. With such influential backing, Salt had felt secure using his own funds to finance Belzoni's operations, and had no doubt he would be adequately recompensed. Salt, however, waited in vain for an official expression of gratitude for the head of Young Memnon, which he and Burkhardt had sent as a gift to the British Museum, expecting at the very least a letter of thanks from the Foreign Secretary, Lord Castlereagh. There was a long silence. He did not even hear whether the head had arrived safely. Though disappointed, he was not deflected from his purpose by what he no doubt put down to a bureaucratic oversight.

Salt thought of himself as engaged in a nationalistic struggle to maintain the interests of his country in Egypt against those of the French. Drovetti had plundered the Nile Valley in search of the finest treasures for the museums of France; he had been encouraged and honoured by official visitors and in the writings of French travellers for his great services to his country. Salt had taken the war to the enemy's camp. He had managed to restrict French activities; he had taken over the east bank of the Nile. Through the agency of Belzoni he had recovered Young Memnon, opened the great temple at Abu Simbel, and discovered the finest tomb in the Valley of the Kings. He had sent gifts to the British Museum, honouring his promise to one of its most distinguished trustees; he had used up his own capital, and made serious inroads into the 5,000 pounds he had been left by his father in excavations in Upper Egypt. In 1818, when Salt first heard the disturbing news that the trustees were disinclined to take any more antiquities from Egypt, a large collection stood in the grounds of the consulate in Cairo, and many pieces still lay by their sites in Upper Egypt, needing funds for transport.

It was too late for Salt to stop. Indeed, it was at this time that he increased Belzoni's allowance to keep him working. At a distance no doubt Salt thought the report he had received indicating a change of heart might be mistaken or exaggerated, and he wrote to his friend and patron William Hamilton, then Under-Secretary of State for Foreign Affairs, for advice. Salt pointed out that he had spent so much of his own capital that unless he could dispose of the collection at a satisfactory price he would never be able to retire to England: 'I must be for ever condemned to remain here, which you will allow is no very desirable lot, since saving out of my salary is totally out of the question, so long as a due regard is paid to keeping up the respectability of the consulate.' He told Hamilton that he had for disposal 'two king's statues, as large as life, in wood, such as Herodotus testifies were placed in their tombs; and also some cows, and other animals' heads and small figures . . .' Salt went on to make what was probably his first mistake, claiming that his statues threw light on the sculpture of the Egyptians, and 'prove their claim to great excellence in the art, and which satisfactorily demonstrate that the Greeks borrowed the rudiments, if not more, from this extraordinary people'.

Although Hamilton was sympathetic to Egyptian antiquities,

and had even written one of the first serious works on the subject, he was also deeply involved in classical sculpture, having, as secretary to Lord Elgin, helped negotiate the purchase of the Elgin Marbles. This had caused a minor scandal, not because the Marbles were thought to have been stolen from Greece, but because they were expensive. Public expenditure on Greek sculpture had to be justified, and Hamilton was sensitive to any suggestions that the sculptures might not be unique. The trustees, having pressed for large outlays of funds over the past two years for the Townley Marbles (28,200 pounds) the Elgin Marbles (35,000 pounds), and the Phigalaean Marbles (19,000 pounds) were also vulnerable to any claim that the sculptures did not represent the perfection of human artistic achievement.

Salt then made his second mistake. He wrote to Hamilton stating that the value of his collection was difficult to calculate, but mentioned parenthetically that he had been pressed to sell them to the Count de Forbin for the King of France, but had refused what he knew would be a handsome price because he would be 'sorry to see such articles out of England'. Salt went on to ask for government help in shipping the pieces to England, and said that he would happily accept a valuation by Hamilton himself, or any other persons the government might care to appoint. To assist in the valuation, Salt appended a list of prices he thought might be fair, adding that these were only to be regarded as 'their supposed value; but in this I am likely to be much mistaken, as I do not at all know how such antiquities might sell: indeed, such as these have never been seen in Europe.'

Salt's tentative valuations do not seem unreasonable in hindsight: a colossal head of Thothmes III from Karnak for 500 pounds; an arm to go with it for 50 pounds; two lion-headed statues for 400 pounds; a seated statue of Sethos II from Thebes for 800 pounds. The most valuable item on the list was the sarcophagus from the tomb of Sethos I, and this presented Salt with the greatest problem. It was, he wrote, 'impossible for me to estimate, but I should think between three and four thousand pounds, being in alabaster, of unequalled workmanship'.

Although Salt's letter was written privately to Hamilton, he tactlessly showed it and the list to several of the trustees, including Sir Joseph Banks. Sir Joseph, bruised from the con-

troversy over recent expenditures on Greek sculptures, and perhaps feeling a little guilty that his encouragement of Salt had
landed the Museum with a further claim on its cash, wrote a
crushing letter to Salt:

Dear Sir,
Though in truth we are here much satisfied with the Memnon, and consider it as a chef d'oeuvre of Egyptian sculpture; yet we have not placed that statue among the works of
Fine Art. It stands in the Egyptian Rooms. Whether any
statue that has been found in Egypt can be brought into
competition with the grand works of the Townley Gallery
remains to be proved; unless, however, they really are so,
the prices you have set upon your acquisitions are very unlikely to be realised in Europe.

The idea that a 'chef d'oeuvre' of Egyptian sculpture could not
be regarded as 'Fine Art' did not originate with Sir Joseph
Banks, who was wealthy, influential, and had a small reputation
in the field of natural history, but was hardly an arbiter of taste.
The idea in fact reflected the prejudices of the classically educated leaders of society, particularly those of the trustees of the
British Museum, who were concerned with maintaining the
standards of their institution, and raising those of the public.
The problem confronting the trustees was a familiar one: the
Act that had established the Museum had stipulated that 'free
access . . . be given to all studious and curious persons'. But, as
one trustee noted, 'a general liberty to ordinary people of all
ranks and denominations, is not to be kept within bounds. Many
irregularities will be committed that cannot be prevented by a
few librarians who will soon be insulted by such people, if they
offer to control or contradict them.' An administrative expedient
was introduced to maintain the letter, while contradicting the
spirit, of the law: all visitors had to present themselves at the
porter's lodge and fill in a register of their name and condition
for the scrutiny of the librarians before being issued with a
ticket. As this process could take several weeks, it defeated many
simply by exhausting their patience.
The numbers of applicants increased, however, and the practice of taking parties round at a brisk canter in a breathless half-

hour, during which all conversation was discouraged, was introduced. This prompted a protest from a Birmingham visitor in 1785:

> In about thirty minutes we finished our silent journey through the princely mansion, which could well have taken thirty days. I went out much about as wise as I went in, but with this severe reflection that, for fear of losing my chance, I had abruptly torn myself from three gentlemen with whom I was engaged in an interesting conversation, had lost my breakfast, got wet to the skin, spent half a crown on coach hire, paid two shillings for a ticket, been hackneyed through the rooms with violence . . . I had laid more stress on the British Museum than on anything else which I should see in London. It was the only sight which disgusted me . . .

By 1810 'persons of decent appearance' were permitted to 'tarry in the apartments or Gallery of Antiquities without any limitation of time', and there was a subtle change of emphasis when the trustees stated that their aim was to further 'Science and the Arts', not to gratify 'the curiosity of . . . multitudes . . . in quest of amusement'. In the context of this aim, the Egyptian antiquities constituted a problem: most people sought the amusement and *frisson* of staring at a mummy or a lion-headed lady rather than frigid rows of classical stone statues. It could have been the sheer popularity and curiosity value of the Egyptian antiquities that prejudiced the trustees against them – and perhaps a need to assert the superior artistic merit of the Greek and Roman collections.

It was an unfortunate climate of opinion in which Salt found himself operating; in May 1819 he received a letter from his friend William Hamilton, accompanying that of Sir Joseph Banks and adding:

> I can only unite with Sir Joseph in recommending you not to dig too deep in search of the hidden treasures of Egyptian sculpture, for in these economical times, John Bull may be easily induced to withhold his purse strings, even at the risk of losing the unique monuments which you have

discovered.

Salt was confined to Cairo during a bout of the plague when he received these letters. His hopes of financial security, and perhaps even of honours, were gone. The sudden change of heart from London was all the more galling because it seemed to have been precipitated by Salt's innocent price-guide that he had sent to Hamilton, emphasising that it may well be wide of the mark. In fact, it had been passed from hand to hand among the astonished trustees, and poor Salt was labelled 'a dealer', and 'a second Lord Elgin' because of it. He had lost what he valued even more than his capital: the good opinion of those at home.

There was, however, one possible way to recover his dignity, and Salt immediately took it. On 28 May 1819 he wrote four letters. The first was to Sir Joseph Banks, offering his complete collection to the British Museum without any conditions whatever, expressing merely the hope that the trustees might see fit to reimburse him his expenses, and that his services might not be overlooked by the government. The second letter was to the Right Honourable Charles Yorke, Salt's patron at the Home Office, telling him of the offer, apologising for 'a foolish list' of valuations, and explaining his financial predicament. He had, he wrote, originally taken the appointment as consul-general on the assumption that he would receive, like his predecessor Colonel Misset, a pension at the end of his service. He had since learned that Colonel Misset's pension was attached to his duties as resident, not as consul-general, and had been told he must not build on any such expectation. Since 'there was no chance of saving anything out of my Consular salary, compatibly with what I conceive to be a duty – the keeping up such an establishment as may secure the respectability of my station, and afford the necessary accommodations to travellers of condition', he saw himself as being condemned to the privations of Egypt for life. Despite this appalling prospect, and the relief that could be afforded by selling his collections to the French, Salt wished only to donate them to the British Museum. 'To this step I have not only been led by my own inclination to serve the public, which has overbalanced all selfish considerations in my mind, but from a desire to comply with your wishes . . .' There is no reason to suppose that Salt's patriotism was disingenuous; he was aware, however, that the officials in line for government rewards are those who demonstrate a devotion to the national interest, without hope of receiving them.

The other two letters were to Salt's friends Lord Mountnorris and William Hamilton, informing them of the action he had taken. To William Hamilton he was a little more specific about his hopes. While protesting that 'rather than forfeit Sir Joseph's, Mr Yorke's, or your good opinion, I would certainly give up all the antiquities in the universe', he went on to 'rest thoroughly satisfied in the thought that Government may some day or other remember my services and enable me, by some future arrangement, to spend my latter days in Europe'. To surrender all claim to his collection in the mere hope of future favours was a bold step. Salt, confined to his house while the plague raged around him, could do nothing but await the results.

Meanwhile he was able to settle his affairs with Belzoni, rounding up the 169 pounds he owed him to 200, and adding a few items from his collection he felt he could spare. Salt records that Belzoni 'seemed quite a satisfied man, and expressed a hope in parting that we should continue friends'. For the first time in their relationship the consul must have envied Belzoni, for he was on his way to be lionized in London.

Belzoni's name had been championed in the capital by the *Quarterly Review*, a widely read journal that had publicised his triumphs over the French along the Nile Valley. These stories delighted a readership that enjoyed a waspish treatment of French claims to scholarship in Egypt, from which even the magnificent volumes of the *Description de l'Egypte* were not exempt:

Everyone knows that, with the army of Egypt, the French despatched a little army of savants to celebrate and to settle 'that ancient and fertile country of the Ptolomies', of the entire conquest of which they made no doubt. These ... when driven out of their promised Canaan by British arms, displayed no less diligence in getting up a national trophy in the shape of an enormous book to perpetuate their own and their patron's renown, and which, for the number of square feet in one of its pages, has no parallel in the annals of bookmaking.

The *Quarterly Review* had announced the gift of the head of Young Memnon to the British Museum, saying that through the efforts of Salt and Belzoni the institution was likely to become the richest depository of antiquities in the world. The *Review* had been delighted to publish Salt's comments on Belzoni's superiority over the best of the French: 'In fact, his great talents and uncommon genius for mechanics have enabled him, with singular success . . . to remove colossal fragments which appear, by their own declaration, to have defied the efforts of the able engineers who accompanied the French army.'

In response to the astonishing claim by M. Jomard, editor of the *Journal des Savants*, stating that the French, having made so many sacrifices to unveil the antiquities of Egypt, should be regarded as their real owners, the editor of the *Quarterly Review* opposed the deeds of Belzoni:

> We do not suppose that Mr Belzoni is a man of much education or deep science; but he certainly possesses a deep talent for research and unwearied perseverance . . . From the exertions of such a man, the British Museum is likely to become the first repository in the world for Egyptian Art and Antiquities; and we trust that every possible encouragement will be given to those exertions by rewarding him liberally for what he has done and by promises of future rewards proportioned to the sum of his discoveries.

The founder of the *Quarterly Review* was the publisher John Murray, and so it was naturally to the office of this enthusiast for the exotic that Belzoni took the manuscript of his book, *Narrative of the Operations and Recent Discoveries within the Pyramids, Temples and Tombs, and Excavations in Egypt and Nubia; and of a Journey to the Coast of the Red Sea, in Search of the Ancient Berenice; and Another to the Oasis of Jupiter Ammon*. Murray realised this was an ideal time to publish the book: the head of Young Memnon stood in the British Museum, a striking advertisement for his author, other antiquities were on their way, and Belzoni, who, from his career onstage, was sensitive to the rewards of publicity, planned an eye-catching exhibition in the centre of London.

Egypt was in the public consciousness: the French expedition to the Nile Valley, and the publication of the *Description* had stimulated public interest, sparking off what has been called the 'Egyptian Revival', although some architectural historians claim that interest in Egyptian or mock-Egyptian culture had remained alive in Europe since the early Renaissance. Egypt, however, never caught on as a national fad: it had neither the prestige of the Greek and Roman antiquities, nor the nationalistic overtones of the Gothic style. And yet, even in the 1790s, before Bonaparte set out, a billiard-room had been designed for Cairness House in Aberdeenshire with mock hieroglyphics around the chimney piece, the friezes and doors, and a fireplace built like the entrance of a tomb. During the years of the French occupation in Egypt, before their discoveries had been trumpeted to the world, Thomas Hope had assembled the furniture and decorations for his 'Egyptian Room' at the mansion in Duchess Street, London. Here, visitors were shown a closet or boudoir in which a mantlepiece in the shape of an Egyptian portico stood beneath a tent of cotton drapery; there was an 'Egyptian chair' featuring crouching priests and a winged Isis; a frieze of Egyptian figures, and a mummy in a glass case. Wedgewood was producing a wide range of sphinxes, and canopic jars and vases with Egyptian motifs from the 1770s, and there was a tendency for interior designers to play with combinations of telamoni, stelae, obelisks, sphinxes, and scarabs.

The British involvement in Egypt and highly publicised victories over the French gave a boost to fashions redolent of the mysterious East. In 1807 Robert Southey complained:

At present, as the soldiers from Egypt have brought home with them broken limbs and ophthalmia, they carry an arm in a sling, or walk the streets with a green shade over the eyes. Everything now must be Egyptian: the ladies wear crocodile ornaments and you sit on a sphinx in a room hung round with mummies, and the long black lean-armed long-nosed hieroglyphical men, who are enough to make children afraid to go to bed. The very shopboards must be metamorphosed into the mode, and painted with Egyptian letters, which, as the Egyptians had no letters, you will no doubt conceive must be curious.

When Belzoni set out to launch himself in London, society had been titillated with Egyptian and was ready for more substantial excitations. Belzoni found the ideal location for his exhibition in the Egyptian Hall, Piccadilly, which had a façade said to be based on Denon's drawings of the temple at Dendera. In fact, the lower windows were in the shape of the Step Pyramid, the door was flanked by a pair of chubby and un-Egyptian lotus columns, and above it stood an enormous pair of statues that only the sculptor could identify as being Isis and Osiris. Inside the gallery was supported by columns banded with lotuses, hieroglyphs, and Hathor heads, and the ceiling was decorated with signs of the zodiac.

Inside the Hall Belzoni set up full-size models of two of the chambers in Sethos I's tomb, and a scale-model over fifty feet long of the entire complex. There was also a four-foot-high model of the Second Pyramid in wax, and another that showed the passages and chambers of the interior in a cutaway section. There was another model of the temple at Abu Simbel on a scale of one-to-thirty; around the walls stood statues made of plaster of paris – Osiris, Horus, and the jackal-headed Anubis – with the pharaohs worshipping them and offering gifts, all brightly coloured to re-create the impressions Belzoni had sketched in Egypt. There were as well the genuine antiquities: statues of the lion-headed Sekhmet, mummies, and glass cases filled with smaller objects such as 'vases containing the bowels of mummies', pieces of ancient palm-tree rope, and ancient shoes, papyri, and fragments of tombs, statues and sarcophagi.

The exhibition got off to a promising start: London was filling up in anticipation of the summer Coronation, and the Egyptian Hall was well situated on the south side of Piccadilly opposite the junction with Old Bond Streeet, where the carriages tended to set down and pick up passengers. On opening day of the exhibition, 1 May 1821, 1,900 people paid their half-a-crown admission and crowded through the hall. *The Times* delivered a ponderous judgement in favour:

Every eye, we think, must be gratified by this singular combination and skillful arrangement of objects so new and in themselves so striking . . . The mechanical ingenuity and indefatigable diligence by which Mr Belzoni has been enabled thus to transport to the arena of European con-

troversy the otherwise immoveable excavations of Egypt reflect no less credit upon him as an artist than his sagacity
and success in discovering the subject matter of this extraordinary exhibition has distinguished him above all European travellers in modern times.

The exhibition ran for over a year, and became a fashionable
meeting place where, as Lady Blessington wrote, persons of
quality came 'merely to pass away an hour, or in the expectation
of meeting their acquaintances'. The relics of the Nile also
worked their magic on more sensitive souls, and the poet Horatio
Smith was moved to compose 'An Address to the Mummy in
Belzoni's Exhibition':

And hast thou walked about, (how strange a story!)
In Thebes's streets three thousand years ago,
When the Memnonmium was in all its glory,
And time had not begun to overthrow
Those temples, palaces and piles stupendous,
Of which the very ruins are tremendous.

The poet longs to converse:

Speak! for thou long enough hath acted dummy,
Thou hast a tongue – come, let us hear its tune:
Thou'rt standing on thy legs above ground, Mummy!
Revisiting the glimpses of the Moon.
Not like thin ghosts or disembodied creatures,
But with thy bones and flesh and limbs and features.

But the Mummy refuses to answer:

If the tomb's secrets may not be confessed,
The nature of thy private life unfold:
A heart has throbbed beneath that leathern breast,
And tears adown that dusty cheek have rolled:
Have children climbed those knees and kissed that face?
What was thy name and station, age and race?

During the summer of 1821, while Belzoni was mixing with high society in London, consorting with royalty at the Masonic lodge of which he was a member and dining with Sir Walter Scott at Almack's Assembly Rooms in St James's, his backer, Henry Salt, lay in Cairo reduced to a skeleton by typhus fever. His letter to Sir Joseph Banks remained unanswered, his unconditional offer to the British Museum of the whole of his collection unacknowledged.

On receipt of his explanations of the misunderstanding caused by his valuation list, Salt's friends and patrons in London had rallied round. William Hamilton, Lord Mountnorris, and Charles Yorke all wrote to Banks, urging him to press for acceptance of Salt's offer and for reasonable compensation. Banks was optimistic: although he protested that Salt's apology for the price list did not cover his motivation for sending it in the first place, he said that he would put the matter to the next meeting of the trustees, adding he had little doubt that the offer would be 'instantly accepted'. Banks, however, was by this time seriously ill, and died the following year without receiving a decision.

Henry Salt had found solace of a sort in Egypt. He had long felt a serious absence in his life, which he expressed to Lord Mountnorris in August 1818:

The greatest want, however, which I feel is the society of a wife. My affections are strong and I want objects around me whom I can love. Had I children, I should be happy; but to stagnate thus at a distance from all science, literature, arts, knowledge, delicacy and taste, is a punishment almost sufficient to drive one mad. But think what we will of it the wheel must go round . . .

In October 1819, Salt had at last married. His bride was the sixteen-year-old daughter of Mr Pensa, a reputable merchant of Leghorn, Italy who had brought his family with him when conducting business in Alexandria. Salt met and married the girl there, and immediately fell ill on his wedding day. He had to be transported in the governor's carriage to Rosetta, where he was met by a surgeon from Cairo and taken there to die. The doctors had no hope of his recovery, and only Salt's determination to enjoy a marriage he had so long looked for seems to have pulled him through.

Throughout 1820 Salt's health was poor, and he asked permission to take leave in England to recuperate. Leave was granted in December of that year, but political tensions made it difficult for him to leave his post: Indian ships were blockading ports along the Red Sea, and there were fears of a rupture with Russia. Salt decided to stay in Egypt until international affairs had settled. He spent the little time he had away from his sick-bed cultivating the pasha, and attending, so far as his health allowed, to his marital duties. In November 1820 he wrote to Lord Mountnorris, 'My lady, you will be glad to hear, is in a promising way; she has had one mishap of two months, but has now, I am happy to say, got over the third month.'

Salt also was able to arrange for a cargo of his antiquities to be sent to London. Although still unsure about their ultimate destination, he engaged an agent, Bingham Richards, to house them in the British Museum until he should be able to return to London and settle the matter. In the meantime Salt continued to augment the collection. Laid low again by typhus in the summer of 1821, he decided to head for the cooler air of Aswan accompanied by his interpreter Yanni. There he had a profitable time arranging for the transport of an obelisk for his friend Banks, as well as exploring the tombs around Thebes, where Yanni managed to unearth some previously unnoticed private tombs, including one of a 'royal scribe', which yielded additions to Salt's collection:

> I have got the statue of himself and wife, his colour-stand, pallet and a scarabee, set as a ring, with his name. Yanni has also discovered an Egyptian chair, in fine preservation, like those drawn on the walls of the Kings' tombs. It is inlaid with ivory and ebony, and is of a very handsome form, being put together entirely with wooden pegs instead of nails or other fastening: he has likewise found the fragments of a harp, from which it will be very easy to restore that instrument . . .

These treasures were shipped to the consulate in Cairo, and Salt waited with them until the settlement of the war between Greece and Turkey allowed him to leave the consulate, take them home, and sell them to the British Museum.

Back in London the trustees showed no signs of reaching a conclusion on Salt's offer of his collection when the Turkish frigate *Diana* arrived in the Port of London carrying the loveliest object so far recovered from the Nile Valley: the translucent-white, alabaster sarcophagus from the tomb of Sethos I.

Bingham Richards had instructions from Salt to deliver the sarcophagus to the British Museum. However, before he could even unload it from the *Diana*, Belzoni had arrived to put in a claim. In terms of his agreement with Salt, Belzoni was entitled to one-half of whatever the sarcophagus raised in excess of 2,000 pounds. The three-year period during which the sarcophagus should have been offered to the British Museum had elapsed; Belzoni had a firm offer from France of 3,000 pounds. The British Museum, therefore, was not authorised to receive the sarcophagus unless it matched his offer. Richards was at a loss. He persuaded the agents of the *Diana* to delay unloading, and wrote in all directions for help. William Hamilton replied that he should follow Salt's instructions; Lord Mountnorris pointed out that the sarcophagus had been admitted free of duty because it was intended for the national collection, and if it were sold on to France, duty would be payable probably in excess of the differences between the British Museum valuation and the 3,000 pounds offered to Belzoni. Charles Yorke raised an essential point to which no-one else had made reference, and which Salt seemed inclined to fudge: Salt would never have obtained the sarcophagus were it not for the 'public character with which he had been invested by the British Government and the influence derived from thence on the mind and intentions of the Visir Mohammed Ali'. Because the sarcophagus had been obtained at least in part through the exercise of British official influence, it would not be appropriate to allow it to be exported.

The deciding letter came from Richards' father, to whom Richards had written in anguish, pointing out that if Belzoni had indeed secured an offer of 3,000 pounds, then he might be sued should he pass it on to the British Museum for less. Richards senior took the view that the agreement between Salt and Belzoni was irrelevant, and that even if Belzoni turned up on the wharf carrying 3,000 pounds in cash, it would be wrong to hand over the sarcophagus because this might lay his son open to an auction for damages from the trustees of the British Museum.

Clearly the position of an agent handling the shipment of antiquities was as hazardous as that of the agent who originally dug
for them. Poor Richards bowed to parental advice and sent the
sarcophagus to the British Museum.

Belzoni of course wanted to get his hands on the sarcophagus
in order to add it to his highly successful exhibition at the Egyptian Hall. So keen was he that he wrote to the trustees, offering
to surrender his interest in the sarcophagus if they would let him
exhibit it for twelve – or even six – months. It took the trustees
two months to consider Belzoni's request, and when they finally
did so, they avoided reaching a decision by writing to Salt and
asking what he wanted done.

Salt, in the meantime, was growing anxious. Two years had
passed since he had offered his collection to the British Museum
and there had been no reaction. On 10 May 1822 he wrote to the
trustees repeating his unconditional offer to donate the entire
collection, which had grown in the meantime. Salt made the
point that it had cost him 'upward of £3,000' to put it together;
that he had spent his patrimony on accumulating it and that he
had no other means of support for himself and his family in failing health: 'I have, therefore, to throw myself entirely on your
liberality and shall be perfectly satisfied with whatever you may
determine in my favour.'

This was, of course, pure cant. Salt wrote only a couple of
weeks later to Richards telling him that he had appealed to his
influential friends, Lord Mountnorris, Charles Yorke, and a
trustee, William Bankes, asking them to press for a fair
remuneration for him, and explaining further:

It may be right to tell you in confidence, that I hope to get
four thousand pounds from the Government, or otherwise I
shall feel myself aggrieved. Should it be five thousand, I
shall be highly satisfied. You know, I believe, that I was
offered for the sarcophagus ten thousand dollars (about two
thousand pounds) in Egypt by Mr Drovetti; and the same
offer was repeated to me by a Prussian traveller, Baron
Minutoli, who begged me, should the Government not take
it, to let him have the refusal. In France, I could get at least
double what I have above stated for my Collection, though,
as Mr Yorke observes, 'this is not exactly a fair argument'.

Richards was given power of attorney to act on Salt's behalf, and told the trustees that the sum of 5,000 pounds would be acceptable for the collection and the sarcophagus together. As Belzoni had told them he could get 3,000 pounds for the sarcophagus alone, simple arithmetic decided the trustees to offer 2,000 pounds for the collection without it – though it took them an entire year to work this out. At a meeting chaired by the Archbishop of Canterbury on 14 February 1823, the offer of 2,000 pounds was officially made and the sarcophagus was declined.

Belzoni, however, was no longer available to negotiate the sale of the sarcophagus. He had spent a fruitless year threatening law suits against the British Museum, trying to get possession of the sarcophagus, and passing the time by travelling around Europe accepting the adulation of the public.

On returning to England in the summer of 1822, Belzoni arranged for the sale by auction of the contents of his exhibition at the Egyptian Hall, and did reasonably well: the huge model of Sethos' tomb went for 490 pounds, two slightly imperfect lion-headed statues of Sekhmet for 380 pounds and one other in good condition for 300 pounds. Even the wax models were sought after, that of the temple of Isis at Philae fetching twenty-eight pounds, and of Abu Simbel twenty-four pounds.

These sums helped Belzoni make his way around Europe for another tour, and early in 1823 he handed over power of attorney to the Rev. George Adam Browne, a Fellow of Trinity College, Cambridge. Belzoni then presented the red granite sarcophagus cover given to him by Drovetti to the Fitzwilliam Museum, and set off to discover the source of the Niger. He died of dysentry on his way to Timbuktu on 3 December 1823.

For a time it seemed that the sarcophagus would fail to find a buyer. In desperation Salt wrote that Richards should sell it for 1,500 pounds, if only he could sell it soon. The British Museum waxed hot and cold, and in February 1824 a firm offer of 2,000 pounds was received from Mr John Soane. Before finally disposing of the sarcophagus, Richards wrote to the trustees on 2 April 1824, offering it to them for the same price. It took them only eight days to come to the wrong decision, and they declined on 10 April. A month later, on 12 May 1824, the sarcophagus was placed in Soane's house, where it can still be wondered at today.

The year 1824 was a bad one for Salt. He lay ill for most of the early weeks, and as Easter approached his wife gave birth to a child. She developed a fever, and the doctor was only able to attend her briefly before being called away to see to his own wife, who had the plague. Twenty days later the doctor himself died of the plague, and Salt's wife sank into a coma from which she never recovered. Then the baby died. Salt was so distressed at losing his wife, and so weakened by his own illness, that he felt he could no longer look after their daughter Georgina, then two years old, and he sent her to Leghorn to be cared for by his wife's family. Henry Salt had lost those closest to him, and was once again alone in a foreign land.

Salt seems to have taken refuge in his work: the consul in Alexandria died in October, and he had to do both jobs without any increase in salary. He also wrote a poem called 'Egypt', which he had published privately in Alexandria. It is long, turgidly philosophical, and best left to the obscurity into which it instantly sank.

Salt was hurt that the fame attached to the discoveries and depredations he had financed along the Nile Valley had been claimed by Belzoni, and he made a bid for recognition as a scholar. He sent an 'Essay on the phonetic hieroglyphics of Young and Champollion', with plates, to Richards, instructing him to have it published as quickly as possible: 'I wish it to be immediately printed, even should it cost me a hundred and fifty pounds.' Sadly there were delays and Champollion's *Précis du Système Hiéroglyphique* appeared before the 'Essay', which was not published until 1825.

Salt's collecting continued, with the assistance of the faithful Yanni, and by early 1825 he managed to assemble another cargo of antiquities. This time, too cautious to send them off to the British Museum, he shipped them to his relatives in Leghorn. He wrote on 15 June to his agent Richards in London:

I have collected, and my collection is now at Leghorn, antiquities to the value of four thousand pounds: the finest collection of papyri existing, the best assortment of Egyptian bronzes, several paintings in encaustic, and rich articles of gold and porcelain – in fine, what would make the collection at the Museum the choicest in the world, as an Egyptian collection; and this I would willingly present at once to the

Museum, could I obtain a pension of £600 like H – on which to retire.

Salt was still looking for the security of an income that would allow him to settle in England. Had the British Museum trustees considered for a moment the state of his health, they would have ventured confidently on a pension that would have cost them very little. But Salt was not inclined to bargain this time, and wrote again to Richards, 'It would be a great pleasure to me that it should go to England; but no more of dealing with the British Museum – the Soanes are the people for me.'

It seems likely that the Museum trustees were not given the chance to consider this offer. Less than a month after it was made, Salt wrote again to Richards to say that an agent was examining his collection in Leghorn on behalf of a royal purchaser who seemed likely to be far more generous and less devious than the trustees. Ironically, the royal purchaser was none other than the king of France, whom Salt had spent his career in Egypt intriguing against, and from whose clutches both he and Belzoni had worked ceaselessly to secure the antiquities. Salt had sent his collection to his brother-in-law, Peter Santoni, with the advice that he expected to raise at least 150,000 francs for it; Santoni was able to impress the king's agent sufficiently to arrange a sale for 250,000 francs (10,000 pounds). The sale was completed in April 1826, and the money was paid to Salt over a period of four years.

Salt was not to have the pleasure of receiving it; he died of an intestinal infection on 29 October 1827. His body was buried in Alexandria, and an epitaph was written by his cousin, the Rev. Thomas Butt, son of the uncle by the same name whose introduction to Lord Valencia in Fuseli's Gallery had launched Salt on his career in Egypt:

His ready genius explored and elucidated
the Hieroglyphics and other Antiquities of this Country.
His faithful and rapid pencil,
And the nervous originality of his untutored verses,
conveyed to the world vivid ideas
of the scenes which delighted himself.
In the midst of his important duties and useful pursuits,

> he was, in the forty-eighth year of his age,
> and after a short illness, summoned, as we trust,
> to his better and eternal home, on the
> twenty-ninth day of October,
> in the year of our Lord 1827.

Salt's agent in Egypt, Yanni, was still amassing a collection there, which was sent to Leghorn only three weeks before Salt's death. This was eventually shipped to England and auctioned at Sotheby's in Wellington Street in 1835. Miscellaneous items from the sale catalogue echo the strange variety of objects over which Salt, like other early impresarios of Egyptian excavation, laid a bizarre claim to ownership through an assumed cultural superiority or, perhaps, on the simple and ancient principle of 'finding's keeping':

2. Forty figures of various Deities in porcelain, some very minute .... 9s.

10. The Hawk with human head .... 8s.

75. A small Basket, containing the right hand of a female mummy, having on the second finger, a scarabeus set in silver .... 19s.

170. Various Eyes of Mummies, inlaid in alabaster ..... 5s.

215. A small Bell, of gold, found on the neck of the mummy of a boy .... Thebes. £6.6s.

321. Six pair of Earrings of red composition of different sizes .... £1.11s.

343. Pair of Eyes, set in bronze, fine, taken from a mummy found at Memphis .... £6.8s.

354. A small goose, of blue composition, on a gold ring .... Memphis. 17s.

363. A piece of Cufic Money, in gold .... 15s.

407. Collection of seven Carpenters' Tools consisting of two different hatchets with wooden handles; three chisels and two knives .... £16.5s.

522. Three specimens of Bread .... £1.6s.

929. A boy's play Ball, the inside made of a husk of corn, the outside of leather, very curious.......................... 14s.

1200. A pair of Sandals, beautifully painted .. Mempis. 17s.

The culmination of the excitement each day was the sale of the mummies, always left to the end so the buyers would linger:

149. The Mummy of a small Child, 2 feet 10 inches high, in its case, in which is represented the portrait, very curiously painted, with rings on the ankles, wrists and arms ... £36.

150. The Mummy of Female of high quality, 5 feet 4 inches high, with its case highly painted and ornamented .... £105.

852. The Mummy of a Royal Personage, in two cases .... £320.5s.

1269. The Mummy of a Dancing Girl, in a high state of pre-servation, 5 ft high .... £28.5s.

There were altogether 1,270 items in the auction, including coins and medals, statues in wood, stone, and bronze, manuscript rolls of papyrus, scarabei, ornaments in gold, and idols in porcelain. The sale took nine days and raised a total of £7,168.18s.6d. This, added to the £2,000 paid by the British Museum, the £2,000 paid by John Soane for the sarcophagus, and the £10,000 from the King of France meant that the Salt Estate benefited to the tune of over £21,000 from the excavations funded by the first British antiquarian collector and diplomat in Egypt.

Drovetti, who had been in the game rather longer, did even better. Initially he had problems disposing of his collection, which had been made under the flag and inspiration of France, because the French clergy were against the purchase of anti-quities that might undermine the authority of the Bible. Although Drovetti had offers from England – Salt even tried to persuade him to sell to the British Museum – and Germany, Drovetti maintained like Salt that he would sell only to the nation he represented in Egypt. Finally, also like Salt, he ran out of patience and sold his first great collection to the king of Sardi-nia for 400,000 lire (over 13,000 pounds), which went to found the Egyptian Museum at Turin. Then, Charles X, having ascended the throne in September 1824 with the intention of re-kindling the ancient glory of the monarchy, purchased Drovetti's second collection for 250,000 francs (10,000 pounds). A third collection was sold to the Berlin Museum in 1836 for 30,000 francs.

Drovetti ended his days in Turin, the city where he had served as a military judge, and whose internationally famous collection of Egyptian antiquities he had supplied. He died in 1852, confined to a mental asylum.

By the time Salt's and Drovetti's great collections were being installed in the museums of Europe, they had acquired a significance that went beyond the sensational and the exotic. They were witnesses to a past which, for the first time in the modern age, was beginning to be understood: the system of writing in which it was extensively recorded had been discovered.

Chapter Four

The Fox, the Hedgehog, and the Colonel

THE BICKERING THAT WENT ON over Drovetti's and Salt's collections seems less baffling when we remember that neither the collectors nor the museums knew what they were fighting about. The statues were there to be seen – some even had names – but who these kings and queens were, when they had reigned, and what they had achieved was unknown, because at the beginning of the 19th century the language that contained the answers to these questions was not understood.

At the time this language was not even recognised as writing. The word 'hieroglyphics', used to describe bands of images and symbols, in fact is from the Greek for 'sacred carving' not 'sacred writing', which is 'hierographics', a word that was not used until 1835 when decipherment had been achieved.

The Greeks thought hieroglyphics enshrined the ancient and occult wisdom of Egypt, which was accessible only to the priests, who had forgotten the secret of decipherment before the conquest of Alexander the Great. Hieroglyphics were thought to be the dumb witness to a lost revelation. They carried an aura of magic: if only the right rituals could be performed, the correct words intoned, the primeval power they once had might be recovered.

In the 17th century a Jesuit professor had set himself the task of deciphering the symbols. Athanasius Kircher was a specialist in the natural sciences and an unbridled polymath: he was lowered on a rope into the crater of Vesuvius after the great eruption of 1630 to discover its cause; he had invented an adding machine, a speaking tube, an aeolian harp, and a magic lantern; he wrote treatises on medicine and earthquakes, and he made a special study of the classical languages.

Kircher seemed destined to reveal the secrets of nature to mankind, and, when he first came upon them during his student days, he was determined especially to tackle the mystery of the hieroglyphics. Whilst in Rome as professor of mathematics at the Collegio Romano, he undertook the decipherment of the texts on the various Roman obelisks. One text, referring to the Emperor Domitian, reads (as we know today): 'CAESAR DOMITIA-NUS, living for ever'. Father Kircher's elaborate translation is so wide of the mark that it is frequently quoted for light relief:

The beneficient being who presides over generation, who enjoys heavenly dominion and fourfold power, commits the atmosphere by means of Mophtha, the beneficient atmos-pheric humidity unto Ammon, most powerful over the lower parts. . .

There continued to be flurries of pseudo scholarship that occa-sionally brought hieroglyphics to the attention of antiquarians: in 1762 the Abbé Tandeau maintained they were arbitrary signs used as ornaments to the buildings and statues on which they were found, and were not intended to convey ideas or words. Tandeau was opposed by the occultist Chevalier de Palin, who in 1802 revealed that he had at last penetrated the mystery: if the psalms of David were translated into Chinese and then written out in the ancient characters of that language, then all the in-scriptions and papyri in Egypt would be reproduced. In 1806 the matter seemed again to be settled when Joseph Von Hammer-Purgstall published his translation of *Ancient Alphabets* by Ahmeed Bin Abuker Bin Wahshih; but the author turned out to be a charlatan, and the book no more than a series of reveries on cabbalistic signs. The French Egyptologist and numismatist Marie-Alexandre Lenoir published his *Nouvelle Explication des Hiéroglyphes* in four volumes between 1809 and 1821. In them Lenoir pointed out that hieroglyphics were simply a form of Hebrew, but this revelation fell on stony ground, as did that of

Count Caylus, who in 1812 declared that *he* had finally managed to decipher the hieroglyphics covering the portico of the temple at Dendara. They were none other than the 100th Psalm of David, inviting the people of Egypt to enter the house of God.

The first definite step towards a translation of hieroglyphics was made in a paper published in 1761 by the antiquarian Abbé Jean Jacques Barthélemy. The abbé suggested that the hieroglyphic signs found enclosed in oval rings were probably royal names, an idea that also occurred to Charles de Guignes, a French orientalist who was after evidence to support his theory that China had once been a colony of Egypt, and had derived its writing from the Egyptian. Another scholar sometimes credited as the originator of this key notion was the Danish linguist George Zoega, who published a study of the obelisks in 1797 – *De Origine et Usu Obeliscorum* – in which for the first time accurate facsimile copies of the texts were reproduced.

The final revelation came when the block of black basalt roughly three feet long and twelve inches thick, dragged from the mud of the Nile delta at Fort St Julien by Captain Bouchard and claimed for Britain by General Hutchinson, became available for scrutiny. The Rosetta Stone was to provide the final answers, but not before there was a prolonged scholarly fracas in which the British and French continued to fight the battle of the Nile.

The first assault was made on the stone's Greek text, which yielded with few difficulties to Professor Porson in London and to Dr Heyne in Germany. There was even collaboration between these scholars and the French Institute, and blanks in the text caused by damage to the stone were filled and the whole translated.

There remained the demotic and hieroglyphic texts, which, everyone agreed, were versions of the Greek. The French fielded Sylvestre de Sacy, an Arabic scholar and the most distinguished orientalist of the day, who was able to announce in 1802 that he had identified, in the demotic text the groups of letters that corresponded to the proper names of Ptolemy, Arsinoe, Alexander, and Alexandria. The Swedish scholar and diplomat Johan David Akerblad studied with de Sacy in Paris, and then, under the patronage of the Duchess of Devonshire, went on to work on Runic and Phoenician inscriptions in Rome. Akerblad had a

copy of the Rosetta Stone texts with him, and managed to identify all the proper names in demotic that occurred in the Greek,
and also the alphabetically written words for 'Greek' and 'temples'. He even attempted to draw up an alphabet of the demotic,
but failed to realise that the vowels occurring between conso-
nants were suppressed, a practice common in oriental languages,
and was not able to make further progress. Significant improve-
ments on Akerblad's alphabet were made by an English scholar,
whose achievements were particularly galling to the specialists in
the field because he was, only late in life, and then only in-
cidentally, a linguist.

Thomas Young was the son of an affluent Quaker mercer and
banker. Having made up his mind as a schoolboy that success
was simply a matter of application, Young pursued his interests
through disparate fields of knowledge, managing to distinguish
himself in all of them. He studied medicine in London and Edin-
burgh, was awarded a Fellowship of the Royal Society at the age
of twenty-one, and went on to a doctorate in physics at Gottingen. His biographer records that, being free from those dis-
sipations into which young persons often fall, Young's energies
were channelled into horsemanship, bodily exercise, and 'feats of
personal agility, in which he excelled to an extraordinary
degree'. As well he was a skilled musician, and contributed
articles to the *Gentleman's Magazine* on Greek criticism, chemical theories, botany, and entomology.

Young, however, was no dilettante. He carried out important
original research in the field of optics, being the first to recognise
astigmatism in the human eye, and discovered the wave theory
of light, anticipating Fresnel. At the age of twenty-eight he was
made Professor of Natural Philosophy at the Royal Institution in
1801. As well he reviewed books regularly for the *Quarterly Review*, and in 1813 was sent a copy of *Mithridates*, a study of
Asiatic languages by the German philologist Adelung. This first
awoke Young's interest in hieroglyphics, and when in the following year his friend Sir William Rouse Boughton brought back
some fragments of papyri from Egypt, Young set to work translating them, taking the papyri and a copy of the Rosetta Stone
inscriptions with him to Worthing, where he spent the summer.

The Greek inscription on the Rosetta Stone ends with the
order:

... that this decree shall be engraved on a hard stone, in
sacred characters, in common characters, and in Greek; and
placed in the first temples, and in the second temples, and
in the third temples, wherever may be the sacred image of
the king, whose life is for ever.'

This confirmed that the three bands of writing were all translations of the same text. With the systematic precision of the
scientific investigator, Young set out to find the correspondences
between them. He noticed that two groups of signs in the second
and tenth lines of the demotic inscription seemed to correspond
with the words 'Alexander' and 'Alexandria' in the Greek, which
gave a possible seven characters identified. He then noticed a
small group of letters recurring in almost every line, which it
seemed reasonable to equate with the word 'and'. The next most
commonly repeated group of letters occurred as frequently in
Greek, so the translation of 'king' was established. Using the
same method, Young discovered that a group of characters
occurred fourteen times in the demotic, and eleven times in the
Greek; he managed to translate 'Ptolemy', and later 'Egypt'.

Having established points of coincidence between the texts,
Young then wrote the demotic text over the Greek, matching the
words he knew, not forgetting that the demotic was written from
right to left. Using this method he was able to work out an alphabet for the demotic script that appeared consistent. In his researches Young was helped by correspondence with de Sacy and
Akerblad, and it could be held that he was merely advancing the
discoveries they had made. De Sacy and Akerblad, however,
worked only on the demotic text. No one yet had made a serious
assault on the hieroglyphics; this Young was determined to do.

He at first assumed that the demotic writing might have descended from a source common to both Egyptian and Coptic, and
so studied Coptic in order to trace the original alphabet. He
abandoned the search, however, when he noticed that a number
of the demotic characters seemed to be imitations, in a cursory
style, of the very clear pictures in the hieroglyphics. There were
shapes in the demotic text that could not possibly be alphabetic,
they seemed so clearly derived from the delineation of objects in
the hieroglyphics.

This led Young to postulate that the two forms of writing were intimately related, and that they might be simply the pictorial and cursive forms of the same signs. He also turned against the pervading opinion that the hieroglyphic consisted mainly of phonetic elements; that, like the demotic, it was a form of writing, that represented sounds rather than objects, and so could be understood by discovering its alphabet. He made a further advance by realising that different characters could be used to represent the same sounds – the principle of homophony. In an article he wrote for the 1819 supplement to the *Encyclopaedia Britannica*, Young proposed a vocabulary of over 100 characters. Although he made mistakes of detail, the method and main conclusions that he was the first to reach led to the eventual success of decipherment of the hieroglyphics.

There was no national outburst at the publication of Young's findings. They were, after all, extensions of de Sacy's and Akerblad's work, in an area remote from public interest. Young continued his work in medicine, physics, astronomy, Greek literature, and mathematics.

He was travelling to Rome and Naples in the autumn of 1821 when he came upon the collection of antiquities Drovetti had sent to Leghorn. He asked to be allowed a cursory inspection, and noticed among them a stone bearing the traces of an inscription in both Greek and demotic. Realising the importance of what seemed to be a second Rosetta Stone, Young asked Drovetti's agents for permission to copy the stone, but they were unable to agree without Drovetti's permission.

Young then wrote to the agents offering to pay for an artist from Florence to make two copies of the stone. The copies would be the property of Drovetti, and would remain with the agent until Drovetti decided whether or not he wished to sell them, and to whom and for how much. Young even offered to let the copies remain in Drovetti's collection, on the sole condition that if the stone were ever sent from Leghorn by sea the copies should be retained at Leghorn until the stone had arrived safely at its destination. It was a generous offer, but on hearing of the stone's significance, Drovetti refused to risk reducing its commercial value by allowing it to be copied.

The following year, 1822, Young was invited to attend a meeting in Paris of the Academy of Sciences at which the famous physicist August Jean Fresnel read a paper on the laws of the interference of light, in which he paid generous tribute to Young's work in the subject. The pleasure Young received from this demonstration of the even-handedness of French scholarship was dimmed slightly when later the same week he attended a lecture at the Academy of Belles Lettres. He was invited to sit beside the author of a paper on Egyptian writing, in which his own achievements seemed to be echoed but unacknowledged. The paper was hailed as a revelation, and its author, Champollion, as a genius.

'The Fox', wrote the Greek satirist Archilochus, 'knows many things – the Hedgehog one big thing.' Young was a fox. By the time he had published his discoveries on hieroglyphics, there had also appeared in the learned journals articles by him ranging from the manufacture of iron and the habits of spiders, to the calculation of the rate of expansion of the supposed lunar atmosphere. These articles were of course in addition to Young's main writings in medicine and the physics of light. He wrote sixty-three articles for the *Encyclopaedia Britannica* on subjects ranging from annuities to weights and measures, and did not take up the study of Egypt until he was forty-one years old, the age at which his principal rival in the field died.

Jean-François Champollion, on the other hand, was a hedgehog. Born in 1790 in the little country town of Figeac, the son of a French bookseller, he had an unremarkable start in life; but there were those who remembered that the corneas of his eyes were yellow from birth, like those of an Egyptian baby, his complexion sallow, and his face remarkably Oriental. Legend has it that as a schoolboy Jean-François was taken to the home of Fourier, the mathematician who had accompanied Bonaparte to Egypt, and was shown papyri and the hieroglyphic inscriptions on stone tablets there. 'Can anyone read them?', he asked. When Fourier shook his head, the boy declared, 'I am going to do it. In a few years I will be able to. When I am big.'

Champollion's biographers also have recorded the story about the visit of the famous phrenologist Dr Franz Joseph Gall to Jean-François' home. Dr Gall felt the bumps on his head and declared him a linguistic genius. There was at the time some evidence of Champollion's ability that the good doctor may well have been told: the sixteen-year-old schoolboy had already learned Arabic, Syrian, Chaldean, and Coptic, as well as Latin and Greek. He also had shown an early awareness of his own distinction by drawing up a history of the world entitled 'Chronology from Adam to Champollion the Younger'.

At seventeen years old Champollion had already written a book entitled *Egypt under the Pharaohs*, and had begun studies in Paris with de Sacy. Here he learned Sanskrit, Arabic, and Persian before going on to master Coptic; the latter was learned so effectively that he kept his journals in that language. At the age of nineteen Champollion was made Professor of History at the University of Grenoble, where he wrote plays and political satires with a strongly republican slant. This recommended him to Napoleon during the Hundred Days, and resulted in Champollion's banishment from the University for traitorous activities when the Royalists triumphed. He returned to Grenoble in 1818, but was threatened again with charges of treason in July 1821, when he fled from the University.

In the same year he published a memoir on some texts from the *Book of the Dead*, in which he seemed convinced that the hieroglyphic system of writing worked symbolically, and did not represent sounds. One year later Champollion gave his lecture to the Académie, published as 'Lettre à M. Dacier, relative a l'alphabet des hiéroglyphics phonétiques'. It was hailed by French scholars as a breakthrough in the struggle for decipherment of the hieroglyphics, and has been regarded so internationally since then.

Whether or not Champollion had read and been influenced by Young's article in the *Encyclopaedia Britannica* it is impossible to establish; he always denied that he had. The publication of the 'Lettre' prompted the *Quarterly Review* to enter the lists on behalf of the priority of Young:

> ... we may say, without at all derogating from the merit of M. Champollion's indefatigable labours, that whether we weigh their value in the scales of utility or novelty, we find little or nothing in them that can repay him for the persevering siege which he has conducted against the pot-hooks of Egypt, for just so many years as the Greeks sat down before Troy ...

The *Review* goes on to remind its readers that Akerblad and

A contemporary view of Napoleon,
surrounded by the savants, inspecting a mummy.

The Battle of the Pyramids in 1798 left many
Bedouin and Mamelukes dead.

The temple at Edfu,
almost totally submerged in sand.

Bernardino Drovetti, the most energetic collector
of his day, rests his hand on the brow of a sphynx.
He is surrounded by native assistants
who helped him control excavations
in the Nile valley on Mohammed Ali's behalf.

Above: A red granite sphynx from Thebes, one of the jewels of Henry Salt's collection, now in the Hermitage Museum, Leningrad.

Below left: Bust of Ramesses II, from Henry Salt's collection.

Below right: Giovanni Belzoni, the flamboyant 'Patagonian Sampson', wearing local dress.

Right: Sir Hans Sloane, whose collection formed the basis of the national British Museum.

Below: The Egyptian Room in the British Museum as it eventually took shape, and survives today.

Above: The Egyptian Hall in Piccadilly,
with a front modelled on the temple at Dendera.

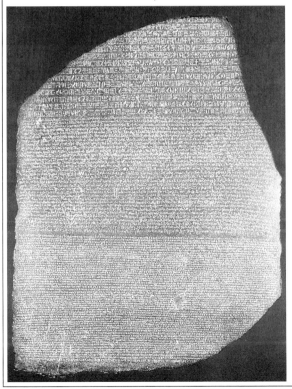

Opposite: The Rosetta Stone,
with hieroglyphs above,
demotic script in the centre,
and Greek below.

Left: Thomas Young, who made
the first essential deductions
in the decipherment of
the Rosetta Stone.

Below: An engraving of the
Circular Zodiac from the ceiling
of the temple at Dendera,
removed to France by Lelorrain
and now in the Louvre.

Jean-François Champollion.

Baron von Bunsen, who encouraged
Lepsius in his Egyptian expedition.

A magnificent painting by David Roberts
of the temple at Dendera, dated December 1838.

Left: Richard Lepsius,
leader of the Prussian expedition
of 1842-48.

Below: The Prussian eagle flies
before the pyramids at Giza.

others began the construction of an alphabet, that Young carried on and extended it to hieroglyphics, and that Champollion was merely extending the principle adopted by them:

> That M. Champollion has little or no claim to originality in what he seems to think a discovery and which we are sure his countrymen will blazon forth as such, will appear from the following passage in Dr Young's account of Egypt, written some years ago.

Printed beneath is the text of a portion of Young's *Encyclopaedia Britannica* article in which he identifies the hieroglyphic signs for the letters that form the name 'Ptolemy' on the Rosetta Stone. Champollion was to object that Young did not get them all right, but the point made by the *Quarterly Review*, that Champollion was extending a principle rather than announcing a new discovery, seems valid.

The following year, 1823, Young published his farewell to the subject with the provocative title; 'An Account of Some Recent Discoveries in Hieroglyphical Literature and Egyptian Antiquities. Including the Author's Original Alphabet as Extended by Mr Champollion.' Young claimed he had always published the results of his researches not 'from an impatience of being the sole possessor of a secret treasure; but because I was desirous of securing, at least for my country . . . the reputation of having enlarged the boundaries of human knowledge and of having contributed to extend the dominion of the mind of man over time, and space, and neglect, and obscurity'. He would have been happy to remain in relative obscurity, but the sudden fame of Champollion had dragged him into the public eye, and he felt himself justified in endeavouring to obtain 'while I have yet a few years more to live and to learn, whatever respect may be thought due to the discoveries which have constituted the amusement of a few of my leisure hours'.

In a letter dated 13 September 1823, Young confirmed he would not publish any more Egyptian texts, partly because of the expense, partly because the material was being exhausted, and partly because 'Champollion is doing so much that he will not allow anything of consequence to be lost.' In 1824, the following year, Champollion staked his claim for sole credit for deciphering the hieroglyphics in a substantial volume entitled 'Précis du Système Hiéroglyphique des Anciens Egyptiens . . .', which contains 465 pages of text and a generous appendix of plates and illustrations. Champollion deals with rival claims in the introduction, stating that his own discoveries were so well substantiated that in announcing them he feared not so much they would be contradicted, as that others would try to share the honour of having made them. This had, indeed, happened; not of course in France, but abroad. Although he was disposed to forgive such pretensions which were based on the spirit of patriotism, the author had to oppose the claims in the interests of truth and scholarship. Champollion then set about attacking Young with vigour, attempting to show he never had understood the phonetic basis of hieroglyphics, and that the few translations Young had made were lucky guesses rather than the result of linguistic research.

There is little doubt that Champollion learned more from Young than he was prepared to admit, and that the discoveries which were announced with such a flourish, and which have since been celebrated among Egyptologists, were less a sudden revelation than a patient and skilled extension of existing research. However, it would be as useless to attempt to diminish Champollion's great achievements as it would be to perpetuate the image of a genius working in isolation, which he and his supporters sought to promote:

With the force of an earthquake the illustrious Frenchman overthrew the puny edifices of his predecessors; and from that hour, the Annals of Egypt, her time-honoured chronicles, her papyri crumbling in the dust of ages ceased to be mysteries! The 'Veil of Isis' – 'the curtain that no mortal hand could raise' – which, for 2000 years had baffled the attempts of Greeks and Romans, with the still more vigorous efforts of modern Egyptologists – was lifted by CHAMPOLLION LE JEUNE.

With these words the retired American Consul in Cairo warmed his Boston audiences in 1844, twenty years after Champollion had burst on to the scene (and only fifty years after the Boston Tea Party had sparked off a bout of international rivalry).

George R. Gliddon, who described himself as 'one of CHAM-
POLLION's disciples', was in Egypt when Champollion's revelations were made, and noted the stunned silence that followed,
'Like the atmospheric stillness that follows the thunderclap,
genius seemed paralysed by the portentous aspect of the truth.'

The silence was due less to the fact that scholars were dazzled
by Champollion's sudden revelations than that their entrenched
positions made them unreceptive to his ideas. Members of the
Institute of Egypt who had accompanied Bonaparte were still in
senior positions, unwilling to be taught by a young republican
upstart who had never set foot in Egypt. The Christians too were
uneasy about the progress of an investigation into an Egypt that
had thrown up no evidence of the Israelites' sojourn there or of
the Exodus. And the classical scholars scorned the use of the in-
tellect and funds in such a barbaric pursuit.

Champollion was rewarded for his scholarly successes in
France by being sent in 1824 on a mission to study the Egyptian
collections in the museums of Turin, Leghorn, Rome, Naples,
and Florence. His republicanism was so far forgotten by Louis
XVIII, and later by Charles X, that he was appointed Con-
servator of the Egyptian collections at the Louvre, and engaged
by the French government to value and purchase the antiquities
that Drovetti and Salt had sent to Leghorn.

However news of the British activities in Egypt began to filter
back to Paris, and Champollion was concerned lest France
should be displaced from her position as Mother of the Arts and
Patroness of Egyptology. An expedition to be led by Champollion and accompanied by four French artists was mounted to re-
claim Egypt for French scholarship. A slight difficulty arose
when it was learned that the Grand Duke of Tuscany planned a
similar expedition, but the situation was arranged tactfully when
the Italian expedition was planned as an exactly equivalent force,
headed by the distinguished orientalist Professor Ippolito Rosselini, a follower of Champollion, who was to be accompanied by
four Italian artists. Since the scholarly aims of the two expeditions were the same, it was decided they should unite for the sake
of economy, and they sailed for Alexandria in the same vessel.

The arrival of the joint expedition was noted by George Gliddon, who was in Cairo in 1828: it 'added new fuel to the flame of
antiquarian jealousy which, for thirty years, had characterised

the archaeological devotees of England and France'. Champollion regarded all other scholars as interlopers on what was his own exclusive field of endeavour, and he made it clear that anyone found recording or expounding hieroglyphics in Egypt was trespassing. The British scholars, who had been beavering away for years before Champollion arrived, were afraid to meet him in case he should allege that everything they published subsequently was a result of that meeting. This resulted in many comic incidents in which the British, hearing of Champollion's approach, would duck out of sight to avoid accusations of personal contact.

The skulduggery that had characterised a generation of national rivalry along the Nile Valley was brought into play during Champollion's visit as well. The British had noticed that a slab of basalt that formed the lintel of a dilapidated mosque in Cairo was inscribed with what seemed to be a trilingual inscription, similar to that on the Rosetta Stone. They applied to Muhammad Ali for permission to remove the slab in the interest of Egyptology, and made the application in the approved manner through the British consul, offering to restore the entire mosque as compensation for the favour. Drovetti, however, heard about the application and persuaded the Pasha to reject it on the grounds that removing the lintel would be a sacrilege. Muhammad Ali, having refused the British on so pious a pretext, realised he therefore could not allow the French to take the slab.

Matters would have rested there had someone not taken Champollion to see the stone. The resulting fuss was so great that Drovetti was called on to exercise his special talents in the field. This he did by applying to Muhammad Ali's son, Ibrahim Pasha, for permission to move the stone without of course mentioning that his father had already refused. Ibrahim granted the request, stipulating only that the local people be told that the Pasha wanted the stone for himself, which would involve less scandal than if it were taken by foreigners. There were no secrets in Cairo, however, and the British soon heard of the plan. They went at night to the old mosque and removed the lintel, carting it off in triumph to the consulate. There was a tremendous row and Ibrahim persuaded his father to force the British to surrender the stone to the Egyptian government. This caused less distress than might be imagined: examination of the stone revealed that it was mutilated beyond being of serious value. Facsimile copies were made and sent to London, and the British returned the original without a qualm to the mosque. The stone ended up in Paris. The main thing Champollion learned from it was something of the technique of besting a rival in the international skirmishing over the antiquities of Egypt.

He learned quickly. When the joint expedition camped in the Valley of the Kings, taking over the tomb of Ramesses VI as their headquarters, Champollion decided that the reliefs on the tomb of Sethos I would grace his collection at the Louvre, and set about having them cut out. Joseph Bonomi, English sculptor and draughtsman, heard of this and wrote to Champollion in protest:

> If it be true that such is your intention I feel it my duty as an Englishman and a lover of antiquity to use every argument to dissuade you from so Gothic a purpose at least till you have permission from the present Consul General or Mohammed Ali.

Champollion replied with *hauteur*:

> I am also performing a duty as a Frenchman in telling you that, as I do not recognise any authority in Egypt but the Pasha's, I have to ask no other permission, much less that of the British consul, who certainly does not make the ridiculous claims that you put forward for him. If I succeed in obtaining better workmen than those they have sent me from Cairo, to whom I can entrust this delicate operation, rest assured, Sir, that one day you will have the pleasure of seeing some of the beautiful bas-reliefs of the tomb of Osirei in the French Museum. That will be the only way of saving them from imminent destruction and in carrying out this project I shall be acting as a real lover of antiquity since I shall be carrying them away only to preserve and not to sell.

A new morality was being introduced along the Nile: it was perfectly correct to steal the Egyptian monuments, so long as the thieves were not motivated by the desire for personal gain. This altruistic plundering became immediately popular, and even affected Bonomi who, on receipt of Champollion's reply and hearing that Rosselini was hacking away for the benefit of the museum at Florence, joined in and had a section cut out for the British Museum.

All three men excused their pilfering on the grounds that they were preserving antiquities for the future admiration of the world, and that if left in the temple the reliefs would soon be destroyed by the rains. Champollion, however, wished to prevent others making free with the antiquities of the Nile Valley, and wrote a letter of protest to Muhammad Ali deploring the trade in antiquities and suggesting that government controls be introduced on excavations and the export of relics. This was to bear fruit, but not before he had persuaded Muhammad Ali to send one of the two obelisks from the front of the temple at Luxor to Paris as a memorial to Bonaparte's troops. It was transported in 1830 to Paris on a special barge named the *Dromadaire*, and on 25 October 1836 was erected in the Place de la Concorde with great ceremony, attended by King Louis-Philippe and 200,000 spectators.

On 15 August 1835 a government ordinance was published in Egypt that should have put an end to such ceremonies. The preamble noted that the museums and collectors of foreign powers were so hungry for the antiquities of Egypt that there was a danger all her ancient monuments would vanish to enrich other countries.

And yet it is well understood that, not only do the Europeans not permit, in any circumstances, the export of similar objects from their own countries, but wherever antiquities are found they hasten to send off scholars to seize them. And these men almost always easily obtain them for miserable sums which satisfy the cupidity of their ignorant owners.

Since these ancient treasures contribute to the glory of the land which possesses them, and since Egypt contains abundant riches, the government thinks it expedient:

1. That the future export of antiquities of all kinds should

be severely prohibited.

2. That all such objects which the government already possesses or shall come to possess through future excavations
and research, be deposited in Cairo in a special place . . .

3. That not only should it be expressly forbidden, in future,
to destroy the ancient monuments of Upper Egypt but
government should take measures to ensure their preservation everywhere.

The ordinance stated that all excavations should cease, and that
the provincial governors should enforce the suspension of work
through armed inspectors. All the ports should be watched to
prevent the future export of antiquities; an inspector should be
appointed to supervise the enactment of the restrictions all over
Egypt; and official notification be sent to all the representatives
of European powers in Egypt so they could ensure the co-oper-
ation of their nations . . . and the appointment of an inspector to
enforce its provisions by travelling around the important sites.

The decree was a well-intentioned piece of legislation that
could have put an end to the international struggle to despoil the
monuments of the Nile Valley. However, at that time the
sovereign power of Egypt lay with an individual whose passing
interest in Egypt's antiquities soon faded, and who chose to override the laws that prevented him from gratifying the whims of
those he sought to impress. The conservation of Egypt's monuments was quietly forgotten for an entire generation.

After the hieroglyphics were deciphered successfully, there remained one great mystery of ancient Egypt that had taxed the
minds and imaginations of men down the centuries: the origin
and purpose of the pyramids. There was no shortage of theories.
Herodotus, writing in 445 BC, had identified the builder of the
Great Pyramid as King Cheops, reporting that the Egyptian
priests had described its construction to him, when labourers
were forced to work in groups of 100,000, relieved only every
three months over a period of twenty years. The sum spent on
radishes, onions, and garlic for the workforce was marked in
Egyptian characters on the Pyramid, and was translated to Herodotus as 1,600 silver talents. Herodotus also reports the story

that as the King's money began to run out he ordered his daughter to prostitute herself to contribute to the building costs. She was so successful in her profession that not only did she finance the completion of the Great Pyramid, but by asking each of her visitors to contribute one stone as well as cash, she amassed enough material to erect her own.

Herodotus correctly identifies the builders of the second and third pyramids as Chephren and Mycerinus, but writes that the Egyptians hated the two kings so much that they called the pyramids the pyramids of the shepherd Philition, who grazed his sheep in the area.

The Greek historian Diodorus Siculus, who visited Egypt in 60 BC, was astonished by the absence of any workings in the sands around the Great Pyramid, 'so that the whole fabric appears to have been placed on the surrounding sand, not gradually, by the workmanship of man, but by the instantaneous agency of a Deity'. The Egyptians, he reported, had many wondrous stories about this, but Siculus recorded the more sober information that the operation was carried out over twenty years by a workforce of 360,000 men.

Pliny, writing a century later, thought the Pyramids an 'idle and foolish exhibition of royal wealth', and explained that they were built simply to exhaust the treasures of the kings of Egypt to frustrate their successors or rivals. No one, continues Pliny, should admire the pyramids as towering memorials to the work of kings because the smallest and most beautiful was built by a prostitute, Rhodope, who was a fellow slave of Aesop. It is, Pliny thinks, a greater wonder than the pyramids themselves that a prostitute should have been able to raise enough funds to build one.

It was accepted generally by the classical writers that the pyramids had been built as memorials, or tombs to the kings. An alternative theory attributed to St Gregory of Nazianzus was popular in the Middle Ages, which claimed that the pyramids had been built by exiled Jews as massive warehouses for the storage of grain.

The Great Pyramid was visited regularly by travellers down the centuries, and was known to have an interior passage and a well. It was famous as the last of the Seven Wonders of the ancient world, enigmatic and indestructible. The only serious

plans on record for its demolition were the brain-child of Ibrahim Pasha, the Viceroy of Egypt who in 1854 was persuaded by
an African magician that the Pyramid contained great treasures.
The Pasha decided to fill up the well with gunpowder and blow
it up, but was dissuaded by the Venetian consul, who told him
the explosion would endanger Cairo.

By the time Frederick Norden entered the Great Pyramid in
1737, the number of visitors was so great that 'the channels on
the northern and southern sides were blackened by the smoke of
torches, inserted from time to time by travellers'. But the Pyramid's well remained unexplored. Captain Caviglia, the Genoese
trader, employed by Henry Salt, finally cleared out the rubbish
and connected the well with the subterranean chamber in 1818.
That same year, Belzoni was the first modern European to enter
the pyramid of Chephren. Much remained to be done, however,
before the secrets of the largest constructions on earth were revealed. This required a man of vision, with a resolute cast of
mind.

Richard William Howard-Vyse was a military man. The son of
General Richard Vyse, he had married the daughter of Field
Marshall George Howard, and had assumed the additional name
and arms of his wife's family. He was Member of Parliament for
Stoke Poges in 1807, and again from 1812 to 1818. He was made
Hon DCL at Oxford University in 1810. By the year 1835, when
he first visited Egypt at the age of fifty-one, this background, together with a firm Christian faith and a handsome competence,
had produced a man with a certain confidence in his own
opinions.

On the subject of the pyramids, Vyse's opinions had been influenced by the writings of Jacob Bryant, an English antiquarian
whose reputation has not flourished since his death in 1804.
Bryant believed that the pyramids were the work of the shepherd
kings, the descendants of Ham, who, because of their apostasy,
had been expelled from Babel and dispersed around the world to
Greece, Carthage, and even as far as America, where traces of
their buildings remained. They were an extraordinary people, of
the same race as the cyclops, and, like them, given to roaming
around the earth and erecting enormous and baffling architectural structures. Vyse associated these people with the
Philistines, and believed their history was evidence of the hand

of God at work in the world:

> These tribes seem formerly to have been living instances of
> Divine retribution as the dispersed Jews are at present.
> They appear at last to have been entirely destroyed . . . and
> the Pyramids remain, enduring yet silent monuments of the
> matchless grandeur of this extraordinary people, of the cer-
> tainty of Divine justice, and of the truth of revelation.

It is an indication of the criteria that Colonel Vyse applied to historical research that he found Bryant's theories convincing,
above all because of the author's 'profound conviction of the
truth of Revelation and of the unerring justice of the Almighty'.

When Vyse applied to the British consulate for permission to
begin investigating the pyramids, he was introduced to Captain
Caviglia, who presented himself as a British subject whose home
port was Malta. Caviglia's experience in excavating around the
pyramids, along with his habit of reading and quoting the Bible,
may well have recommended him to Vyse, who agreed to employ
him to supervise the work. The money was to be put up by Vyse,
Colonel Campbell, the British consul-general, and Charles
Sloane, the vice-consul. Caviglia was given *carte blanche* at the
hotel for his personal accommodation, and for any stores he
should need to carry out the excavations. Having exacted a
promise from Caviglia to write should anything of interest turn
up, with a curious indifference to the momentous investigations
he was initiating, Vyse set out for a tour of Upper Egypt.

His long, slow journey up the Nile Valley convinced Vyse that
this was a land indeed blessed of the Lord, as foretold by the
prophet Isaiah. At the island of Philae, where the river broadens
out into a vast lake, he found it impossible to contemplate unmoved

> . . . that mighty and wonderful stream, the sources of whose
> periodical visitations are veiled in the same obscurity which
> still involves the history of those powerful nations whose in-
> dustry once clothed its banks with fertility; and whose
> science, called into action by superstitious enthusiasm en-
> nobled them with buildings of such matchless beauty, that
> the very ruins have for successive ages commanded uni-

versal admiration.

At Thebes Vyse was sorry to observe that a gunpowder magazine was being constructed within a mile of the ancient buildings, and thought the approach to Luxor, which once must have been truly magnificent, had been disfigured by the accumulations of sand and rubbish, and 'by the loss of the obelisk taken to Paris which has destroyed the effect of the one remaining'.

Vyse was angered by the destruction of the monuments, and frequently complained that people were pulling them down to get at the stones even in areas where there was plenty of easily available building material. He lamented that many of the interesting objects described by earlier travellers had been destroyed; but, with the curious ambivalence that seems to have afflicted other ardent nationalists in Egypt, in the same paragraph that he records his lamentation at the loss of ancient monuments, he was able to end:

It is to be regretted that the obelisk from Thebes has not been erected in this country as a monument to Lord Nelson: it would have been a more appropriate and glorious record of his fame than any sculpture which modern times can produce.

Thebes, however, also convinced Vyse that the ancient Egyptians had preserved something of the glory of antediluvian man. He recalled that it was possible to infer from Homer and ancient mythology that

... together with longevity, mankind were originally endowed with superior intellectual and bodily faculties ... and that the arts had arrived at great perfection before the deluge; and it may reasonably be inferred that many of them survived that great event. The power and skill displayed in the different magnificent sepulchres, in the pyramids, and in many other stupendous remains of remote antiquity, appear, therefore, less surprising ...

At Dendera, where Vyse visited the most publicised of the temples along the Valley in 1836, he was again shocked by the destruction, noting that 'in proportion as what is called the civilisation of the country extends, these noble edifices become more and more delapidated, and that neither perfection of art, nor antiquity are any protection when materials are wanted, either for public buildings or private palaces.'

Although Vyse demonstrated an assumed cultural superiority common among English gentlemen abroad at the time, he was sensitive to another common affliction of the English that they refused to recognise: the inability to speak the local language. Vyse often refers to his sense of frustration at not being able to communicate diplomatic niceties when being entertained by, or making a request to, a local dignitary; and complains that his interpreters tended to leave out all inessential graces. He took the trouble to record an incident that occurred when visiting the governor of Asyut, 'which shows the foolish mistakes that may arise in this country between persons who cannot understand each other'. He was riding through the bazaar accompanied by the governor's janissary and attendants, when at a gateway he met an Arab officer:

> . . . who called out with much earnestness and made violent gestures for me to stop and to get out of the way. His horse was rather troublesome and, as the one I road was the same, I concluded that he was afraid of their coming into a collision. I knew perfectly well, however, that I could easily prevent any accident and accordingly passed through the gate, keeping on the left hand and making signs to him to keep on the other side, at the same time giving him the usual salutation; when, to my surprise, he became more excited and talked louder than ever. I was afterwards informed that what I intended as a civility he took as an affront, and that he had been insisting that I should wait, in order that he, being a Mohametan, might go first through the gate.

Although the janissary urged Vyse to report the man to the governor, he records simply and with humility that he refused. Vyse could, however, be roused by an affront to his national pride: when he later was told on sailing down the river that a boat moored on the eastern shore and flying the English flag was owned by an Arab and had no European aboard, Vyse insisted on boarding it to haul the flag down. He was stopped by the appearance of a Maltese, who claimed the right to sail under the flag. Vyse recorded the incident to report to the consul-general with the comment that he was not prepared to tolerate a practice that 'exposes the flag to disgrace from the misconduct of the Arabs who sail under it'.

Colonel Vyse had served under Wellington, and was particularly sensitive to the encroachment in Egypt of the influence of the French. They were, he writes, a nation 'whose interests have always been and must necessarily be hostile to those of Great Britain'. He also reports that any casual observer in Egypt is aware of the extent of French influence in the country. It is likely that Captain Caviglia was aware of the views of his employer, and felt reasonably safe reporting to Vyse that the slow progress he had achieved at the pyramids was in part due to the envy and interference of the French. When Vyse returned, however, he discovered that the labour he had been funding to investigate the pyramids was being used chiefly in excavating the mummy pits between the Sphinx and the Second Pyramid. Caviglia had changed the direction of the work because, he said, he felt it likely the pits would yield objects of great value to the scientific world. They were certainly more likely to yield valuable and saleable antiquities than the pyramids, and at a fraction of the effort, but Vyse was not concerned with making a profit, and had agreed that all objects discovered under his firman belonged to the Pasha. There followed a period of wrangling reminiscent of that between Salt and Belzoni, during which Caviglia claimed he was a partner in the venture, not an employee, and that although Vyse may have the money, he had the necessary skills. They parted company with rancour, and Vyse set about supervising the work himself.

Initially it must have seemed to Vyse that there could be few problems in handling the labour. Even-handed justice, firmly and impartially applied, won universal respect; and a highly successful career as a professional soldier had bred a self-confidence in his abilities as a leader of men. He worked out a table of just wages, and in return the men, women, and children worked from sunrise to sunset, with an hour for dinner. Those employed inside the pyramids were paid higher wages, and there was a bonus of double pay when any discovery of consequence was made.

Not only did this system result in the villagers earning more money than they had ever possessed in their lives, but, notes Vyse, while employed by him they were exempt from the compulsory and unpaid public work on the nearby canal. He had every expectation of being received as a benevolent despot.

He was, however, to be disappointed. The labour straggled along each morning, many only managing to get to the digging by seven or eight o'clock; theft was common; the reis had the habit of including on the payroll men who turned up only to receive their wages. And, far from treating Vyse with respect, his employees seemed to put all their energies into outwitting him. His journal sadly records the incident one evening when 'a lad was brought in on a man's shoulders, apparently half dead; his white cap and forehead were matted with blood and sand; and he was said to have fallen down the whole depth of the shaft in the Third Pyramid.' Vyse found him lying insensible on an earthen bank with an old man who claimed to be his uncle, sitting by him to keep off the flies. Vyse immediately sent to Cairo for a doctor, but then, turning round suddenly, he saw that the boy had opened his eyes and shut them again as soon as he was noticed. A second time Vyse caught the boy talking to the man with him, but as soon as he appeared the lad fell back unconscious on the ground. Vyse then told the man he could carry on nursing the lad if he chose, but he would not be paid for it. The man replied that in that case he had better take his patient to the village, and they set off, to be met by a large crowd of lamenting villagers who carried the boy home. It turned out that the boy had grazed his head against the side of a shaft and was otherwise unharmed. 'Such', comments Vyse, 'was the conduct of these wretched people; and instances of similar behaviour were continually recurring.'

The expectations Vyse had brought to the work – that people who were treated fairly, in his terms, would respond with loyalty and gratitude – were steadily eroded during the whole period of the excavations, and his final judgement on the work force is a testament to the triumph of experience over hope:

Yet with all the advantages of regular wages and exemption from severe labour while employed at the pyramids, of attention to their comforts and to any little accidents that might occur and of medical aid and of food to the sick and likewise of a positive prohibition of severe measures and of corporal punishment, these unhappy people were totally insensible of the kindness shown to them. Indeed, on the contrary, they practised every possible imposture and deceit to obtain money, food, medicine, etc., and at last their insolence and idleness arrived at such a pitch that the only alternative was to give up the work . . . I am certain that, in the present state of things, no business can be carried out without the dread of corporal punishment.

Vyse was lucky in engaging the services of John Shae Perring, an engineer who held the position of assistant manager of public works to the Pasha. Vyse and Perring surveyed all the pyramids at Giza, and then went on to Saqqara, Dashur, and Meidum. When they began, the interior of the Great Pyramid had been explored, and the Second had been opened. Vyse succeeded in opening the Third Pyramid – that of Mycerinus – by using controlled explosions of gunpowder, for which he has been much criticised. Ironically, the explosions were wasted on the Third Pyramid: having blasted his way almost to the centre, Vyse chanced on the true entrance by removing a few loose blocks on the northern side. He then discovered why the tunnels made from above had not been successful: the burial chamber and the passages leading to it were all underneath the pyramid, not inside. The chamber already had been opened by tomb robbers, and the long blue vessel they found inside contained only the decayed remains of a man. There was a sarcophagus without a lid, which Vyse resolved to send to the British Museum because it would have been destroyed if left in the chamber. The men managed to roll the sarcophagus on trucks to the bottom of the entrance passage, and then to lever it out, 'which, considering that its weight was nearly three tons, was an arduous undertaking'. At last it was cased in strong timbers and placed on a merchant ship, which, however, was lost off Carthagena in October 1837, and remains today on the seabed with its ancient cargo.

In the detailed account that Vyse published of his work there is no record of permission being obtained for the export of the sarcophagus. He does, however, make it clear that all antiquities found at the pyramids were the property of the Pasha, and that everything was sent to Colonel Campbell at the British consulate, with instructions that applications be made to Borghos-Bey, the private secretary to Muhammad Ali, for the articles Vyse wished to take to England. A list does not include the sarcophagus, but only such items as, 'three broken earthenware pots; five small glass bottles; three wooden birds; nine broken pieces . . .'

Vyse brought his collection back to England and presented it to the British Museum in 1888. He left Perring to continue surveying the pyramids at Vyse's expense, and supervised the publication of the records of his work in London. These were the most exact and comprehensive surveys of the pyramids to be published in the 19th century, and remained standard works of reference down to modern times. Although in the histories of Egyptology Vyse's name is linked with the use of gunpowder and violent methods of excavation, the damage he inflicted was minor, and the results he achieved a major contribution to knowledge. Vyse deserves a better reputation, not least because his ambitions in Egypt were unusual: he sought to enlarge neither his personal reputation nor fortune, nor that of this country, but only the extent of human knowledge.

Chapter Five

Culture Contact

THE INTERNAL SECURITY THAT FOLLOWED Muhammad Ali's rise to power, and his encouragement of foreign enterprise brought a fresh influx of travellers from Europe to Egypt. After 1808, the British leisured classes were able to wander again along the Nile Valley. Sir Archibald Edmonstone, Bart. approved of the changed political situation:

Since the distracted tyranny of the Mameluke Beys has been replaced by the sturdy despotism of the Turkish Pashas, the government has assumed a degree of strength and security almost unknown before: the consequence is that not only have the fellahs been reduced to a state of perfect subordination; but even the Berbers of Nubia, who join Egypt on the South, and the wandering Arabs, who long infested its borders on the West, have been rendered tributary and dependent.

Sir Archibald, who had explored two oases in 1819-20 dressed in Mameluke costume ('an immense pair of cloth trowsers, red slippers, and a turban of white muslin') was unconcerned with the commercial scramble for antiquities that was going on around him. He spent his hours along the Nile copying inscriptions in Greek, and making notes in his journal about interesting native habits and customs with which to divert the reading public at home.

The concerns of Jean Baptiste Lelorrain, engineer, were of a more practical nature. He had been commissioned by the French collector and antiquarian Louis-Sebastien Saulnier to remove the magnificent Circular Zodiac relief from the ceiling of the temple at Dendera and ship it back to Paris. France's justification for the commission seems to have been that the beauty of the carving had so excited the artistic sensibilities of General Desaix, and had been so exquisitely reproduced in the great *Description de l'Egypte*, that it had 'in a way become a national monument'. On applying for his firman Lelorrain was diplomatic enough to conceal the object of his visit from Muhammad Ali, and presented himself as just another foreign voyager with a thirst for knowledge.

When Lelorrain arrived at Dendera, he found a group of English visitors sketching the zodiac, and so he went to Thebes where he bought a few antiquities to give the impression he was a casual tourist with an eye for minor curiosities. Then, having put the story about that he was in poor health and planned a few weeks recuperation by the Red Sea, Lelorrain doubled back to Dendera and set to work cutting out the zodiac.

The zodiac was carved on blocks of stone three feet thick, and Lelorrain used gunpowder to blast holes, and then a foreman and forty workers cut it out using chisels and saws. After three weeks of working day and night, the blocks were removed and dragged on rollers to a boat. The captain announced that the waters were too low to attempt to sail such a heavy load north at that season. Lelorrain, however, had been in Egypt long enough to realise that the man had been bribed by the English. He simply asked the captain how much he had been offered, met the price of 1,000 piastres, and they set sail. Halfway to Cairo they were stopped by an English agent with an order from the Pasha's grand vizier forbidding them to carry away the stones. Lelorrain ran up the French flag, defied the opposition to board his vessel, and sailed on. At Alexandria the English and French consuls both tried to prevent Lelorrain from loading the zodiac, realising what an impressive addition it would make to their own collections. Lelorrain held out, however, and the blocks were shipped safely to France, sold to Louis XVIII for 150,000 francs, and reassembled in the Louvre.

Saulnier's account of the operation, published in 1822, explained to the world that his motives for commissioning the removal of the zodiac to France were inspired by aesthetic altruism: the Wahhabis of Arabia, he wrote, were threatening Egypt, and should they successfully invade, they would destroy all her ancient monuments: 'It is from this peril, which is not entirely imaginary, it is from all the destructive forces described above, that the circular zodiac of Dendereh has happily been snatched to be placed under the protection of European civilisation.'

In 1822, the year the zodiac was installed at the Louvre, the French mineralogist Frédéric Caillaud, who had returned from Egypt with a collection of more than 500 objects, published in London his account of his travels along the Nile Valley. He bemoaned the destruction that other countries were inflicting on the ancient treasures of Egypt: 'Indeed, had the monuments nothing to fear but the water and the seasons, they might exist for ages, but they have to encounter the violence of the Turks . . . and yet more, the hands of certain Europeans. I shall mention no names, but merely observe that they are not French . . . '

The attitude was at least consistent: from the first years of Anglo-French rivalry in the plundering of Egyptian antiquities, each nation had blamed the other for the damage both were inflicting. In the years following the publication of Caillaud's book, Champollion was touring the major sites, protesting against their desecration while arranging for the shipment of the Luxor obelisk to France. On his travels Champollion met Lord Algernon Percy, 4th Duke of Northumberland, who, with his companion Major Orlando Felix, was apparently absorbed in the copying of tomb inscriptions; they took time off from their academic preoccupations, however, to gather a collection of antiquities eventually amounting to over 2,000 objects.

There were also travellers in Egypt in search of aesthetic experience. The romanticism that affected the arts at the beginning of the 19th century drew its inspiration from a scorn of urban man, an idolisation of the noble savage, an intoxication with religious mysticism, and the visceral appeal of vanished or primitive cultures, including Egyptian. The leading Romantic poets of the time all dabbled in Egyptiana: the closing words of Shelley's 'Ozymandias' (1818) powerfully evoke the silence and desolation of the desert scene:

Nothing beside remains. Round the decay
Of that colossal wreck, boundless and bare
The lone and level sands stretch far away.

Keats was fitfully entranced by Egypt: seven of his poems
appearing in the same year refer to it or to Cleopatra, including a
sonnet 'To the Nile'. As for Byron, his plans to visit Egypt date
back to a trip to Athens in 1811, when he had obtained a firman to
enter the country but was distracted by Greece. In 1819 he persuaded the publisher John Murray to add a few stanzas to the
first Canto of 'Don Juan':

What are the hopes of man? Old Egypt's king
Cheops erected the first pyramid
And largest, thinking it was just the thing
To keep his memory whole and mummy hid;
But somebody or other rummaging,
Burglariously broke his coffin's lid:
Let not a monument give you or me hopes,
Since not a pinch of dust remains of Cheops.

Benjamin Haydon, a close friend of Keats, painted large,
detailed canvases on epic themes, of which five were on Egyptian
subjects. He researched these by visiting the Egyptian rooms of
the British Museum, the sarcophagus of Sethos I at the Soane
Gallery, and consulted 'everything Aegyptian in the Musaeum'.
He spent most of his time between 1823 and 1826 on 'Pharaoh
dismissing Moses at dead of night, on finding his first-born dead
at the Passover', a subject that inspired him because, as he
recorded in his notes, 'a Sphinx or two, a pyramid or so, dark
and awful, with the front groups lighted by torches, would make
this a subject terrific and affecting. It combines pathos and sub-
limity.'
The dark and the awful, the pathetic and the sublime that
attracted Haydon and others to Egyptian themes were used by
architects of the time in a style that has been called 'Commercial
Picturesque'. The Egyptian Hall in Piccadilly, which had
housed Belzoni's exhibition, was an early example. There was
also an Egyptian House in Penzance that resembled it, with cor-
bel-arched windows, torus mouldings, and a scattering of

winged discs, which was built as a museum and geological repository. The 'Egyptian style' was much favoured for such
places as being redolent of high antiquity. It was also thought to
suggest strength, solidity, and durability, making it highly suitable for mills, railway stations, and bridges. The Brighton Chain
Pier of 1823 and the Clifton Suspension Bridge at Bristol, designed in 1831, both have Egyptian features, Brunel's scheme for
Clifton including pylons with sphinxes and winged orbs on top
of them, as well as decorations of hieroglyphics, a *tout ensemble*
that was greatly admired.

Even the manufacturers of the industrial north sought to
spiritualise their satanic mills with echoes of Egypt. The Temple
Mills in Marshall Street, Leeds, were built with a front based on
the Temple of Edfu and a factory block derived from Dendera.
The interior columns had palm and papyrus capitals, and the
roof had a layer of earth sown with grass so sheep could graze
above; this had to stop when one of the sheep fell through into
the machines.

Egyptian motifs had been common in funerary architecture
since the Renaissance, but in the early 19th century they
acquired a new prominence. Under Napoleon the great and
beautiful cemetery of Père-Lachaise in Paris was laid out, and
many of its most distinguished monuments are Egyptian in style.
The standard house-tomb comprised a subterranean vault with a
chapel above, often ornamented with Egyptian motifs. The
tomb of Gaspard Monge, erected by the pupils of the École
Polytechnique, is rich in Egyptiana, befitting a memorial to the
senior of Bonaparte's savants. Père-Lachaise quickly became
famous as a model for public cemeteries, and was widely copied.
An 'Essay on Cemeteries', published in the *Architectural Magazine* in 1837, observed that 'The Egyptian Style, from its massive breadth and colossal proportions, has sometimes been
adopted for mausoleums, and, I believe, occasionally for buildings connected with enclosed Cemeteries, probably on account
of the idea of duration and strength which naturally connect
themselves with Egyptian remains.' The author, however, goes
on to mention a reservation expressed earlier about the practice:
'. . . it is as well to cultivate a preference for the Gothic style,
since it is a fact, which nothing can alter, that this is Christian
architecture, and the Classical and Egyptian belong equally to

paganism.'

The 10th Duke of Hamilton, however, was unaffected by the misgivings of his fellow Christians. In 1837 he paid 600 pounds for a sarcophagus that had been shipped to France by Champollion, not for exhibition, but to receive his own remains. The Duke commissioned a vast mausoleum in the grounds of Hamilton Palace, which *The Times* described as 'believed to be the most costly and magnificent temple for the reception of the dead in the world – always excepting the pyramids', and had himself interred there, his body first having been embalmed by Joseph Pettigrew, author of *A History of Egyptian Mummies*.

Aside from individual eccentricity, the sober municipal authorities and commercial concerns also were swayed by the increasing popularity of the Egyptian fashion. In 1839 the London Cemetery Company built the 'Circle of Lebanon Catacombs' at the Cemetery of St James in Highgate, in which a stucco-faced range of house-tombs in the Egyptian style surround a great Cedar of Lebanon. The entrance, a corbelled arch flanked by Egyptian columns with guardian obelisks, leads to an 'Egyptian Avenue'. The 'Glasgow Necropolis', laid out in the early 1830s, contains several tombs with Egyptian features, as well as an obelisk with inscriptions and Egyptian vaults for the storage of bodies pending the building of permanent tombs. Several other places at this time incorporated Egyptian themes into their cemeteries: Kensal Green, Norwood, Brompton, and Bradford.

Undoubtedly the most bizarre scheme was that of Thomas Willson who in 1824 proposed the erection of a vast pyramid in the centre of London to house five million bodies. It was to be constructed of brick, faced with granite, occupying an area the size of Russell Square, and would 'tower to a height considerably above' that of St Paul's Cathedral. The cost was estimated at 2,583,552 pounds. Since all the vaults within the structure were to be sold as freehold at prices ranging from 100 to 500 pounds each, the estimated profit was calculated to be 10,764,800 pounds. However, despite Willson's claim that 'This grand Mausoleum will go far towards completing the glory of London', and despite its clear profitability and the fact that it would be ornamental, vandal-proof and hygienic, financial support was unforthcoming and the grand design remains unfulfilled.

Most of the poets, architects, and artists who drew inspiration from Egypt never got around to actually visiting the place. Some of the most famous were satisfied with a perfunctory tokenism, like the pyramids that J.W. Turner occasionally placed on the horizons of his biblical landscapes. There were, however, some artists who had the means and the leisure to seek out the real thing, and it is perhaps not surprising that their lives became interconnected.

Frederick Catherwood, who is best known for his drawings of the Maya monuments, visited Egypt during 1823-4 and met Robert Hay, a Scottish antiquarian and traveller, in Malta on his way home. Hay was so impressed by Catherwood's tales and drawings that he set off for Alexandria, and spent the next twelve years visiting the Nile Valley in the company of artists and scholars. One of them was Joseph Bonomi, a sculptor and draughtsman, who, having been introduced to Egypt by Hay, spent the next eight years there assisting the researches of visiting scholars, among whom was the man who first stimulated popular interest in Egyptology in Great Britain.

John Gardner Wilkinson had been introduced to the mysteries of hieroglyphics when a schoolboy at Harrow, the headmaster at the time, Dr George Butler, being a friend and former student of Thomas Young. Having left Exeter College, Oxford without taking his degree, Wilkinson was visiting Italy for his health, in accordance with the fashion of the day, when he met Sir William Gell, antiquarian, with whom he had corresponded on the subject of hieroglyphics, and was persuaded to devote himself to Egyptian archaeology.

Wilkinson had a small income, and at the age of twenty-four was able to visit Egypt in 1821 remaining there for the next twelve years. During this time he visited every significant archaeological site, making careful and skilled drawings. He studied Arabic and Coptic to help him translate the hieroglyphics, and, independently of Champollion's work, arrived at many of the same conclusions.

Working for the most part on the hieroglyphics and without government assistance, Wilkinson was able to identify many royal names, and produced the first reliable chronological order of the kings and dynasties. He also drew up the first comprehensive plan of ancient Thebes, produced an unsurpassed wealth of drawings and paintings from the tombs, and wrote his monumental, wide-ranging, and highly successful *The Manners and Customs of the Ancient Egyptians. Including their Private Life, Government, Laws, Arts, Manufactures, Religion, Agriculture, and Early History, derived from a comparison of the early paintings, sculptures, and monuments still existing, with the accounts of ancient authors*, which appeared in three volumes in 1837. Bonomi had prepared the illustrations.

The previous year *Manners and Customs of the Modern Egyptians* by Edward William Lane had appeared in London. The work sought to do for the modern Egyptians what Wilkinson was to do for their ancestors. Of all the Englishmen who donned linen drawers and kaftan, ate sheeps' eyes, adopted Arabic names, and generally tried to submerge their Englishness, Lane is among the most scholarly and readable. Son of a Hereford parson, he was destined for the church via Cambridge, but abandoned the plan after a short visit to that city. After a few years in London, where he learned drawing, engraving, and Arabic, in July 1825 at the age of twenty-four he set out for Alexandria in a brig that nearly foundered in a gale off Tunis. His biographer records that having sent the incompetent master to his cabin, Lane had himself lashed to the wheel and navigated the brig safely into Malta. Once in Egypt, Lane displayed the same courage and independence by attempting to live as an Arab:

I have associated, almost exclusively, with Muslims of various ranks in society: I have lived as they live, conforming with their general habits; and, in order to make them familiar and unreserved towards me on every subject, have always avowed my agreement with them in opinion whenever my conscience would allow me, and, in most other cases, refrained from the expression of my dissent, as well as from every action which might give them disgust; abstaining from eating food forbidden by their religion, and drinking wine etc; and even from habits merely disagreeable to them; such as the use of knives and forks at meals. ... While, from the dress which I have found most convenient to wear, I am generally mistaken, in public, for a Turk.

Wilkinson became famous by revealing the secrets of a long-dead civilisation. Lane, like the social anthropologists of the later 19th century, acquired status because of his familiarity with a culture that was alien and exotic. He carefully observed and noted every aspect of the Egyptian way of life, making a series of drawings by using a camera lucida, which threw an image via a prism on to a black plate where the image could be sketched.

The publishers Lane offered his observations on Egypt to turned the book down on the grounds that there was insufficient interest at the time. Fortunately Lord Brougham saw its possibilities, and recommended it to the Society for the Diffusion of Useful Knowledge. The book was a commercial success, passing through four editions in the first ten years. This was perhaps not due entirely to a widespread interest in anthropology; there is a comment in the introduction that might have caught the reader's attention: 'The heat of the summer months is sufficiently oppressive to occasion considerable lassitude, while at the same time it excites the Egyptian to intemperance in sensual enjoyments; and the exuberant fertility of the soil engenders indolence . . . '

Early Victorian society did not shrink from diverting itself occasionally with revelations of the 'intemperate sensual enjoyments' of foreign peoples. Indeed, there was a keen interest in the exploits of those who broke with impunity the taboos of polite society, and Lane was clearly well placed to reveal them. He describes not only the outward show of Egyptian culture – the houses, dress, social habits, games, public festivals – but also the hidden world of the harem and bedroom. There are revelations about the preparation and smoking of hashish and opium, the secret rites of the dervishes, the practice of circumcision, and charms against the evil eye. He writes with enthusiasm about the allure of Egyptian women: 'The eyes, with very few exceptions, are black, large, and of a long, almond form, with long and beautiful lashes and an exquisitely soft, bewitching expression: eyes more beautiful can hardly be conceived . . .' The secrets of their makeup are revealed in detail, and the instructions they receive for becoming instruments of pleasure to their husbands. Many a *frisson* must have occurred in the Victorian breast at the observation that, 'The libidinous character of the generality of the women of Egypt, and the licentious conduct of a great number of them may be attributed to many causes; partly to the cli-

mate, and partly to their want of proper instruction and of innocent passtimes and enjoyments.'

As well as the enchantments of sensual pleasure, there were
those of the supernatural. Lane was able to testify from personal
experience that the occult powers of the ancient Egyptians had
been passed to their modern descendants. He once visited a magician in Cairo, taking with him as directed a mixture of frankin-
cense and coriander seed. This was burned in a chafing dish, and
a young boy, 'not arrived at puberty', was brought in to stand by
it. In the palm of the boy's hand the magician drew a 'magic
square' containing numerals which, if added up in vertical, horizontal, or diagonal rows, came to fifteen. In the centre of the
square the magician poured a little ink, and told the boy to gaze
into the blot. Lane was then asked if he wanted to call up any
person, living or dead. He chose Lord Nelson. Immediately the
boy saw a man dressed in black European clothes who seemed to
have lost his left arm. This was impressive, though inaccurate,
and Lane asked helpfully if perhaps the image in the blot could
be as in a mirror, so left appeared right; the magician confirmed
that this was indeed so.

The sobriety of Sir John Gardner Wilkinson, who was
knighted after the publication of *Manners and Customs*, was
never in question. In *Modern Egypt*, published in 1843, his view
is uncompromisingly that of the Englishman abroad, and contrasts sharply with Lane. Wilkinson's book had of course a different aim, being a comprehensive guide-book for travellers. It
seeks to equip the foreign tourist in Egypt with the information
necessary for a successful visit, rather than to enlighten the
curious. The book is superbly wide-ranging. Wilkinson eval-
uates the various routes and hotels on the way to and within
Egypt, and gives hints on how to avoid the rapacity of the boat-
men and donkey drivers. There is a wealth of carefully researched information on the history and layout of every major
archaeological site along the Nile Valley, as well as down-to-
earth practical advice for the traveller, such as the suggestion
that the first thing to do with a boat after hiring it is to sink it to
drown the rats.

Wilkinson's *Modern Egypt* contrasts most sharply with Lane's
Modern Egyptians in its attitude to the Egyptians. Wilkinson
gives the traveller minute and exact advice on the wages appro-

priate for various classes of servant, and constantly warns against the malpractices of those in his employ. After the first few days sailing in the boat that you have hired and sunk, for example, it is a good idea to order one of the native servants 'at night or under the plea of bathing' to examine the keel for logs of wood that are sometimes tied across it to slow it down, increasing the length of the voyage and hence the hire charges. According to Wilkinson, Egyptians may be perfidious and grasping, but the English traveller has to get used to the notion that even the Egyptian beggar thinks of himself as a superior person.

Wilkinson's drawings were admired for the fidelity with which he reproduced the monuments, inscriptions, and wall paintings that he studied; Bonomi, who helped prepare them for publication, was a draughtsman, Lane an engraver. Until this time the function of the artist on expeditions was to act like a camera and record without distortion. The first artist to visit Egypt who regarded himself as a professional painter, in the sense that he earned his living by painting, was David Roberts.

Roberts was the talented first son of a Scottish shoemaker, who found his way into the art world through working as a scenic artist in the circus and the theatre. His paintings retained a theatrical quality throughout his career, and would all be perfectly at home on the set of romantic opera. Roberts sought out subjects in dramatic settings that allowed him to fill large canvases with glowing colours. One of his earliest commissions was 'The Departure of the Israelites from Egypt', which he chose himself, he wrote, 'more as a Vehicle for introducing that grand, although simple style or architecture "the Egyptian" than for any other reason.' The painting shows tens of thousands of people departing from the house of bondage, gazed upon by the Egyptians from the hanging gardens of their rich palaces. There are rich and sombre colours, but the architecture is not very accurately Egyptian, being Graeco-Roman after the style preferred by Denon and most of the early 19th-century travellers. A vast, colonnaded building occupies the left side of the picture, and stretches into the distant mists, which are pierced by steeply angled pyramids. The picture has a megalomaniac quality, characteristic of the visionary painters of the age. Its reception was so enthusiastic that Roberts was able, in the year of its first exhibition, to give up painting scenery for the Covent Garden

Christmas pantomine and devote himself to higher things.

In 1838 Roberts made a pilgrimage to the source of his inspiration. Having presented himself to Colonel Campbell, he set off on a trip up the Nile accompanied by Captain Nelley of the 99th Regiment, a retired sugar planter from the British West Indies, the myopic and gouty Mr Vanderhorst, and a mysterious 'Mr A' they had picked up in Cairo. They chartered a boat to take them to the second cataract, at a charge of fifteen pounds a month for a crew of eight, for three months. They arranged to have the boat sunk to drown the rats, and bought a Union Jack to fly at the mast-head. While not an exploratory voyage – there were few risks, and many other foreign tourists had led the way – it introduced the reality of Egypt to a painter whose imagination had long been fed by visionary notions:

> To the eye of a painter nothing can exceed in beauty these craft skimming along the river with their white sails spread and shivering in the wind: their little cabin on the deck reminds me of the high quarters and sterns of the Dutch shipping that from a boy upwards has been the object of my admiration in the sea pieces of Vendervelde and Backhuysen. They are on a small scale certainly, but with their picturesque baskets . . . and the still more picturesque costumes of the men they are superior even to the Dutch.

Roberts, who never forgot his humble beginnings above the cobbler's shop, took some pride and pleasure in acting the British gentleman abroad:

> . . . there is to me the gratification of being for the first time commander of a vessel with a crew of eight or nine men at my disposal. I now and then look up to the British ensign with no little degree of pride, as some vessel passes me with her tattered flag with its Arabic inscription or the Pasha's with its crescent and star.

One day, above Edfu, the sense of national superiority seemed to evaporate when the Pasha's flag, attached to the Pasha's steamer, hove into view. Roberts and his companions decided the Pasha's must be the first steamer to ascend the Nile, so they gave it three hearty cheers, 'English fashion until the old rocks of Hagar Sil-sila rang again'. They had letters of introduction to the Pasha, and went into a frenzy of activity at the possibility of presenting them. The Pasha's steamer stopped midstream opposite the place where Roberts' boat was anchored. Interpreting this as a sociable gesture, they set off in hope of an audience. They were met by a Scottish engineer who said they had been ordered to stop to find out what all the shouting was about, and, hearing Roberts' explanation, went below to get up steam. The Pasha Muhammad Ali kept below decks, and Roberts' party was forced to make a hasty and undignified exit as the steamer moved forward.

Roberts noted in his journal that the Pasha had refused to appear because he thought them to be a 'set of swaggering Englishmen'. Apparently the young Egyptians who were sent to England to study came back with what the Pasha called a 'swagger of independence', which was not to his taste.

Roberts and crew sailed on down to Karnak, where Roberts felt that the spontaneous enthusiasm of the French army, as recorded by Denon, must have been affected because there was nothing to get excited about from a distance. 'It is only on coming near that you are overwhelmed, as it were, with astonishment; you must be under them and walk around them.'

He made a study of the Great Hall, a long perspective of columns, with the priapic god Min standing proudly on the left-hand near column, but deprived of his erect member in deference to the sensitivities of the age. Roberts lamented the absence of the obelisk, removed from its rightful place in the sun after thirty-three centuries to decorate 'a spot in Paris which has been stained with a 1,000 crimes'.

The group went on to the island of Philae, which, like all travellers before him, Roberts found spellbinding, a 'paradise in the midst of desolation'. He made a dramatic study of the island at sunset, with the light streaming through the ruins, and wrote that it made him homesick: 'Its ruins, even at a distance, are more picturesque than any I have seen; perhaps this may be owing to the high barren rocks by which it is surrounded. To me it brought recollections of "my fatherland" by reminding me of the first descent upon Roslin Castle.'

The furthest point south that Roberts reached was Abu

Simbel, where he stayed for three days sketching the great temple. He found the four great statues, though battered, to be awe-inspiring, and feared they might be 'not only destroyed by relic hunters but covered with such names as Tomkins, Smith, and Hopkins', and such people who have 'the effrontery to smear their stupid names on the very forehead of the god'.

Once back in Cairo, through the intervention of Colonel Campbell, Roberts managed to get a firman from the governor giving him permission to draw interiors of the mosques in the city. The only condition was that he should do so properly dressed. He shaved off his mutton-chop side-whiskers and grew a heavy moustache, wore a large turban and Turkish baggy trousers, an abba – a sleeveless coat – and a broad sash that covered the lower half of his chest. He decided he made quite a 'tolerable Turk'. For Roberts, of course, the great excitement was being the first European artist to have the privilege of drawing inside the mosques. This was not strictly true, since the larger mosques had been open to visitors since the beginning of the century, but Roberts could claim to be the first professional artist to be given official permission to take his pick of the mosques in Cairo.

He was always conscious of being in a special position and worked hard to justify it: 'I am the first artist', he wrote, 'at least from England that has been here . . . The French work, I now find, conveys no idea of these splendid remains.' His delight in Egypt was expressed in the vast portfolio of drawings that he amassed in Cairo, which he wrote enthusiastically to a friend about:

> I do not mind stating to you that I think them (you will say natural enough) the most interesting that has ever left the country, I mean as artistical drawings and having been familiar with allmost every work on ancient Egypt previous to my coming out I should say that those mighty remain yet to be done both with regard to showing their Magnitude and ellegant formation . . . all of which I have vanity enough to suppose, I cannot say done justice to, for no painting can do that, but I think I have approached nearer the thing than any hithertoo anything near the thing would take years . . .

David Roberts stands far above all the artists who worked in or on the subject of Egypt at this time, both in the sheer quality of his work and in its skill and presentation. His book *Egypt and Nubia*, containing a collection of fine lithographs from his work, was published in 1846-9. It became widely popular, achieving some distinction from the fact that among its original subscribers were Queen Victoria and the Archbishops of Canterbury and York. The illustrations, all beautifully drawn, and presented with a high degree of accuracy, only failed Roberts when his taste for the theatrical took over. The original painting of one of them, 'A Recollection of the Desert on the Approach of the Simoon', is a dramatic composition showing the Sphinx with a pyramid behind it, bathed in the vermilion glow of a setting sun. The Sphinx shows its left profile, and the sun sets centre-stage, which is an impossible angle since the Sphinx – the embodiment of Ra-Herakhty, the rising sun – faces due east. The juxtaposition of the pyramid is also inaccurate. Holman Hunt was appalled by Roberts' licence, but Charles Dickens, to whom Roberts presented the original painting, was delighted with it and pronounced it 'a poetical conception'.

Like Lane and Wilkinson, Roberts was a highly individual personality who worked alone. The extent of these men's understanding of Egypt was limited by their preconceptions and the restrictions of time and money, yet each accomplished an enormous amount of work despite those limitations.

In the early 1840s there were plans for an expedition for which there would be no impediments, for it came to advance the reputation of an ambitious European power.

Frederick Wilhelm IV came to the throne of Prussia in 1840 with a reputation as a man of liberal leanings and a taste for the antique and the picturesque. He was the lifelong friend of Baron Christian von Bunsen, scholar and diplomat, who spent the 1840s at the court of St James in London, and wrote the five volumes of *Egypt's Place in Universal History*. Having kept up a regular correspondence with Bunsen, King Frederick was aware of the reputations that England and France were making in the fashionable field of Egyptian discoveries, and of the internationally admired collections at the Louvre and the British Museum. It was, King Frederick decided, time for Prussia to advance human knowledge, as well as national status. Accordingly, King Frederick ordered the mounting of an expedition to

Egypt that was to be the largest and best organised in the history of the exploration of that country.

On the advice of Bunsen and the elderly scholar Humboldt, the King appointed Karl Richard Lepsius, lecturer in philology and comparative languages at the University of Berlin, as leader of the expedition. Lepsius had spent four years touring the Egyptian collections in England, France, Holland, and Italy, learning the art of making squeezes and tracings of inscriptions, as well as engraving on copper and lithography – all of which were to serve him well in Egypt.

The expedition left from England, where Lepsius had signed up Joseph Bonomi as well as the English architect James Wild. They arrived in Alexandria in September 1842.

Through the good offices of the Swedish consul-general, who was looking after the affairs of Prussia in Egypt, they were granted an audience with Muhammad Ali. The Pasha declared himself delighted with the vases that Lepsius brought as gifts from King Frederick, and even more honoured to receive a personal letter. The Pasha 'showed himself brisk and youthful in his motions and conversation; no weakness was to be seen in the countenance and flashing eye of the old man of three and seventy springs'. Lepsius asked how the Cairo Museum, established by the law of 1835, was getting on. The Pasha replied that it was not flourishing because of the many unjust requisitions made of him in Europe; he then consented to a firman giving Lepsius unlimited right to excavate and to make whatever collections he chose.

On 15 October, the entire expedition celebrated the birthday of King Frederick by making their first visit to the Great Pyramid. They rode in a long procession, and had a simple breakfast in one of the nearby tombs while the workmen erected a large tent, brought from Cairo:

I had it pitched on the north side of the pyramid, and had the great Prussian standard, the black eagle with the golden sceptre and crown, and a blue sword, on a white ground, which had been prepared by our artists within these last few days planted before the door of the tent.

About thirty bedouins were assembled at the foot of the Pyramid, and on the signal for the climb to begin, each member of the expedition was seized by several bedouin and hoisted up the steps to the pinnacle:

> A few minutes afterward our flag floated from the top of the oldest and highest of all the works of man with which we are acquainted and we saluted the Prussian eagle with three cheers for our King. Flying towards the south, the eagle turned its crowned head homeward towards the north . . .

The expedition stayed for three years in Egypt, carefully and methodically recording its findings. They spent six months at Memphis and seven at Thebes, where Lepsius expressed his gratitude to Wilkinson and Hay for restoring some of the old houses that the expedition took over as living quarters: 'At the extremity of the court there is still a single watch tower, whence the Prussian flag is streaming, and close by it a little house of two stories, the lower of which I myself inhabit. Space, too, is there for the kitchen, the servants, and the donkeys.'

During the winter season, which Lepsius called the 'season of sociability', they had visitors every week from Europe. England, he wrote, 'of course was the most represented', the French being less frequent.

By the early 1840s the Nile Valley had ceased to be the remote and perilous region of half a century before, and was on its way to becoming the well-beaten tourist trail we know today. The expedition was particularly well sited at Thebes for the second of their annual celebrations:

> In the jewel of all Egyptian buildings, in the palace of Rameses Sesostris, which this greatest of the Pharaohs erected in a manner worthy of himself and the god . . . on a gently rising terrace, calculated to overlook the wide plain on this side, and on the other side of the majestic river, we kept our beloved King's birthday with salutes and flags, with chorus singing and with hearty toasts that we proclaimed over a glass of pure German Rhine wine.

What the Egyptian labour thought of all this carousing around the ancient temples is not recorded; no doubt by this time they were used to the strange ways of European visitors. Lepsius does not seem to have had the difficulties with his employees that others had experienced. Perhaps he did not trouble to record them, or perhaps his status symbol had the effect he ascribed to it: 'I wear also a broad-brimmed, grey felt hat, as a European symbol, which keeps the Arabs in proper respect.'

The research was meticulous, the records comprehensive, and the Lepsius expedition has gone down in history as having changed the character of Egyptian exploration by bringing order out of chaos. But this was not its only aim; Lepsius records that its royally sanctioned purpose was 'an historical and antiquarian research into, and collection of the ancient Egyptian monuments in the valley of the Nile and the peninsula of Sinai'. The expedition did not neglect its acquisitive duty and sent home a total of 15,000 antiquities and plaster casts, which formed the Berlin collection, including three complete tombs from the region of the Great Pyramid, which were carefully taken to pieces and embarked by four workmen specially sent from Berlin for the purpose.

In shipping his antiquities down from the southern provinces, Lepsius was supplied with government boats from Mount Gebel Barkal to Alexandria, which caused friction with excavators from other countries who were forbidden by law to export their finds, or even to claim them as their own. The justification Lepsius gave for this unusually extensive plundering of the ancient monuments was in line with the new morality of selfless contribution to a greater good:

> For as we did not, like many of our rivals, dig out and remove the monuments, which had mostly been hidden below the surface, in haste by night, and with bribed assistance, but at our leisure and with the open cooperation of the authorities . . . and we were not in danger of allowing [our judgement] to be dulled by self interest, as we did not select the monuments for ourselves, but as the agents of our government, for the Royal Museum, at Berlin, and therefore for the benefit of science and an inquiring public.

Lepsius was made Professor at Berlin University in 1846, soon after his return, and eventually Keeper of the Egyptian Collections. He published the epigraphic and other illustrated material from the expedition in 1859, in the twelve vast volumes of the *Denkmaeler aus Aegypten und Aethiopien*, probably the largest work on Egypt ever produced.

With Lepsius' massive publication and those of Lane and Wilkinson, the international reputations of Prussia and England in the field of Egyptology were in the ascendant. By the time the *Denkmaeler* appeared, however, the control of Egyptian archaeology had passed from them and firmly into the hands of the French. A national, and then a world-wide, conscience had finally been awakened concerning the destruction of monuments. An organisation at last was created to conserve and protect them; its founder and director has been described as 'the most titanic figure in the whole history of Egyptology'.

Chapter Six

The Jealous Eye

UNTIL THE MID-19TH CENTURY Egypt was free territory for competing European collectors and museums. Individual pioneers working at the digs bargained with the fellahs and the dealers in open competition with each other. As Howard Carter, discoverer of the tomb of Tutankhamun, wrote, 'Those were the great days of excavating. Anything to which a fancy was taken, from a scarab to an obelisk, was just appropriated, and if there was a difference of opinion with a brother excavator, one laid for him with a gun.' Then, through the efforts of one man, came a great change: the law forbidding the export of antiquities, which had been a dead letter for twenty years, was enforced; sites were inspected; unauthorised excavation was forbidden. This one man took control of the entire Nile Valley, from the Delta to the second cataract. Egyptian archaeology became his personal preserve, within which, on one famous occasion, the Pasha himself claimed only second place. The childhood of Auguste Mariette, unlike that of his distinguished compatriot Champollion, seems to have been innocent of portents. The son of a marine lawyer in Boulogne-sur-Mer, Mariette showed an early talent for drawing and a general aptitude for his studies, but seemed to have no particular focus to his ambitions. He went to England while trying to decide what he wanted to do with his life, and taught French for a year in a private school in Stratford-on-Avon. Next Mariette turned his artistic talents to commercial use by designing ribbons in Coventry, but soon after returned to France at the end of 1840 to teach at the college in Boulogne where he had been educated.

Mariette dabbled: he designed and painted scenery for college plays, receiving rapturous notices in the local paper; he then began to write articles on local history, branching out into the arts with essays on the death of Giotto, a history of French song, a prose elegy on the death of the Duke of Orleans, and even a poem in celebration of the erection of a statue to Napoleon, which he called 'Apothéose de Napoleon'. In 1842 Mariette published a romantic novel, *Hassan le Noire*, which betrayed no hint of literary talent. That same year he was bitten by the Egyptian duck – the phrase he used to introduce the story of his first contact with Egypt: 'The Egyptian duck is a dangerous animal. It greets you in a kindly way, but if you let yourself be taken in by its innocent air and associate with it in a friendly manner, you are lost: one blow with its beak, it inoculates you with its venom, and you are an Egyptologist for life.'

It happened that the painter Nestor L'Hôte, who had accompanied Champollion on his expedition to Egypt, was Mariette's cousin. L'Hôte had died of dysentery there, and his papers were returned to the family. Many of these were drawings of monuments containing inscriptions in hieroglyphics. Mariette, who knew nothing of the subject but had the reputation as a budding intellectual, was asked to sort them out.

Immediately fascinated, he set out to teach himself the rudiments of Egyptology. For seven years Mariette worked alone in his spare time, using the few published books available in an effort to understand the inscriptions. He was seriously hindered by the great *Description de l'Egypte*, which the Museum of Boulogne had purchased, because he assumed that the superb plates were accurate transcriptions of the hieroglyphics. Naturally he found contradictions and inconsistencies in them, and almost gave up the attempt to learn. Many years later Mariette realised that the artists of Napoleon's expedition, confident that nobody would ever succeed in translating the language, had improvised occasionally and made up sections of the hieroglyphic inscriptions to suit their own designs.

In 1847 Mariette described and identified the Egyptian holdings of the Boulogne Museum in his *Catalogue analytique des Monuments composant la Galerie égyptienne du Musée de*

Boulogne, which brought his name to the attention of a circle wider than the readership of the local paper. Most influential was Charles Lenormant, who had been to Egypt with Champollion and was Professor of Egyptian Archaeology at the College de France. Lenormant was so impressed by Mariette that he managed to get him a minor job at the Louvre. In 1849 Mariette moved to Paris. He was then twenty-eight.

Although his menial post was a step down from being a college teacher and minor celebrity at home, Mariette was excited to be out of the provinces at last and in the centre of Egyptian studies. He was given the job of cataloguing new Egyptian acquisitions, and of sticking the papyri on to board so they could be handled without damage. His position, he was warned, was a temporary one, and he was paid very little. His letter of appointment, however, while regretting these inconveniences, reminded Mariette that he would have the pleasure of working in the presence of the Egyptian monuments, and the satisfaction of being of personal service to a great institution. He tried to augment his salary – he was by this time married and had three small daughters – by offering to catalogue and organise the whole collection of papyri in his spare time; he was refused on the grounds that, as he was already in receipt of a monthly salary, it would be inappropriate for the Museum to pay him any more. Civil servants do not have spare time.

Mariette had brought his family to live with him in Paris. A friend who visited him found him sitting in a half-furnished apartment, at a large table covered with books, with one daughter on his knee and two others playing around his ankles. Mariette announced that 'I never work better than like this. I love to feel my little world close to me.' For the rest of his professional career he was to surround himself, through all dangers and discomforts, with his 'little world'.

Working hard to understand the papyri he was asked to catalogue, Mariette acquired an expertise that was to land him his first commission in Egypt, which was inspired by the notorious exploits of two English collectors.

Robert Curzon, 14th Baron Zouche, scholar and traveller, had toured Egypt, Syria, and Palestine in 1833-4 searching for manuscripts in the monastic libraries. At Alexandria he had been offered hospitality at a Coptic monastery, and had returned it by plying the monks with large quantities of raki, leaving his hosts befuddled and taking with him a fine collection of manuscripts. Five years later, the Rev. Henry Tattam – a distinguished Coptic scholar, and Rector of St Cuthbert, Bedford, and Great Woolstone, Berks. – found time to leave his pastoral duties long enough to visit the same monastery. Using the same method of anaesthetising the custodial faculties of the monks, he departed with the rest of the library. Although this caused something of a scandal in academic circles, the reputation of the Rev. Tattam remained wholesome enough for him to be appointed Chaplain in Ordinary to Queen Victoria, and to receive honorary doctorates from the Universities of Dublin, Gottingen, and Leiden.

Mariette was instructed to search for manuscripts in the same locations, though not necessarily using the same techniques of acquisition. Money speaking as loudly as raki, the sum of 6,000 francs was voted for the expedition to finance the collection of manuscripts. Mariette suggested that as a subsidiary aim he might do a little excavating on the side 'to enrich our museums'. This was approved.

As it turned out, the subsidiary aim of the expedition became its principal one. As soon as he landed in Egypt in September 1850, Mariette discovered that all of the manuscripts from the Coptic monasteries had been sent by order of the patriarch to Cairo and placed in one large room out of reach of foreign adventurers. As a further precaution, it was said that the doors to the room had been walled up. The patriarch received Mariette with great charm – he was after all an official representative of the government of France – and offered vague promises of future help. Mariette quickly saw that he was prevaricating, and abandoned all hope of acquiring the Coptic manuscripts.

Mariette was entertained by the French colony in Cairo: Arnaud Le Moyne, the consul-general; Linant de Bellefonds, an explorer and artist who had searched for gold in the service of Muhammad Ali and been rewarded with the title of bey; and Antoine Clot, also a bey, who Muhammed Ali had appointed surgeon-in-chief in Egypt. Mariette noticed that displayed in their gardens were sphinxes of a type he had seen in Alexandria. When he found a similar one at the house of antiquity dealer Solomon Fernandez and remarked on it, he was told that all of the sphinxes came from the same place: Saqqara.

Mariette decided to begin his excavations there, and recorded how one day he came across the half-buried head of a sphinx exactly like the ones he had seen in Cairo and Alexandria:

> At that moment a passage from Strabo came into my memory: 'One finds also at Memphis a temple of Serapis in a spot so sandy that the wind piles up the sand in heaps under which we saw sphinxes buried, some partially, some up to their heads, from which we could guess that the road to the temple would not be without danger if we were surprised by a gust of wind'. Doesn't it seem that Strabo had written this phrase to help us find again, after 18 centuries, the famous temple consecrated to Serapis?

He decided that the sphinxes he had seen in his friends' gardens, and the ones he found buried at Saqqara, could be part of the avenue of sphinxes that led to the Serapeum at Memphis. All he had to do was follow the line of sphinxes to discover the temple:

> I forgot, at this moment, my mission. I forgot the Patriarch, the convents, the Coptic and Syrian manuscripts, even Linant-Bey himself. And so it was that, on the 1st November 1850, at one of the most beautiful sunrises I have ever seen in Egypt, thirty workmen found themselves reunited under my orders, close to the sphinx which was going to bring about so complete a disruption of my stay in Egypt.

Mariette was hazarding a great deal on a hunch. The money he had been given was specifically intended for the purchase of papyri; the excavations on which he planned to spend it were not only incidental – they were both expensive and illegal. The Ordinance of 1835 was still in effect in Egypt, whereby all excavation was forbidden without a firman, and all antiquities discovered on Egyptian soil were the property of the government. It was, however, treated as an ineffective piece of window-dressing. At Saqqara alone there were at the time excavations scattered around the plain being financed by the consul-general of Austria, by the antiquities dealer Fernandez, by the German missionary the Rev. Rudolph Leider, and half-a-dozen lesser lights, none of whom had formal permission. They would hardly welcome a rival on the site, and would tolerate Mariette only if he remained unsuccessful. Mariette, on the other hand, needed a swift and eye-catching success to convince the officials in France that their money, if misdirected, was not being wasted.

As he had hoped, the excavations revealed a line of buried sphinxes twenty feet apart from one another. For two months the workmen battled with the shifting sands to uncover them. By mid-December they had found 134 in an avenue heading due west, which seemed to lead inevitably to the hidden temple. Then, suddenly, there was a gap. The workmen dug to a depth of fifty feet but found nothing. It seemed the avenue just stopped and led nowhere. Mariette's gamble had lost.

On Christmas Eve Mariette discovered that the line of sphinxes turned abruptly at right angles and headed south. There was a further surprise when, instead of a sphinx appearing at the regular distance of twenty feet, they uncovered the seated statue of the Greek poet Pindar, and close by a group of rather battered Greek philosophers meditating, seated on a semi-circular bench. It was disappointing to come upon Greek sculptures at what seemed to be the culmination of an avenue of Egyptian sphinxes, but Mariette pressed on with the work. He soon managed to uncover two temples, one Greek and one Egyptian, the latter with the name Nectanebo, one of the last of the native Egyptian rulers of antiquity. The great temple of Serapis remained undiscovered and his money had started to run out.

Mariette hoped that a report of his findings might help the officials of the Ministry of the Interior to accept the news that the money they had advanced for the purchase of manuscripts had been swallowed up by the sands of Saqqara, and send him some more. Accordingly he made careful drawings of the excavations, and sent them with full details to Paris by hand of the French consul in Alexandria, who was going on leave. To keep the work ticking over, Mariette sold a few pieces of jewellery he had found in the temples, and raised loans from the merchants of Alexandria, and his consul, Arnaud Le Moyne. The news of his successes spreading rapidly among his rivals, the intrigues against him began.

An official complaint that the law was being flouted was made to the Pasha by the Rev. Leider who had a reputation for driving a hard bargain for his own illegal purchases of antiquities, made in the intervals between unsuccessful attempts to convert the Copts to Protestantism. The Pasha was rumoured to be about to interfere, and Mariette, who had built himself a small two-roomed house at Saqqara, took to flying the French flag to render it inviolate. Once he was approached by four horsemen in the service of a local chief, who demanded he hand over all of his discoveries in the name of the Egyptian government, but he drove them off 'with blows of the courbash'.

In Paris, the Committee for National Museums of the Ministry of the Interior sat to hear a report on Mariette's activities in support of his claim for more funds. In spite of the irregularities of his behaviour, they were powerfully swayed by its reasoning:

> In spite of the circumspection and the prudence which have presided over the operations of the French explorer, the alarm has been raised among foreigners. It would be difficult to prevent them from approaching the temple. To suspend or to stop the researches which have been conducted with so much success, would be to hand over to rival museums that which it is our duty to preserve for the national collection. These motives decided the Finance Committee to propose a credit of 30,000 francs . . .

The credit was approved, the French consul in Cairo was notified of it and of the specific purposes to which it was to be applied: 'for the excavation of a temple dedicated to Serapis, discovered among the ruins of Memphis, and for the transport, to France, of the objets d'art which come from it.'

While delighted to be solvent, Mariette was disconcerted by the communication because the objets d'art that he was being paid to send back to France belonged by Egyptian law to the Egyptian government. And Abbas-Pasha, nephew of Muhammad Ali, who had assumed the government of the pashalik, was less pliant than his uncle in the matter of firmans. The French consul decided that the official communication, together with the obvious work that Mariette was engaged in at Saqqara, made it advisable to apply, if belatedly, for official permission. He did so in a manner calculated to appease the Pasha: 'M. Mariette does not in the least contest the rights of ownership of the Viceroy over all the monuments which are on Egyptian soil and undertakes in advance to take away nothing which he has already discovered or will in the future discover.' The firman was granted by Abbas Pasha, subject to two conditions expressly written into the 1835 law but not previously insisted on: all portable objects discovered by Mariette were to be handed over to the officials, and five guards were to be stationed at the excavation sites to supervise operations.

Mariette was completely frustrated by the situation, he being caught between the directives of his native and his host governments. The firman meant he could legally continue with his excavations, but the French Ministry of the Interior would hardly look kindly on his spending their 30,000 francs on acquiring treasures for the Pasha. Mariette suspended the work to give the impression of pliancy, and Abbas Pasha in return compromised by ruling that the French could keep all they had discovered up to the date of the firman, as long as all subsequent finds were handed over to his officials, according to the law.

At this point the situation was further complicated by the discovery at Saqqara, while negotiations were still going on, of the massive underground mausoleum of Apis. It surpassed all expectations. Behind a magnificent sandstone door lay a communal sepulchre, in which the bulls, which had been the incarnation of Apis, were buried. Twenty-four enormous granite coffins were found in a long gallery with corridors and rooms branching off to each side. The gallery was littered with stelae, broken statues, and treasures of all kinds. By good fortune the Pasha's inspectors happened to be away from the site when the entrance was discovered, and Mariette ordered it to be buried and kept secret. Whatever the final official agreement between the diplomats and the Pasha, Mariette decided he had to make his own arrangements.

He installed a work-room in the temple of Nectanebo, and during the day, under the eyes of the official inspectors and following lists approved by them, began packing all the items that had been ceded to France. A secret, wood-lined shaft led from this room to a chamber above. At night, the treasures from the Serapeum were passed down the shaft, to be packed and hauled away to Alexandria by donkey. As each tomb was cleared Mariette made an official report of its discovery, and led disappointed officials through its empty chambers.

For months the deception was kept up. Mariette was able to send back to the Louvre a magnificent collection, including the gold and jewellery of Khaemwese, son and co-regent of Ramesses II, discovered in a tomb where, Mariette recorded, the sand still bore the imprints of the funeral workmen.

Because it became impossible to keep up the pretence that all the tombs were totally empty, Mariette employed a colleague, inappropriately named Bonnefoy, to make copies of the stelae and figurines found in the Serapeum for the Pasha's collection, and even turned his own hand to a few hieroglyphics. Mariette also supported the flourishing industry in fakes by discreet purchases for the national museum in Cairo. So long as appearances were kept up, officialdom was content and the inspectors were co-operative. The Pasha showed his personal satisfaction by ordering official help to be given to the sailors on board the *Labrador* and the *Albatros* in loading crates of contraband treasures for the Louvre.

The European population of Cairo was split over Mariette's activities. His supporters included Clot-Bey, Linant-Bey, the consul, the Italian painter Vassali, who was trying to make a living painting the Pashas, and Pruner, a doctor, anthropologist, and assistant to Clot-Bey. Against him were the dealers – the Rev. Leider and Fernandez – as well as the consuls-general of England and Austria, Charles Augustus Murray, and Baron von Huber, who repeated to everyone who would listen that the 'Frenchman at Saqqara is nothing but a thief.'

There were problems on the site: once Mariette was given poison in his food by a servant and nearly died, and attempts were occasionally made to ambush him. However, these were the normal hazards of a successful dig, and he enjoyed the status of Chevalier de la Légion d'Honneur, to which he had been elevated in recognition of his discovery on 16 August 1852.

The German scholar Heinrich Brugsch, who had been sent to Egypt by the Prussian government, joined Mariette at Saqqara to help with the Serapeum inscriptions. The two men became close friends. Brugsch lived with Mariette's family and described the living conditions there:

About thirty monkeys lived around the house or camped on

the roof . . . snakes crawled along the floor, tarantulas or scorpions crawled along cracks in the walls, enormous spiders' webs hung from the ceiling like flags. As soon as night fell, bats, attracted by the light, came into my little room through the shutters and disturbed my rest with their spectral flight. Before sleeping, I tucked my mosquito net under the mattress and commended myself to the grace of God and all the saints while the jackals, the hyenas, and the wolves howled around the house.

Mariette laughed at all the inconveniences of his situation, reported Brugsch, the only sadness in his life being the thought that one day he would have to leave his little hovel and return to France. The day eventually came when, after shipping a little over 7,000 antiquities to Paris, Mariette decided to follow them and enjoy the reputation his discoveries and successful contrabanding operations had won him. There was, however, one further commission to perform before he left. The Duke of Luynes was intrigued by a passage in Pliny in which the poet reports that the Egyptians thought of the Great Sphinx as the tomb of an ancient king called Harmais, believing it to be constructed from materials that had been transported to the site. Pliny did not believe the story because he knew the Sphinx was carved from a natural outcrop of rock. The Duke, however, wondered if possibly the tomb of the king might either be inside the body of the Sphinx or nearby. The undiscovered tomb of an Egyptian king merited a small outlay, and the Duke sent 6,000 francs to Mariette and asked him to find it.

Mariette discovered signs of a stone way leading to the south, away from the natural alignment of the Sphinx's body, and decided to follow it. He came upon a granite enclosure, inside which were the walls of a temple. He decided it could only have been built by the kings who built the pyramids, and began clearing it to the foundations, in the hope of finding an inscription. But the paved floor of the temple was twenty-seven feet down, the sands were loose and shifting, and there was an enormous amount of debris to clear away.

The money ran out again, and Mariette wrote to the Académie des Inscriptions to ask for government assistance. The Secretary made application to the Minister of State, who pursued the argument most likely to loosen the purse strings: national pride. The Minister reminded the officials that the discovery of the Serapeum head meant 'a renewal of the glory of France in Egypt, just at the time when a member of the Berlin Academy had carried out there the name of Prussia with a certain eclat'. Now Mariette was on the verge of another great discovery:

> . . . and the Academie is very disturbed to learn . . . what treasure from antiquity France is in danger of losing, for want of a little money. How many regrets shall we have if this gold-mine, acquired by France through the law of having first discovered it, should become the property of other nations who would not hesitate to take possession of it and exploit it for their own profit.

The Minister was unhappy about advancing further government funds to scientific expeditions because they seemed to find it impossible to keep proper accounts, and Mariette was certainly no exception. The request was passed on to the Director General of Museums, who agreed to the 'positively last subvention' of 10,000 francs. By the time it arrived in Egypt, Mariette had already spent the money, through advances arranged by the consul, and work had to stop while the temple lay half uncovered. As Mariette was later to discover, just beneath the sands, only ten days work from the place where he abandoned the dig, lay the magnificent diorite statue of the king who had built the Second Pyramid. 'A few hundred francs more,' he wrote, 'and the statue of Chephren would today be in France.'

The Louvre welcomed Mariette back and appointed him Assistant Keeper in the Department of Egyptian Antiquities in 1855. He was given permission to visit other European museums, the better to understand and classify his own discoveries, and began in Germany, where Brugsch returned the modest hospitality he had enjoyed at Saqqara. King Frederick William IV, who had demonstrated his interest in Egypt by financing the Lepsius expedition, and who, unknown to Mariette, had sent with Brugsch an anonymous contribution to the work at the Serapeum, invited Mariette to dinner, and bestowed on him the honour of the Red Eagle third class.

Back in Paris, Mariette wrote a study of Egyptian religion as revealed in the inscriptions he had found in the Serapeum. In the work, Mariette tried to show that the Egyptians believed in one God, and that Apis was the incarnation, born of a virgin mother, miraculously conceived without an earthly father; Apis was the Word, on pilgrimage for a time on earth in the form of a bull. Applying concepts such as the Virgin Birth to Egyptian religion smacked of the mystical writings of the mid-19th century rather than the output of a serious Egyptologist, and Mariette's superior at the Louvre, de Rougé, a devout Catholic, was not pleased. Mariette was advised to turn to less controversial areas for his future work.

He visited Turin in May 1857 to examine the collections there, and was fêted by the Museum and by royalty. The King conferred the order of Saints Maurice and Lazarus on him, and the Academy of Sciences of Turin elected him a correspondent. Mariette was already a correspondent of the Academy of Fine Arts at Rio de Janeiro, and had been elected to the Society of Antiquaries in London. In fact, he had become one of the most widely known and respected French Egyptologists abroad. In Paris, however, he found no chance of further professional advancement. The key position was Keeper at the Louvre, and the Museum made it clear that Mariette could only be promoted to this post on the death or transfer of the present incumbent, de Rouge, who showed no sign of moving, was only ten years older than Mariette, and in rude health. His salary of 4,000 francs as Assistant Keeper was all he had to support a family that seemed to increase every year.

One solution was to leave the expensive living in Paris and head for Egypt. As the months passed, Mariette often thought of the Arab proverb, 'He who has once drunk the waters of the Nile will always thirst after them.' He told his friends that he was finding it difficult to concentrate on his work at the Louvre. He would settle down in his office to translate an inscription on an antiquity he had brought back, and as he handled the object he was transported back to the site where he had discovered it, breathing again the clean air of the desert and hearing the cries of the workmen. He would suddenly hate the whole business of translation, de Rouge, the Louvre, and everything around him and long to be back in Egypt. It was out of these frustrations that Mariette conceived the idea of working not for the Louvre, but

reamed of setting up a service to protect the
...1 the interests of science – a service of which,
...ld be the head.

...me early in 1857. Prince Napoleon, cousin of the
...s something of an embarrassment to the Second
...ng restless, cynical, and resentful of Napoleon III's
...wer. Fortunately, the Prince loved to travel. The
E...   / was always ready to encourage him to be abroad on any
pretex., and when the Prince expressed an interest in Egypt,
everything was done to further the realisation of a whim which
would take him out of France for five or six months.

Mariette's old enemy Abbas Pasha had been assassinated by
his own troops, and Said Pasha, his successor, was keen to improve relations with the European powers. He was also under
the influence of the French diplomat Ferdinand de Lesseps, who
had known him since his youth, and so France was once again in
favour, and a visit from the Emperor's cousin would be welcomed.

De Lesseps told the Pasha that the Prince was a lover of
beautiful things and of ancient history. He would therefore ex-
pect to be shown around the excavations of the Nile Valley by
someone who could explain their significance, and to leave Egypt
with a collection of antiquities worthy of his dignity. The Archduke Ferdinand Maximillian of Austria had paid a visit two years
before, and insisted on leaving with the best part of the Cairo
collection, so there was a precedent – of which the Prince was
aware – for heaping the finest of Egypt's antiquities on royal
visitors. The only man who could conduct Prince Napoleon on a
tour, and who would have the energy and organisation to amass a
fitting collection for him to take away, was Mariette. Said Pasha
asked de Lesseps to persuade Mariette to return to Egypt.

There was some discomfort in the invitation. Mariette was
being invited back to Egypt not as the director of a conservation
service for ancient monuments as he wished, but as the quarter-
master for a touring Prince. Instead of enforcing the law forbidding the export of monuments, he was being engaged to flout it.
De Lesseps, who knew of Mariette's ambitions, wrote to him explaining the difficulty of getting the notion into Said Pasha's
head that he had any obligation to look after the monuments.
However, de Lesseps continued, if Mariette made the Prince's

visit a success, he might ask what he would of the Viceroy.

Mariette was granted four months' leave from the Museum and arrived in Egypt in October 1857. Said Pasha greeted him warmly, and put at his disposal a steamboat, the *Samannoud*, with a crew of armed men. Mariette was instructed to sail up river and tell the provincial chiefs that the Pasha forbade them to touch a single antique stone, and to put in prison any fellah who should so much as put a foot inside a temple. Mariette's duties were twofold: to prevent anyone from removing antiquities from the ancient sites, and to collect all the best pieces for the visiting Prince. He set about his work with vigour. He had secured a position undreamed of by the most ambitious of his predecessors: the right to take whatever he wished, as well as the authority to stop anyone else from taking anything at all.

Mariette's sudden pre-eminence was cut short by the news in January 1858 that the Prince had changed his mind and had called off the visit. This communication arrived in Cairo together with a letter from the Louvre informing Mariette that, as he would no longer be required to prepare for the Royal visit, his leave was cancelled and he should return immediately to the Museum, where his desk awaited him.

It seemed to be a hopeless situation: Said Pasha's concern for his country's antiquities sprang purely from a wish to ingratiate himself with the Emperor, and, having lost this opportunity, he had no reason to keep Mariette in his employ. The prospect of returning to the sunless ennui of his unpropitious career in Paris inspired Mariette to write with a proposal that would keep him in Egypt: since the Prince's ambition to visit Egypt was born of a delight in beautiful things, and a deep concern for the early history of man, would the Prince not like to have a collection of the country's finest antiquities as a souvenir of an expedition that had not taken place, but upon which such brilliant hopes had been set?

The private secretary wrote back expressing His Royal Highness's pleasure in Mariette's suggestion, and asking for a list of 'jewels, statuettes, and specimens of Egyptian Art' that could without impropriety be added to Prince Napoleon's already brilliant collection. The list was sent, together with a suggestion as to a small service the Prince might feel inclined to render in return to the future guardianship of such treasures in Egypt. The private secretary's reply was all Mariette could have hoped for: 'Prince Napoleon will not hesitate to let the Viceroy know that, if His Royal Highness were to request from France the help of a savant to establish a Museum fo Egypt, the French government would certainly choose nobody but yourself.'

On 1 June 1858, Mariette was appointed Director of Antiquities in Egypt. He was granted a personal allowance of 18,000 francs a year, the authority to engage colleagues, and the use of the steamboat. Labour for his excavations was classified as public works, and could legally be raised by conscription. He was responsible directly to the Viceroy, and was not allotted a budget, but had the right to apply for funds when they were needed.

Mariette's first duty was to replenish the Cairo Museum, stripped by the Archduke Maximillian, and his first request was for buildings in which to house the nation's present and future collections. He was allotted the warehouses at the port of Bulaq, which had belonged to the steamship company operating between Alexandria and Cairo, but which had been put out of business when the railway opened. Here Mariette installed his friend Bonnefoy as keeper of the antiquities that were to come. There was a low, damp house on the site, to which he brought his family. It was dark, vermin-infested, and falling about their ears, but Mariette, having his 'little world close to him' again, was happy.

While the French community rejoiced, others resented the *arriviste* who took it upon himself to forbid all excavation but his own, threatening the livelihoods of dealers and forgers alike. Mariette spread his work along the entire Valley, and at one time had thirty-seven excavations in progress from the Delta to the first cataract. More than 300 tombs were emptied at Giza and Saqqara; at Edfu Mariette moved an entire village from the roof of the buried temple, exposing the magnificent building for the first time in the modern age; at Thebes he cleared part of the superb edifice of the temple of Queen Hatshepsut at Deir el-Bahri, and discovered the wall depicting the famous 'Hottentot Venus'. This was so admired by the Marquis of Dufferin and Ava, who happened to be visiting at the time, that he took a small force of labour in at night and demolished the wall, hoping to ship the blocks back with other scupltures he had acquired to his family seat at Clandeboye, Ireland. He was discovered, and the blocks were confiscated and sent instead to the Cairo Museum. Across the river at Karnak, Mariette exposed the great temple of Amnun, and removed from there over 15,000 small antiquities. At Abydos, after a brief study of the surface, Mariette astonished the workmen by pointing out to them the line along which they should dig to uncover a boundary wall. When the wall appeared in exactly the place he forecast, the villagers assembled to witness a miracle:

> An old Arab came up and said to him: 'I have never left this village yet I never heard tell there was a wall there. How old are you that you should remember it?' 'Three thousand years', Mariette replied, imperturbably. 'Well,' said the old man, 'to have reached so great an age and yet to look so young, you must be a great saint. Let me look at you.' And, for three days he came to gaze on the great saint, three thousand years old, who, with matchless prodigality, handed out blows of his stick to the workmen who did not work to his liking.

During these years Mariette was all-powerful in the field of excavation. He thought of ancient Egypt, he was to write, as his own personal property, a hereditary fiefdom which he would hand on to his descendants. He travelled everywhere with his wife and eldest son Auguste, whose toys were the statuettes and amulets from ancient tombs, and who referred to the great statues of Thebes as 'les grandes poupées de papa'.

There was, however, a constant threat to Mariette's position. Said Pasha cared nothing for antiquities or for ancient stone statues. He had been persuaded by de Lesseps and Prince Napoleon to set up the Service of Antiquities, but was able at any time to change his mind. The funds that kept Mariette's work going were granted by the Pasha on application and could easily be withdrawn; the collection, which was slowly increasing, could be given away at the whim of a distinguished visitor. But if the Viceroy was insensitive to the needs of scholarship, he could be fired by discoveries that included gold or jewels; Mariette was under steady presssure to produce these, and he did not hesitate to use dynamite to speed up the work.

In February 1859 Mariette heard from his agent at Luxor that an unusually rich sarcophagus had been discovered. It was decorated with gold, and an inscription identified it as that of Queen A-Hotep. Unfortunately, the provincial governor had ransacked the coffin and taken a quantity of gold and jewels, which he planned to send as a gift to the Viceroy to advance his own standing. On hearing the news, Mariette immediately boarded the *Samannoud* and set off up the Nile to intercept the governor's boat. The meeting of the vessels was described by an eyewitness:

> We saw the ship carrying the treasure coming towards us. In half an hour the two steamers were alongside each other. There followed a very heated discussion. Seeing that he was getting nowhere and driven to the limits of his patience by their obstinacy, M. Mariette employed the only methods recognised out here as being effective: he handed out a few hard punches, said he would throw one man into the river, blow the brains out of another, send a third to the galleys, hang a fourth and treat all the rest the same. Thanks to this they agreed to transfer all the antiquities to our ship in return for a receipt.

Mariette was able to arouse the gratitude of the Viceroy by presenting him with a box of magnificent jewellery to adorn himself and his wives; the form that gratitude took was an order to build a new national museum.

The collections at Boulaq were worthy of better housing. George Hoskins, an English traveller who had visited Cairo in 1833, went there again in 1860 and wrote: 'The Museum of Egyptian antiquities collected by Signor Marietti and now very well arranged at Boolak is well worth visiting.' There were, however, very few in the field of Egyptology, either in England or France, who rejoiced. It seemed perverse that an Egyptian ruler should conceive the ambition to hang on to the treasures that were unearthed by European efforts; neither the British Museum nor the Louvre thought it preferable to house, in the remoteness of Cairo and however adequately, treasures that should be admired by the whole world.

At the time both the French and the British were paying court to Said Pasha, and he was careful to balance his favours between them. He had granted his old friend de Lesseps the concession to build the Suez Canal – although Lord Palmerston had managed to delay its ratification at the Porte by two years; on the other hand, he had agreed to let the British set up the Eastern Telegraph Company and the Bank of Egypt. Both countries were offering loans to Said, and each had extended invitations to him to make a state visit. France seemed to have nudged ahead in the diplomatic contest when the Emperor sent a handwritten invitation to the Pasha, by the hand of Mariette. Said was so overwhelmed at the personal honour that he kissed the messenger effusively and offered to grant his dearest wish. Mariette replied that all he wanted was to finish building his new museum. The orders were given.

Mariette was in attendance when the Pasha visited Paris in 1862, and he took some pleasure at being received in high places, though this was tarnished a little by his being forced to accompany Said, to maintain the diplomatic balance, on an extension of his state visit to London.

The group returned via Boulogne, Mariette's home town, where the celebrations so delighted the Pasha that he conferred the title of bey and a pension on Mariette. He also announced publicly that he would be personally responsible for the education of Mariette's children. The future was at last secure.

Six months later, however, Said Pasha died suddenly and Mariette's career in Egypt was once more in jeopardy. Ismail Pasha, who replaced Said, showed no interest in the work of the Service of Antiquities, and had the reputation of needing all the money he could raise for his own extravagances. However Ismail too was keen to modernise and to maintain good relations with the European powers, and so he informed Mariette that nothing would change – funds would be supplied to keep the Service going, and work on building the new museum was to continue.

Supervision of the building work took up most of Mariette's time for the rest of that year. The little time he had left over was spent taking distinguished visitors around the excavations. These included Prince Napoleon, who finally realised his ambition to see the great discoveries his countrymen had made in the valley of the Nile. The weather being uncomfortably hot, the Prince saw very little as he spent his whole time in his luxurious cabin on board the *Menchieh*, only emerging at Philae, where he was roused by indignation at the news that a tourist had damaged the French inscription placed there by General Desaix. The Prince ordered the words to be chiselled out again, and added his personal comment, 'On ne salit pas une page d'histoire.'

When the Museum was finally completed in October 1863, it was one of the most delightful buildings in Cairo. Frederick de Saulcy, Member of the Academy, wrote a report on his visit there for the *Revue Archéologique*:

> Two linked courtyards border the Nile, separated by an ironworked gate. The first one, planted with beautiful trees, holds the residential quarters, including those of Mariette-Bey himself. A delicious gazelle, called Finette, walks freely here, searching eagerly for cigar butts, which are a particular treat for her. Some pretty little monkeys frolic around in her company. The second courtyard is already an integral part of the Museum, for it contains two large sphinxes from Karnak and three superb sarcophaguses in basalt.

There was some difficulty in persuading Ismail to declare the buildings open. Mariette suspected the intrigues of his enemies in Cairo, but the Pasha had always been lukewarm in his enthusiasm for the place, since mummies, however historically significant, are after all just corpses, and he was uncomfortable in the presence of death. The Pasha finally inaugurated the Museum on 16 October 1863, but was careful to avoid crossing the threshold. It became his habit to accompany distinguished visitors to the gates and then wait in the courtyard while Mariette showed them around the buildings.

In 1867 the International Exhibition was held in Paris and the Egyptian entry was in the hands of Mariette. It was a triumph. The Egyptian Temple was crowded with visitors, many of whom, wrote one critic, came to see it out of idle curiosity, but left with a sense of wonder at the civilisation that had produced the magnificent monuments on display. Mariette was promoted to the Red Eagle of Prussia second class, and to Commander of the Légion d'Honneur.

The splendour of the Exhibition, however, caused a turn in

Mariette's fortunes. The Empress Eugénie was so dazzled by the display of jewellery, that she let it be known to Ismail that she would be graciously pleased to receive them as a gift. Taken off his guard, the Pasha could only reply that he would be delighted to accede to her wishes, but added, 'There is someone more powerful than I at Boulaq and you must apply to him.' Mme Cornu, the Emperor's foster sister, was given the task of buying Mariette's consent, and made her request to him in such precise terms that he could not pretend he did not understand: she offered him, in return, the Directorship of the Imperial Printing Office, or of the Imperial Library, a seat as a Senator, a place among the scholars credited with supplying material for the Emperor's *Life of Caesar*. Mariette refused, explaining to Mme Cornu that, dearly as he would love to see the finest antiquities of Egypt safely in France, he had been commissioned to keep them on Egyptian soil, and to protect them against all foreign claims, even those of his fellow countrymen. If he conceded the claims of France today, how would he oppose those of England tomorrow, and of Germany, and of Austria?

It was a courageous decision, not least because Mariette knew that it would win him enemies in France, without gaining him the respect of Ismail, who, like his predecessors, thought that the principal virtue of the treasures of Egypt was their ability to buy the friendship of foreigners. The Service of Antiquities, which operated on different assumptions, began to slide out of favour. Mariette found that the labour he had conscripted was ordered away from his excavations to work on the Suez Canal. He even lost the use of his steamship, which was transferred to other duties and was only returned when he threatened to resign.

Rumours were put about by his enemies in Cairo that Mariette was in league with the Emperor to bring Egypt under French control, and that his paying court to Ismail Pasha had a sinister political motive. Those who were jealous of Mariette's influence, or who had lost income through his enforcing the ban on the antiquities trade, took every opportunity to discredit him. His inability to manage money made it easy to suggest he was mis-applying government funds, and he was always defenceless against auditors. He wrote to a friend at this time:

As I grow older, I turn myself into a philosopher with the

143

whitening of my beard. Before, I used to have periods of dark despair followed by black anger. Today I think of life as a journey by boat with periods of seasickness. When the weather is fine, I go up on the deck and inhale the sea breeze; when its bad I give up and go to bed and vomit . . .

Although it temporarily lost him his labour supply, the building of the Suez Canal turned out to be the occasion for Mariette's rehabilitation with Ismail Pasha. The opening of the Canal was to be an international festival, to which sovereigns and scholars of the civilised world were invited. Ismail had been raised to the rank of Khedive by the Porte, and he was determined to use the glories of ancient Egypt to draw the notables of Europe to Cairo so his prestige with the Sultan would be further enhanced. For this plan Ismail needed Mariette. Suddenly, funds were provided for excavations and for publications, and Mariette was given sole charge of the programme to conduct the guests on a tour of Upper Egypt, and even funds to publish a guide-book to enlighten them.

The occasion was glittering: the Empress Eugénie opened the Canal in the royal yacht *Aigle* on 16 November 1869, and then sailed from Port Said to Suez in four days, followed by sixty-eight vessels of different nationalities. For two months distinguished guests were entertained lavishly by the Khedive, and then passed on to Mariette for tours of the temples. Mariette wrote to his son, 'I've just got back from a tour of Upper Egypt, of Suez, of Saqqara, in the company of so many Empresses and Emperors and Princes and Ministers, I no longer know where I am. The fact is my brains are addled and my legs have given up . . .'

But he had his reward. The Empress Eugénie was charming and attentive, having forgiven him for denying her the jewels, and the Khedive appointed him Commander of the Order of Medjidieh, and announced publicly that he would be paid 4,500 francs a year for the upkeep of his three sons, and a lump sum of 100,000 francs to share between his two eldest daughters. It was a time of clear, not to say brilliant, weather in Mariette's life.

Mariette then was commissioned by the Khedive to provide the story for an opera that was to have its première in the Cairo theatre, built to celebrate the opening of the Suez Canal. The finest and most expensive composers would be approached: Verdi first, and, failing him, Gounod, then Wagner. It took Mariette back to his early dabbling in theatrical design and the romantic novel. He came up with the basic idea for *Aida*, and the synopsis was accepted by Verdi.

For almost a year Mariette was preoccupied with the opera. He travelled to Philae to make drawings of the buildings on which to base his set designs, and copied details of costumes and arms from temple walls, tombs, and statues. He travelled to Paris with his drawings to make sure the sets and costumes being put together were authentic, and found that the professionals had taken over. His original story was being reworked by Camille du Locle, and translated at Verdi's insistence into Italian, with alterations being made at each stage. The sets and costumes were in the hands of theatrical designers who did not welcome Mariette's interference, and Verdi had firm ideas about the music that were not to be deflected by any notions of authenticity. Mariette left the sets and costumes in Paris, which was caught up in the Franco-Prussian War, beginning in July 1870 when the city was under siege.

The Cairo première of *Aida*, which finally took place on Christmas Eve 1871, was a splendid occasion, and Mariette shared in the glory. It began the last decade of his life at a high point, from which he was slowly dragged down by ill-health, the loss of his children, and struggles to keep the Service of Antiquities from falling victim of the extravagances of the Khedive. Mariette was established as a celebrity abroad and was always visited at the Boulaq Museum by travellers of distinction and those involved in Egyptology. The Vicomte de Vogue, diplomat and author, called on him in 1872:

A man of great stature, broadly built, aged rather than old, an athlete, rough-hewn out of the mass like the colossi over which he watched. His high coloured face had a dreamy and morose expression . . . he could easily be taken for a Turkish Pasha. When a visitor crossed the garden, this proprietor would frown, arrogant and annoyed. He would follow the intruder with a jealous eye like that of a lover who sees a stranger enter his beloved's house, or a priest who sees an unbeliever enter the temple.

So jealous was Mariette of the Service and of the Museum he had created, that when de Rougé suddenly died in December 1872, and he was at last offered the position of Keeper at the Louvre, he refused. Along with the offer came vacancies of chairs at the Académie des Inscriptions and the Collège de France, as well as an offer of indefinite leave to allow him to make the necessary arrangements at Boulaq before taking up the appointments. However, Mariette believed that the 'necessary arrangements' at Boulaq involved his continued presence. This was not only to maintain the Service that he had founded, but, of equal importance, to prevent it from falling under the control of another nation. He replied to the offer from Paris:

> Would you now allow that Egyptology, which, until now has been represented in Egypt by a Frenchman, should, in future, be represented by a German? We are now struggling hard in Egypt, against the influence of Germany, which is imposing itself in many directions. Do you really think that I should be the means whereby the Germans manage to get possession of one of the positions they most desire in Egypt?

Mariette stayed on to keep the antiquities of Egypt in the country and under French control. He even persuaded the Khedive not to send the treasures of the Boulaq Museum to Vienna for the Exhibition of 1873, on the grounds that if any of them caught the eye of the Emperor of Austria, Ismail would find it difficult to refuse an Imperial request.

When the American consul-general made an official request to be allowed to export an obelisk, and the request was passed on to Mariette for consideration, his reply showed that his resolve had not wavered since refusing the Empress Eugénie:

> There are two museums in Egypt: one is the Boulaq Museum, the other is the whole of Egypt which, with its ruins spread out on both banks of the Nile from the Delta to the second cataract, constitutes the most beautiful museum that exists in the whole world . . . Why diminish the importance of this second museum which, every winter, the entire world comes here to admire? There is a universal principle in effect in all museums. It is that a museum may receive, but it must never give. Let Egypt demand the Venus de Milo from the Louvre or the Rosetta Stone from London or

any monument from the Abbott Collection in New York. Nobody would hand over such a gift. Why should Egypt be treated differently from other museums?

As Egypt slid into financial chaos, Mariette fought hard for the survival of the Boulaq Museum and the Service of Antiquities. The first of a series of Commissions of Enquiry into the financial condition of the country were held jointly by Britain and France in 1875. Two years later the system of Dual Control was put into effect, whereby an English official supervised the country's revenue, and a French official its expenditure. Ismail's inability to tolerate direct interference led to his organising a military riot in Cairo, and the European powers appealed to his Turkish masters for help. On 26 June 1879, Ismail received a telegram from the Sultan addressing him as the ex-Khedive of Egypt. His son Tewfik was appointed to replace him.

Suddenly, Mariette and the Museum were required to maintain budgets and keep accounts. While the money made available was reduced, at least it was paid regularly, in the form of solid guineas and not promissory notes, and Mariette was still able to run his boat, the *Menchieh*. Work on the excavations was reduced, and Mariette's declining health made it difficult for him to supervise. His last months were spent reorganising the Museum, and trying to ensure that after his death the influence of France on Egyptology would not decline. It seemed certain he would be replaced by Henri Brugsch, his close friend and colleague, and so Mariette reluctantly agreed to a scheme to set up a French Archaeological Mission in Cairo, which would combine Egyptologists and Arabists to maintain influence in the field, should the crucial post of Director be lost to France. The Mission arrived in Cairo at the beginning of January 1881.

Mariette died on 18 January 1881. He was given a state funeral, and was buried in the garden of the Boulaq Museum, just by the front door. That the Museum became the largest and most comprehensive collection of Egyptian treasures in the world is entirely due to Mariette; the government made sure that when its site was relocated Mariette's remains followed. They lie today in a tomb of granite and white marble. Beside this is a bronze statue bearing the inscription: 'A MARIETTE-PASHA L'EGYPTE RECONNAISSANTE'.

Chapter Seven

Sentimental Archaeology

D URING THE YEARS OF FRENCH SUPREMACY in field excavations along the Nile Valley, while Auguste Mariette,
Director of the Service of Antiquities, was contemplat-
ing his growing collections or conducting royalty around his excavations, the founder of British Egyptology was spending his
working days in a small room at the south-west corner of the
Nineveh Gallery of the British Museum.

Dr Samuel Birch was not of a nervous disposition, yet he was
haunted by the conviction that, like the pioneer archaeologists
who struggled against the harsh climate and unyielding soil of
Egypt, he worked in a situation of constant hazard. Despite this
feeling of uncertainty, he directed a vast assembly of monuments
– registering every one of them in his own hand – published over
300 works, lectured widely on Egyptology, and conducted a
vigorous correspondence with scholars all over the world in his
field.

Samuel Birch had no formal education beyond five years at the
Merchant Taylors' School, which he left in 1831 at the age of
eighteen. This is rather surprising since his father had been a
mathematics and classical scholar who was elected to a fellowship of St John's College, Oxford before taking up clerical
appointments. Possibly Samuel had been distracted from his
studies by an interest in Chinese, which he took up at an early
age, and the hope of a post in China may have deflected him
from going on to university.

Samuel put his skills to use in his first job at the British Museum, cataloguing the holdings of Chinese coins. He held what was then called an Assistantship in the Department of Antiquities, which was under the Keepership of Edward Hawkins. It contained almost the entire range of collections that now make up the British Museum. A vast storehouse of miscellaneous materials, the Greek and Roman collections were considered the most valuable. The antiquities from Egypt were still thought of as not quite fine art, but not primitive enough to be ethnographic. The trouble was that nobody had the skills to identify and classify them properly; Hawkins decided to steer the energies of young Birch in just that direction.

He found a ready student. By 1838 Birch was familiar enough with hieroglyphics to produce a monograph on a fragment of coffin presented to the Museum by Vyse and Perring, and even a sketch for a hieroglyphical dictionary. For a time he doubted that Champollion's system was the correct one, but gradually became convinced of its validity by confronting the wrong-headedness of its opponents.

The most valuable work Birch engaged in at this time was the publication of papyri. Originally the trustees of the Museum had insisted that because all papyri were handwritten documents they belonged in the Department of Manuscripts, even though nobody there could understand them. Since Birch, in the Department of Antiquities, was eager to get his hands on them, the 'Hieroglyphic, Hieratic and Demotic Papyri' were transferred in May 1840 to Antiquities. In 1841 the first part of *Select Papyri in the Hieratic Character* appeared. It was a publication that Birch collated and edited, and which represented the beginning of his life-long struggle to make the texts in the care of the Museum available to the scholarly world.

Birch's reputation in that world became international and unassailable. Although he had never set foot in Egypt, he was consulted by the editors of learned journals on papers relating to Egyptian archaeology, and was constantly in demand to help with translations, the preparation of lectures, and the correction of manuscripts. Above all Birch was pestered regularly by dealers in antiquities in search of a pronouncement on the worth of their wares.

Previously, the best way to guarantee the genuineness of an

Egyptian antiquity had been to dig it up. Museums and monarchs, governments and private individuals alike had financed expeditions with the sole intention of acquiring treasures which, because they were taken from the soil, were of unimpeachable genesis. By the mid-19th century, however, the excavations had been so widespread, and so many treasures had found their way on to the market, that the easiest way to acquire them was to buy from the dealers. This demanded expertise of a different kind from that of the field excavator: the need was not to discover but to discriminate, and the skills of the forgers had by this time been finely honed. 'Scarabs', for example, were being turned out by the hundreds in back rooms of the shops of Luxor. These had been disguised skilfully by a covering of glaze made from crushed beads found among the wraps of mummies. The patina of age was added by feeding them to turkeys, whose digestive systems seemed to affect their colouring in much the same way as a couple of thousand years under the soil.

Birch seemed to have an instinct for spotting fakes, perhaps from having developed a familiarity with the genuine objects over many years before the forgeries flooded the market. It was difficult to challenge his opinions, and they became widely accepted as authoritative by both dealer and client. The small back room off the Nineveh Gallery became the source of indispensable authentication in a rising market, and Birch frequently was under siege there.

His views also were canvassed on a matter of increasing public debate. The publicity given to discoveries in Egypt was matched with fierce interest by those concerned with projecting or demonstrating the infallible truth of the Bible. During the first half of the 19th century, criticism from German scholars who questioned the historical accuracy of the Old Testament filtered through to England. This did not have a great impact at first, partly because the church-going public were not fired by the pedantry of foreign intellectuals, and partly because of a settled conviction that the Bible was beyond criticism. In 1830, Dr Thomas Arnold preached that the Christian faith 'which is the guide and comfort of our lives' must not be confounded with 'all questions of science, of history and of criticism'. He added that the Bible could not be properly understood if it is regarded as 'in all its parts of equal authority . . . and like the Koran all composed at one time and addressed to persons similarly situated'.

There was enough public disquiet for the Earl of Bridgewater to bequeath a large sum of money in 1839 to the Royal Society for a series of treatises to be written by experts in theology and science, demonstrating that the Christian religion was compatible with the new discoveries in science. One of the scholars who published a 'Bridgewater Treatise' was the geologist William Buckland, who declared that the Bible did not contain 'historical information respecting all the operations of the Creator'. The age of the earth, as established by geology, and the developments that had taken place upon it, showed that the account of the Creation in Genesis could not be reconciled with the findings of science.

Religious publishing houses joined the fray by producing tracts that called on archaeological evidence to shore up the crumbling authority of the Old Testament. In the 1850s, William Osburn, a member of the Archaeological Institute, published three books in which he cited the wall paintings found in Egyptian tombs as proof that the Israelites had indeed lived there. Canon George Rawlinson, who was to become Camden Professor of Ancient History at Oxford, and who wrote a two-volume *History of Ancient Egypt*, pointed out that modern historical scholarship had made it impossible to treat the campaigns of Caesar on the same footing as the deeds of Romulus, adding that this did not apply to the book of Genesis because it was clear from the chronology that only five generations had elapsed between Adam and Moses, and therefore, 'Moses might, by mere oral tradition have obtained the history of Abraham and even of the Deluge at third hand; and that of the Temptation and the Fall at fifth hand.' He concluded that, 'we possess in the Pentateuch not only the most authentic account of ancient times that has come down to us, but a history absolutely and in every respect true'.

In the same year the final part of a five-volume work that challenged Rawlinson's confident judgement appeared in England. In his great work, *Egypt's Place in Universal History*, Baron Christian Bunsen, whose influence on King Frederick of Prussia had sent Lepsius to Egypt, set out to reconstruct the 'authentic chronology of Egypt' and to 'restore to the ancient history of the world the vital energy of which it has so long been deprived'.

The volumes are ponderous and confused; they might well have sunk without trace were it not that they challenged the authenticity of the Bible and its chronology. Churchmen ridiculed Bunsen's ideas as heartily as unbelievers took them to their hearts. They were given added credence in England by the support of Birch, who had been free with his advice to the author, and had even written the 'Grammar and Dictionary of the Egyptian Language' which appeared in Volume Five.

Soon the established church was being shaken from without by assaults on its doctrines in the name of Darwinism, and from within in the name of progress. In 1860 the publication of *Essays and Reviews*, a collection of seven essays promoting the need for free enquiry, even into religious dogma, divided Christians into violently opposing camps. The essays expressed the belief that the Church of England should come to terms with the critical methods long established in Germany that examined the text of the Bible using the latest techniques of literary analysis and in the light of archaeological discoveries.

With such questions as these being raised, it is hardly surprising that the community of the faithful turned elsewhere for reassurance. The solid evidence of ancient history stood dumbly in the Egyptian rooms of the British Museum, and a stream of visitors demanded that Birch set their doubts at rest by showing them the twenty pieces of silver for which Joseph was sold into slavery, or the library of books which, it was rumoured, had been preserved from the Ark. As the dating of finds in Egypt seemed increasingly to threaten the dates in the Authorised Version, biblical chronology became an obsession and Birch was pestered by eccentrics about every happening recorded in the Bible.

He was promoted to Keeper of Oriental Antiquities in 1860. This was also the year of *Essays and Reviews*, of the Oxford debate on Darwin's theories, and the beginning of a decade in which the battle between science and religion was fought out in England with particular ferocity. It was hardly surprising that Birch was called on by both sides to lend weight to their arguments. Because the Bible made specific references to Egypt and to Egyptian history, those who promoted the cause of the Bible's infallibility looked to the excavations to confirm what was written; their opponents looked for refutations. There was also a

Right: Auguste Mariette,
a drawing made from a photograph
of 1874 – six years before he
actually reached Egypt
for the first time.

Below: Sir James Alexander
studying Cleopatra's needle,
the gift of Muhammed Ali.

MARIETTE EN 1874

D'après une photographie reproduite dans *L'Egypte à petites journées*

The elaborate timber cradle used to manoeuvre Cleopatra's needle
into its position on the embankment in London.

Left: Amelia Edwards, whose book
A Thousand Miles up the Nile
has become a classic.

Below: A drawing by
Amelia Edwards, showing
digging at Thebes.

Sir Evelyn Baring, the British Minister in Egypt – a
man of unusual self-possession.

EXAMPLE OF THE CASING-STONES. OF A PYRAMID, SUPER-POSED ON THE
RECTANGULAR MASONRY COURSES; FROM A PHOTOGRAPH BY PIAZZI SMYTH OF THE SUMMIT OF THE 2ND PYR:

REMNANT OF THE ORIGINAL CASING-STONE SURFACE OF THE GREAT PYRAMID
NEAR THE MIDDLE OF ITS NORTHERN FOOT. AS DISCOVERED BY THE EXCAVATIONS OF COL. HOWARD VYSE IN 1837.

The frontispiece from Charles Piazzi Smythe's
Our Inheritance in the Great Pyramid.

Sir William Flinders Petrie in 1923.

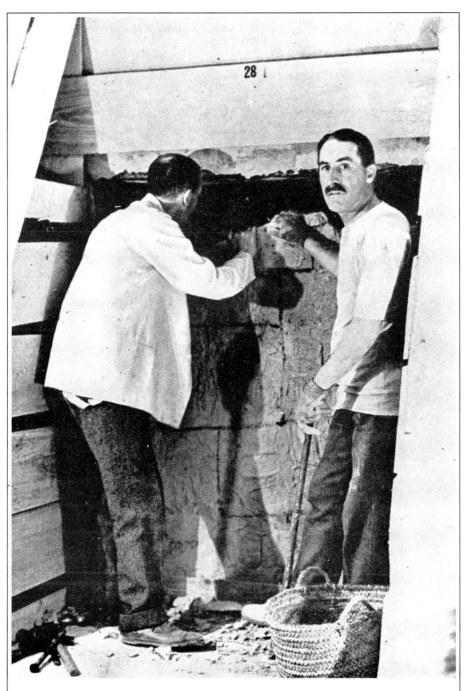

Howard Carter (right) and Lord Carnarvon removing the first stones
from the second sealed door to Tutankhamun's tomb, on 26 November 1922.

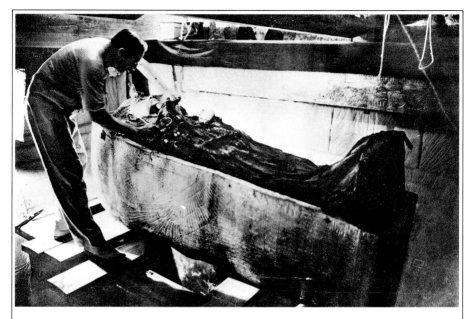

Above: Howard Carter begins to roll back the shroud
which covers the second coffin, after the removal
of the first case cover.

Above: Howard Carter sweeping dust off the second coffin
which still lies in the first coffin case.

tendency for Egyptologists (the word is first recorded in 1859) to promote the culture of ancient Egypt as a high point in human evolution, from which mankind has fallen away.

A view of the ancient Egyptians that was more palatable to biblical scholars was put forward by Birch's junior colleague Reginald Stuart Poole in his contribution to Smith's famous *Dictionary of the Bible*, published in 1863:

> The ancient Egyptians in character were very religious and contemplative, but given to base superstition, patriotic, respectful to women, hospitable, frugal, but at times luxurious, very sensual, lying, thievish, treacherous, and cringing, and intensely prejudiced, through pride of race, against strangers, although kind to them.

Their religion was a sort of fetishism, the lowest kind of nature worship, Poole goes on, and their social organisation had nothing to teach the Israelites: 'The idea that the Law was an Egyptian invention is one of the worst examples of modern reckless criticism.'

Birch seems to have been circumspect in his contributions to the dispute. Although the son of a parson, he remained discreet about his own faith. He would have had much to lose by openly opposing the Church, even though the views of its more reactionary members must have distressed him. In November 1870 he took a step that must have reassured those who had any doubts about his allegiance by calling a meeting together with Bonomi, then Curator of the Soane Museum, and founding the Society of Biblical Archaeology. Its objects were:

> ... the investigation of the Archaeology, Chronology, Geography and History of Ancient and Modern Assyria, Arabia, Egypt, Palestine, and other Biblical Lands, the promotion of the study of the Antiquities of those countries, and the preservation of a continuous record of discoveries, now or hereafter to be in progress.

Birch became the Society's first president, and the council of the Society included six men of the cloth. It was later to number among its vice-presidents Gladstone, Lord Halsbury, and Dean

Stanley.

When pressed about his own religious beliefs, Birch would say only, 'I believe all Science and all Religion.' In his presidential address to the Society on 21 March 1871, he reviewed the progress made in the field, noting that its scope was to diffuse the knowledge of scholars in the field of Semitic archaeology, 'not only in relation to Biblical subjects, but also to the wider history of those great nations of Central Asia which played so important a part in the early history of civilisation, and are so interlinked with the traditions and history of Western Europe'. All previous knowledge of these nations had come from the sacred scriptures or from the early Greek writers, but the discoveries of archaeology, and particularly of philology, had made it possible to 'ascend into the remotest times of antiquity and to examine the contemporaneous monuments of these great nations'. Birch, with some caution and rather surprisingly for the Keeper of Oriental Antiquities, seems to come down on the side of the scriptures. After examination of the monuments, it is possible, he says, 'to test the information they afford by what is known from the pages of the sacred Volume and the Greek and Roman Histories'.

Nothing here to alarm the conservative bishops; even when Birch went on to claim that the progress of excavations in Egypt had been so great that 'it will be impossible hereafter to adequately illustrate the history of the Old Testament without referring to the contemporaneous monuments of Egypt' they might have flinched only at the split infinitive. And the exegetical critics, who were becoming an increasing force in the land, might have taken some comfort in Birch's summing up of the intentions of the Society for Biblical Archaeology: 'Its scope is Archaeology, not Theology; but to Theology it will prove an important aid.' The Society did not seek to prove or disprove the Bible; its proceedings and published materials were on topics geographical, linguistic, archaeological, and of such minute detail that they provided no ammunition for either side.

While the significant research into ancient Egypt was taking place in England, the British presence on the Nile was maintained by travellers and eccentric temporary residents, rather than by camps of archaeologists. In 1861 Lady Lucie Duff

Gordon travelled up the river to Thebes and noted that it 'has become an English watering-place. There are now nine boats lying there, and the great object is to do the Nile as fast as possible.' Lady Lucie took to spending her winters in Luxor, where she rented the Maison de France. This had been built by Henry Salt in 1815, and used by Belzoni in his excavations at Thebes (it was built partly on top of the Temple) and then sold to the French in 1820, later to be used by Champollion and Rosselini on their joint expedition. It had distinguished connections but was hardly luxurious; Lucie mentioned in a letter of 1867 that half of the house had collapsed into the temple below. However it became a centre for British tourists, especially after Lucie's letters home were published in 1865.

There were distinguished guests to be welcomed: Edward Lear called to make a sketch of the French House for Lucie's husband, and in 1869 she was visited by the Prince and Princess of Wales. While her talents lay in observation and description of the contemporary scene rather than the study of ancient Egypt, Lucie played her small part in the distribution of antiquities: she bought them as presents and sent them to her family.

By 1870 there was a regular steamship service between Italy and Alexandria. The trip took only three-and-a-half days – the Roman galleys had taken six. In that year 300 American tourists registered at the Cairo consulate, rallied no doubt by Mark Twain's *The Innocents Abroad*, which had just appeared; Shepheard's Hotel was flourishing in Cairo, and organising regular tours to the pyramids.

One casual tourist of the 1870s was to become a founding mother of British Egyptology. Amelia Ann Blandford Edwards was the daughter of an army officer who had served under Wellington in the Peninsular War. She had a precocious talent for writing, her first published poem being written at the age of eight. She contributed articles and short stories to the *Saturday Review, Chamber's Journal, Household Words, The Morning Post* and *The Academy* in such profusion that, together with her popular books on history and art, and a clutch of early novels, she was able to travel in comfort on the proceeds of her pen. In 1873 Amelia set out on a tour of the Continent, but it rained and she decided to head south in search of the sun. She arrived in Egypt, as she recorded in her book *A Thousand Miles up the*

Nile, quite by chance: '. . . in simple truth we had drifted hither by accident, with no excuse of health, or business, or any serious object whatever; and had just taken refuge in Egypt as one might turn aside into the Burlington Arcade or the Passage des Panoramas – to get out of the rain.'

The refuge was to become an obsession. At first Amelia became caught up in the chase for antiquities: at Saqqara she found the ground strewn with scraps of broken pottery, limestone, marble and alabaster, and scrabbled in the sands in search of treasures, finding only the occasional noseless head among the debris and bleached bones: 'And then, with a shock which the present writer, at all events, will not soon forget, we suddenly discover that these scattered bones are human – that those linen shreds are shreds of cerement cloths – that yonder odd-looking brown lumps are rent fragments of what was once living flesh!'

She was astonished at how quickly her feelings of disgust were overcome, and she soon found herself rummaging among the remains with no more compunction than a professional body-snatcher. The passion for relic-hunting was as contagious as the callousness which accompanied it; she records that the prevailing ethos among travellers in Egypt at the time was for unscrupulous bargain hunting:

> Most Egyptian travellers, if questioned, would have to make a similar confession. Shocked at first, they denounce with horror the whole system of sepulchral excavation, legal as well as predatory, acquiring, however, a taste for statuary and funerary statuettes, they begin to buy with eagerness the spoils of the dead; finally, they forget all their former scruples, and ask no better fortune than to discover and confiscate a tomb for themselves.

At Thebes there was no need to scrabble: the treasures were brought to Amelia's boat by dealers, grave men in long, black robes who produced from hidden pockets pursefuls of scarabs or bundles of funerary statuettes. Most of the offerings were forgeries, but the diggers, the dealers, and the forgers worked together. Only the diggers and dealers were operating illegally, since the legal prohibition on excavation and dealing applied only to genuine antiquities; the forgers had only the tourists' displeasure to fear if they were detected. And detection, by the time of Amelia's visit, was a matter for the experts.

Life in Thebes was filled with incongruities: the mornings would be spent seriously studying the temples, and the afternoons hunting for forbidden treasures: 'I may say, indeed, that our life here was one long pursuit of the pleasures of the chase. The game, it is true, was prohibited; but we enjoyed it none the less because it was illegal. Perhaps we enjoyed it the more.'

Mariette's excavations were being conducted during Amelia's visit and there was an order put forth that all mummy cases discovered should be sent unopened to the museum at Boulaq. One morning Amelia heard that a new tomb was about to be opened across the river, and she leapt into a boat to witness the discovery. The tomb was near the Ramasseum and when she arrived, the governor was already watching the diggers in the pit scraping away the sand from a partially buried mummy-case. Amelia saw the sarcophagus slowly revealed, hands crossed over the chest and inscribed with hieroglyphics. The lid fell away. Inside, a small wooden box lay at the feet of the mummy. This was handed to the governor, who put it to one side, unopened. The mummy case was lifted to the surface:

> It gave one a kind of shock to see it first of all lying just as it had been left by the mourners; then hauled out by rude hands, to be searched, unrolled, perhaps broken up as unworthy to occupy a corner in the Boulak collection. Once they are lodged and catalogued in a museum one comes to look upon these things as 'specimens' and forgets that they once were startlingly human and pathetic lying at the bottom of its grave in the morning sunlight.

While Amelia herself had no ambitions to acquire a mummy, there was what she described as a growing passion for them among Nile travellers at the time; fifteen had been smuggled successfully through the customs house at Alexandria that winter.

Although she had been smitten by antiquities fever shortly after her arrival, Amelia ended her tour of Egypt with a commitment to preserve them, and an admiration for the Boulaq Museum and its founders. She admired Mariette, and regretted that the uncaring pashas had allowed the treasures of Egypt to be carried off to the museums of Europe and America. The riches that remained at Boulaq were for the most part portrait statues of private individuals, funerary tablets, amulets, and personal relics:

> It is necessarily less rich in such colossal statues as fill the great galleries of the British Museum, the Turin Museum, and the Louvre. These, being above ground and comparatively few in number, were for the most part seized upon long since and transported to Europe. The Boulak statues are the product of the tombs.

Mariette had noted in his guide-book, published for the travellers who arrived for the opening of the Suez Canal, that the tomb of Ty at Saqqara had suffered more damage from tourists in the ten years since its discovery than in the previous 6,000, and requested his readers to 'abstain from the childish practice of writing their names on the monuments'. Amelia confessed to having her name painted on the inside of the doorway at Abu Simbel; but she was ashamed of the lapse and regretted the injury done:

> Such is the fate of Egyptian monuments great or small. The tourist carves it all over with names and dates, and in some instances with caricatures. The student of Egyptology, by taking wet paper 'squeezes' sponges away every vestige of the original colour. The 'collector' buys and carries off everything of value he can get; and the Arab steals for him. The work of destruction, meanwhile, goes on apace. There is no-one to prevent it; there is no-one to discourage it. Every day more inscriptions are mutilated – more tombs are rifled – more paintings and sculpture are defaced.

Egypt was ripe for missionary endeavour, and Amelia Edwards had the fire, tenacity, and strong sense of purpose to take up the rôle. On her return to England in 1875 she began to correspond with the leading figures in Egyptology, both to increase her knowledge of the subject and her influence over its future.

The files at the British Museum from this date contain regular letters from Amelia to Samuel Birch. Birch's replies are not preserved, but they must have been prompt and helpful enough to encourage an extended correspondence. Her queries were not all academic. She also pestered Birch for help in acquiring papyrus to add to the small collection of portable artefacts she had smuggled out of Egypt.

It soon became clear that Amelia wanted to rescue Egyptian antiquities from the hands of Mustapha Ali, heir to the throne, as well as from the British Museum. Not surprisingly, she found Samuel Birch unenthusiastic. He has been quoted as having no time for what he called 'sentimental archaeology' – anything that did not have as its primary aim the procuring of objects for the British Museum. When Amelia wrote to him for support in launching the Egypt Exploration Fund, which was to preserve the monuments of Egypt in their homeland, he refused his support:

> I have delayed my answer because of the great difficulty I have always felt about recommending to the Public a sub-scription to make excavations the results of which would have to become the property of the Egyptian government and enriching the Museum of Boulak and I cannot therefore sign the paper you have sent me.

Undeterred, Amelia forged ahead. As a close ally, and some say begetter of the scheme, she had Reginald Stuart Poole, who had contributed to Smith's *Dictionary of the Bible*. Poole was the nephew of Edward Lane, author of *Manners and Customs of the Modern Egyptians*. Lane had been partly responsible for Poole's education, and had aroused in him an early interest in Egyptian antiquities and Oriental coins. Having brought out a book on the chronology of ancient Egypt, Poole was appointed to the Department of Antiquities at the British Museum in 1852 at the age of twenty. In 1866, when the Department was divided and Birch took charge of Oriental Antiquities, Poole was transferred to the newly created Department of Coins and Medals, although he continued to write and lecture on wider aspects of Egyptian history, including its relevance to biblical research. Poole understood that the appeal of Egyptian archaeology at the time consisted almost entirely in its capacity to throw light on the contentious areas of criticism of the Bible. It had not yet caught the imagination of the public, or established itself in academic circles as a discipline in its own right.

Poole and Amelia wrote to several influential people, both lay and of the clergy. Their most important convert was Sir Erasmus Wilson, the eminent and wealthy surgeon. Sir Erasmus recently had spent over 10,000 pounds financing the transport of an obelisk from Alexandria to London, to be erected on the Embankment. Chancing to read *A Thousand Miles up the Nile*, Sir Erasmus had been captivated, and readily offered his enthusiasm and his money to Amelia's proposal if it would help England to recover ground lost to her European rivals. He wrote to Amelia:

France and Germany have always had active and zealous labourers in the field and the scientific character of England demands that she also should be worthily represented. It were vain, perhaps, to hope that an Archaeological Commission, like the Egyptian Commission of France, Germany, and Italy, will ever be despatched by the government of this country to report upon and explore the treasures of the Nile Valley; but it is earnestly to be desired that private enterprise should do something towards vindicating our rational aim to a place amongst the scholars and Archaeologists of Europe.

On 1 April 1882 the announcement appeared in the leading newspapers that England had taken an important step towards establishing itself as a leading nation in the future exploration of Egypt: 'We have great pleasure in announcing that the long-desired Society for the Promotion of Excavation in the Delta of the Nile has at last been constituted under very favourable auspices.' The Society's purpose was to conduct excavations in the Nile Delta, where 'must undoubtedly lie concealed the documents of a lost period of Biblical history – documents which we may confidently hope will furnish the key to a whole series of perplexing problems'. The sponsors of the Society made an impressive team: the Archbishop of Canterbury, plus several bishops; the Chief Rabbi; Lord Carnarvon, the President of the Society of Antiquaries; as well as Robert Browning; Sir Henry Layard, excavator of Nineveh; and Professor Thomas Huxley.

England's enthusiasm had been harnessed and the funds organised; it remained to be seen how ready Egypt was to receive them.

Chapter Eight

Antiquarian Politics

THE YEAR 1882 WAS ONE OF CRISIS in Egypt, particularly affecting the position of Europeans there. During the early years of settlement, they had lived as aliens in a foreign land, clinging together in enclosed districts of Cairo and Alexandria, always in danger of being forced to contribute special taxes and occasionally being pillaged. The reforms of Muhammad Ali, however, followed by the policies of Said Pasha and Ismail Pasha to make Egypt part of Europe had changed the situation of Europeans in Egypt from an oppressed to a privileged class.

The Europeans had come to think of themselves as above the general laws of the country, for example claiming the right to be tried only in consular courts. They were appointed to senior positions in the civil service, and flaunted the superiority of their dress and customs. While European travellers amused themselves by trying to live as Egyptians, the Egyptians who had risen into government circles in Cairo were parading in European clothes. As early as 1846 Edward Lane had noted that Egyptian officials were wearing 'frock coat, waistcoat and trousers, the last as narrow as any of ours'. It was the familiar clash of cultures that occurred in the late 19th century wherever European trade and technology was imported into less developed countries. As elsewhere in the world, in Egypt this clash brought resentment, and eventually open opposition.

Under the leadership of an army officer, Ahmed Arabi, who

called himself 'the Egyptian', a protest movement began, initially against the preference given to Turkish officers, but expanding into a revolt in 1882 against the privileged position of all foreigners in Egypt, including Europeans. The Khedive's government was too weak to suppress the revolt, and instead tried to ingratiate itself by promoting Arabi, then making him Under-Secretary for War, and finally a member of the cabinet.

There were urgent negotiations between Britain, France, and Turkey, but each had a different attitude to the situation, and was too suspicious of the others to reach an agreement on concerted action. Although Tewfik remained in nominal control in Egypt, the army was growing increasingly mutinous, and Arabi was hailed as a national hero. He had at the time no clear or specific aims, only a generalised anti-European stance, which was soon interpreted by the Press as a cry for the regeneration of Islam and Egypt for the Egyptians.

Gladstone was loath to interfere. Egypt did not present itself to the public eye as worth the expense and the risk of a military intervention, and there was also the inevitability of alienating the French. 'My belief is', Gladstone declared, 'that the day which witnesses our occupation of Egypt will bid a long farewell to all cordiality of political relations between France and England.' He was right. However, British capital was invested there, and the investors did not want to lose it; Disraeli had directly involved the British government in Egyptian affairs with his purchase of Suez Canal shares, and, as news of threats to British citizens in Cairo and Alexandria filtered back to London, Gladstone's hand was forced. On 22 May he sent the Mediterranean fleet under Sir Beauchamp Seymour to anchor off Alexandria, where it was joined by a squadron of the French fleet.

The situation was not unfamiliar to the Egyptians: ever since Bonaparte's invasion, every time there had been serious civil unrest in Egypt, warships would be sent from the European powers to anchor off Alexandria, and their presence had helped cool things down. This time, however, they presented a visible and alien threat, which seemed to unite what increasingly was becoming seen as a nationalist uprising.

On the streets of Cairo and Alexandria, Europeans were being hustled and spat on. On 11 June 1882 disturbances broke out simultaneously in three places and fifty Europeans were killed.

Many others, including the British consul, Sir Charles Cookson, were severely wounded.

There was a panic exodus. By 17 June 14,000 Christians had fled the country and 6,000 more were waiting for ships to take them away. The British and French governments both appealed to the Sultan to interfere, and a hurried conference was held in Constantinople; the Sultan did not send a representative and seemed unwilling to support an armed intervention. Then the French withdrew their support and the Italians refused to help. The order was finally given to bombard Alexandria and land an invasion force without allies.

Arabi withdrew to Kafr-Dawar, a few miles from Alexandria. A force of 20,000 men landed and the rebels were defeated at the battle of Tellel-Kebir on 13 September 1882. A small force of cavalry pushed on to Cairo, which was taken without opposition. The British, without firm imperial ambitions in the area, found themselves in command of Egypt.

It had become clear that the staging post of Egypt would be well kept only if placed under the management of a competent licensee, and so, in the face of opposition from the French, who demanded that Britain withdraw from the country or, at the least, set a date for doing so, in 1877 it was placed under the informal supervision of a quite unusually self-possessed civil servant, Sir Evelyn Baring.

Baring was born into a family of distinguished financiers, and was given the education of a well-connected child intended for a military career. As a young artillery subaltern he was first posted to Corfu. In 1872 Baring accepted the appointment of private secretary to his cousin Lord Northbrook, who had been made Viceroy of India. There, his unremitting industry and readiness to give orders earned him the sobriquet 'The Vice-Viceroy'. In 1877 he was sent to Egypt as Commissioner for Public Debt during the operation of the Dual Mandate. His financial skills in this post won him a local reputation for sound management and the post of Financial Member for the Government of India. When the British found themselves in control of Egypt after Tellel-Kebir, Baring was the obvious choice. In August 1883, having received a knighthood, he set sail for Egypt.

Baring's official title was British Agent and Consul General; his general mandate was to restore the authority of the Khedive, and, having steered him for a time in the right direction and re-stored the country's finances, to arrange the withdrawal of the British forces from Egypt. In the meantime the Suez Canal had to be protected, and the route to the Far East kept open.

Baring's major achievements in Egypt were in his control of the finances: taxes were reduced and irksome duties repealed – yet the annual deficit became a surplus, and the capital of the public debt was reduced. The system of corvée, or forced labour, was abolished, yet extensive irrigation schemes were car-ried out, opening wide areas of the Nile Valley to cultivation. In all that he did, Baring was motivated less by a desire to protect the interests of British bond-holders in Egypt than to advance those of the Egyptians. He found it tiresome that this was an atti-tude that seemed never to be remotely understood by the Egyp-tians. It was particularly galling to discover that the French, who, as he saw it, were in Egypt solely to advance their own national interests, were always more popular than the British. The national 'superiority' of the British was as yet undetected by the Egyptians, charmed as they were by the French. In his memoirs Baring analysed at some length the contrasting psychol-ogy and culture of the English and the French, always emphasis-ing the solid worth of the former against the latter's superficial attractions. It speaks volumes for the sober moral worth of the British agent and consul that, holding these views, he was able to turn his own back on the British Museum and give his support to the Director of Antiquities in Cairo, who was a Frenchman.

When Wallis Budge, the most aggressive agent the British Museum ever commissioned to add to its Egyptian collections, called on Baring with letters of introduction, he was met, he re-called, by a cold but civil hostility. Sir Evelyn let it be known that he would not support any scheme for excavations by any agent of the trustees of the British Museum, whether working on their behalf or that of anyone else: 'the occupation of Egypt by the British ought not to be made an excuse for filching antiquities from the country, whether to England or anywhere else.' He then politely but firmly showed Budge the door.

Gaston Maspero, the French Director of Antiquities in Egypt, was educated in Paris where, as a schoolboy and like so many future Egyptologists, he had become fascinated by hiero-glyphics. He made such progress that on the death of de Rougé in 1874 he took over at the age of twenty-eight the position of Professor of Egyptian Philology and Archaeology at the Collège de France, which Mariette had turned down. Maspero considered archaeology a romantic rather than scientific pursuit, seeking to bring to life the peoples of the past; he once wrote that the popular German novelist and Egyptologist George Ebers, whose romantic extravaganza *An Egyptian Princess* had a brilliant success all over Europe, had done more for Egyptology than the scientific memoirs of Lepsius.

Maspero's ambition to write a definitive history of Egypt was interrupted by the French government's decision to open the French Archaeological Mission in Cairo in 1880, and to appoint him the head of it. Having secured agreement to the project, Maspero arrived in Cairo with his staff, ready to set up the new school. However, on Mariette's death he had to abandon it because, to his surprise, he was appointed Director in Mariette's place.

There was little money available and few staff. Maspero seems to have adopted a relaxed attitude, taking over the flat-bottomed brigantine *Menchieh*, which had an engine so archaic that it deserved, he said, a place in the Museum of Arts and Crafts. It was Maspero's habit to have the boat towed upstream as far as Aswan each December, then abandon himself to the stream and head for home. This gave him the advantage of visiting and inspecting minor sites, which, were it not for the whims of wind and current, he would not otherwise have stopped at, and where he picked up monuments which might otherwise have gone unnoticed. He would arrive back each spring with a load of antiquities for the Museum. Then he would leave to spend the summer months in Paris, returning to his duties in the autumn.

In the summer of 1881 the most exciting discovery of Maspero's career as Director was made. He had received reports that a number of royal insignia were appearing for sale in Luxor. They were showing up irregularly and at long intervals, which seemed to indicate that someone had a cache of them and was floating individual pieces on to the market so as not to attract suspicion, and to keep up the price. He sent his assistant Emile Brugsch, disguised as a wealthy tourist, to investigate. Before long Brugsch was offered a statuette that he recognised as genuine and from a royal tomb of the 21st Dynasty. Brugsch paid for it and asked for more, whereupon he was taken to the house of Abd-el-Rasul and shown a collection of mortuary objects from the 19th and 20th Dynasty tombs. Brugsch had Abd-el-Rasul arrested and taken before the local Mudir for an enquiry. Here a flood of testimony came from his villagers, his family, and even minor officials to the effect that he was of upright character, unblemished integrity. Abd-el-Rasul and his brothers were tortured, but they kept to their story. The case was closed. Shortly afterwards, however, one brother revealed that the Abd-el-Rasul family was in league with the consular agent for Britain, Belgium, and Russia, one Mustapha Aga Ayat, under whose protection they had been marketing their finds. In return for immunity and 500 pounds, Mustapha offered to show Brugsch the tomb.

They went to Deir el-Bahri and climbed a steep cliff, until, 180 feet from the plain, they came to an opening in the rocks that led to a shaft thirty-five feet deep. Brugsch was lowered on a rope to the bottom, where he found a corridor that ran 150 feet into the mountain. At the end was a large burial chamber, and wonders beyond his imagination. The official report by Maspero reads:

> Where I had expected to find one or two obscure kinglets, the Arabs had disinterred a whole vault of Pharaohs. And what Pharaohs! Perhaps the most illustrious in the history of Egypt, Thutmose III and Seti I, Ahmose the Liberator and Ramses II the Conqueror. Monsieur Emile Brugsch, coming so suddenly into such an assemblage, thought that he must be the victim of a dream, and, like him, I still wonder if I am not dreaming when I see and touch what were the bodies of so many famous personages of whom we never expected to know more than the names.

Maspero was able to see and touch the Pharoahs because Brugsch and his assistants employed 300 Arabs to load forty kings and other notables on to the aged steamboat and head downstream, followed by a crowd of wailing women and men firing shots in honour, it was said, of the greatness that was past – or perhaps they were mourning the riches they had lost.

Maspero supported Amelia Edwards in setting up the Egypt

Exploration Fund; he was always ready to befriend any organisation that might help with the excavations without carrying off the discoveries. By April 1882 he had learned the politics of his position well, when he refused to co-operate with Schliemann, who had a reputation for aggression and had quarrelled with the Porte over his excavations at Troy. Maspero realised that the delicate situation in Egypt demanded a more retiring personality who would not offend the Egyptians. He wrote to Poole at the British Museum, asking for a young Englishman who he could train, in conditions when 'national vanity' had been 'violently excited by recent events'.

It is taken for granted that Egypt is the premier country of the world, the mother of civilisation both ancient and modern, and that foreigners in spending money for the benefit of the Egyptian Government are doing no more than render due homage to Egypt's superiority: the money is accepted as an act of grace, nothing more. You will appreciate that, holding such views, the minister in office and those who will succeed him have sensitive skins.

Maspero insisted he did not want to spend English money filling his Boulaq galleries, and he would always ensure that the greatest possible number of monuments should be left in situ. In fact he applied the rules with great flexibility, and was known to allow diggers and dealers to keep a proportion of the objects they discovered, as long as they acknowledged the priority of the Museum. If an excavator had been unlucky enough to turn up nothing of value, Maspero would even allow him to take pieces from the Egyptian storerooms as *don gracieux*.

The relaxed pragmatism with which Maspero carried out his duties, as well as his wider interests and admiration of English literature, may well have recommended him to Sir Evelyn Baring. The two developed an amicable, though not personal, relationship. With the British agent's help, Maspero was able to develop the Service of Antiquities until the entire Nile Valley was divided into five administrative districts. A small staff of inspectors made it known that the age of the unfettered entrepreneur was over.

Maspero's supervision of the excavations in Egypt was suddenly cut short in the summer of 1886. His wife had been ill for some time, and was forbidden on medical grounds to return to Egypt. Maspero resigned his post as Director of Antiquities and returned to Paris, missing the arrival in Egypt of the most colourful, extravagant, and dynamic character in the history of British Egyptology: Ernest Alfred Thompson Wallis Budge.

Ernest Wallis Budge was the buccaneer of Egyptologists. Financed and encouraged by the British Museum itself, outwardly a bastion of respectability, he managed to harass and cheat the officials of the Service of Antiquities, and ship home rich cargoes of spoils in the manner of Drake despoiling the Spanish galleons.

As assistant to Birch at the British Museum, while observing the stream of dealers and clients seeking authentication, Budge had learned that antiquities had a commercial, as well as an archaeological, value. As a servant of the Museum, it was as important for him to know the current price of a monument as its place in history. Having acquired the necessary expertise, it was far easier and cheaper to add to the Museum's collection through discriminating purchase than by excavation. To this end Budge dedicated his formidable talents and energies.

Budge's first visit to Egypt was a consequence of the spare-time activities of a distinguished British General. Sir Francis Grenfell, in command of the British troops at Aswan, had taken to relieving the monotony of garrison life by digging in the area. Sir Francis had made a few small discoveries, was curious about their value, and offered to donate them to the British Museum if they would send someone to evaluate them. The proposal attracted the Museum trustees, but they were unwilling to finance it, so they applied to the Treasury for funds to send a representative on an official visit to Aswan. The Treasury consulted the Foreign Office, and the Foreign Office consulted their man on the spot, Sir Evelyn Baring. Given Baring's opposition to the export of antiquities the matter might well have ended there, but, as a good civil servant, he referred the proposal for an official visit to Aswan to his representative there: Sir Francis Grenfell. In his reply Grenfell urged that the great museums of Russia, France, and Germany all had men in Egypt, who were reported to be doing well for their countries. It was unthinkable that the British Museum should be allowed to fall behind, and furthermore the excavations had cost the Egyptian government nothing, since he had financed them himself and was prepared to continue to do so.

Baring agreed to the mission, and Budge was given four months' leave of absence and 150 pounds. He was also instructed to contact native dealers with a view to making purchases for the British Museum. When the Vice-Chancellor of Cambridge University heard of the project, he authorised a further 100 pounds to be advanced to Budge against the purchase of antiquities for the Fitzwilliam Museum.

Budge's first official encounter in Cairo was an unpromising meeting with Sir Evelyn Baring, which made it clear to him from the start that his only hope of success was to cheat the system. Fortunately, Budge left England with a resourceful clergyman, collector, and amateur archaeologist who was willing to show him the ropes. The Rev. William John Loftie's delicate health forced him to pass the colder months of each year in Egypt, where he had developed a taste for scarabs and an eye for forgeries. He had the reputation of a foreign eccentric, and he was rarely cheated. On the evening of the day that Budge had been shown the door by an inflamed British consul, he was taken by the Rev. Loftie to an annexe of the Hotel du Nil, 'much frequented by the better class of native travellers', introduced to the leading dealers in antiquities, and given his first lesson in 'antiquarian politics'.

If Budge had any moral qualms about the chicanery of the underworld he met that evening, they were dispelled the next day when he visited the Boulaq Museum. He found the royal mummies 'laying naked in mean deal cases, glazed with the cheapest of brown glass; a white mist rising from the surface waters of the Nile and condensed on the glass and ran down the inner surface of the cases'. The floor of the Museum was 'reeking wet', and nobody seemed to know or care about the treasures it contained. When Budge asked to see the storehouse containing the objects that would not fit into the showrooms, he was shown a number of sheds called the Magazine, in which were piled coffins and mummies, funerary boxes, tomb furniture, and a multitude of small antiquities from all over Egypt. These had not been registered, and since nobody quite knew what was there, anybody could steal without fear of detection. The Magazine stood in the industrial quarter and was surrounded by work-shops. There was a serious fire risk but no hydrants in any of the buildings. It was immediately clear to Budge that the antiquities of Egypt would be far better off in the British Museum.

He began a conducted tour of the private houses in Cairo where antiquities were stored. His guide was another clergyman whose delicate health forced him to overwinter in the Nile Valley. After his first tour of Egypt, the Rev. Greville Chester had discovered that the Keeper of the Department of Antiquities at the British Museum wanted to buy most of the small souvenirs the Rev. Chester had brought back with him to London, and was prepared to give him a profit on them. The Rev. Chester increased his haul on his next visit, and after a number of years became a regular supplier for Birch and the Museum's Egyptian Collection. The British Museum had encouraged his acquisitiveness, and he repaid them by introducing Budge to his circle of dealers and showing him around their collections so that before setting off up the Nile, Budge would have a clear idea of what was already available to him in Cairo.

At Aswan, Budge claimed, on behalf of the British Museum, Sir Francis Grenfell's share of the results of the excavations. He was told that only a few small things of interest remained, the rest having unaccountably disappeared. The few objects that had survived had been taken by the representative of the Boulaq Museum stationed in Aswan, and sent to the Director of the Service of Antiquities in Cairo. They had never arrived. Budge, thrown back on his own considerable ingenuity, and finding that the promised collection had vanished, decided to dig one up for himself.

Over the following weeks Budge's workmen cleared eighteen tombs in the Aswan area. Having no funds to pay for this work, he managed to persuade General the Hon. R. H. de Montmorency, in command of the British troops at Aswan, that it was a proper function of the British Army abroad to lend a hand to the British Museum. General de Montmorency arranged for tackle, railway plant, and the occasional Corporal of Sappers to keep the natives at work. They had the unfortunate if common experience of all excavators in the region at the time: every tomb they uncovered had already been rifled; they found nothing of value but the lower half of what must have been a fine statue.

Fortunately, less strenuous methods of antiquity collecting were opened to Budge. On his journey upriver, he had been followed by a representative of the Boulaq Museum detailed to check on his movements and prevent him from buying from the dealers. The official spread the rumour that Budge was the totally unscrupulous agent of a foreign institution who would stop at nothing, and had been given unlimited funds to strip Egypt of her treasures. Once it became known that Budge was a rogue and a swindler, who cared nothing for the law and had money to spend, he had no further need to search for antiquities. This was exactly the calibre of man the dealers liked to do business with, and they came up the river in boats by night, pressing him to buy.

For many years the centre of the antique trade had been Luxor, and Budge decided on a trip there to try out his bargaining skills. There were risks involved, even if he managed to shake off the officials of the Service of Antiquities. In his *Guide to Luxor*, Mariette had written, 'Luxor is the centre of a more or less legitimate traffic of antiquities . . . Luxor possesses certain manufactories where statuettes, stelae and scarabi are initiated with a dexterity which often deceives even the most experienced antiquarian.' Amelia Edwards had been waylaid by hordes of dealers on her visit there:

> Some of these gentlemen were Arabs, some Copts, all polite, plausible and mendacious . . . Both sell more forgeries than genuine antiquities. Be the demand what it may, they are prepared to meet it. Thothmes is not too heavy nor Cleopatra too light for them . . . As for genuine scarabs of the highest antiquity, they are turned out by the gross every season. Engraved, glazed, and administered to the turkeys in the form of boluses, they acquire, by the simple process of digestion, a degree of venerableness that is really charming.

Budge would need all his powers of discrimination, finely honed by years of tuition at the hands of Samuel Birch, to emerge from Luxor with genuine treasures.

The dealers at Luxor gave him their account of the market situation: all objects of antiquity in Egypt, whether above or below ground, belonged by law to the Egyptian government. It was unlawful for any native to possess or to deal in antiquities. However, no government had ever tried to enforce this law, and both Mariette and Maspero had bought openly from the dealers – and had used government money to do so. The locals who had been astute enough to get themselves appointed consuls or agents for European powers felt themselves above the law, and often engaged in excavation or trading openly, to the extent that some had even thrown out the officers of the Service of Antiquities who had tried to interfere.

Mustafa Agha, the British Consul at Luxor, had a fine collection at his house; out of a profound affection for the British people, and his ambition to make the British Museum 'the best in all the world', he offered the pick of it to Budge. He also introduced Budge to the members of the Rasul family who had discovered the cache at Deir el-Bahri. They had managed to steal and hide papyri, alabaster vessels, blue-glazed vases, and ivory objects. They were prepared to sell these to the British Museum, partly, it seemed, to have the satisfaction of outwitting the Service of Antiquities. According to the Rasuls, when antiques had been surrendered according to law to the Boulaq Museum, the officers there would refuse to pay the excavation or other expenses as the law provided. Instead they would claim the objects were fakes, hand over a pittance, and then sell them on to foreign tourists. Budge presented himself as the just man who brought salvation to the dealers by offering them a fair price, and to the antiquities by transporting them to a safe home. He left Luxor with a fine collection.

It was at this time that Budge was given an unusual commission by Professor Alexander Macalister, of Cambridge University, who was using physical anthropology to investigate the history of the human race. The Professor needed some ancient Egyptian skulls, and wondered if Budge could supply a few. It so happened that a deep pit had been uncovered containing the mummies of priests of the Third and Fourth Order. As the priests were minor officials, they had not been very well mummified, and their heads were not securely attached to their bodies. Budge ordered a pile of mummies to be crated up and sent off to Alexandria for export. Here they struck a problem. The export of mummies of human remains was against the law of Egypt, and since Budge had declared the crates' contents, they were held up in the custom house in Alexandria. The customs official refused to accept Budge's claim that the skulls were of value in scientific research; the only possible value they could have, he claimed, was as bone manure, and directed that they be so classified. Professor Macalister's specimens finally left Egypt with the official designation 'bone manure', having paid the appropriate duty for manures of one per cent.

Budge had more difficulty with the transport of his treasures. One technique the Service of Antiquities used to frustrate illegal trading was to seize boats suspected of carrying antiquities, a method used by both Mariette and Maspero to add to the collections at Boulaq. Fortunately for Budge, his friend General de Montmorency was still keen to help the British Museum outwit the Egyptian Service of Antiquities, and he simply picked up all Budge's crates and had them taken by official barge, together with the military baggage, to Alexandria.

Sir Evelyn Baring was furious. It was his duty not only to shape the law of Egypt but to ensure that his fellow countrymen complied with it. He sent for Budge, reminded him forcibly that the export of Egyptian antiquities was forbidden by law, and ordered him to return to the dealers all the objects he had bought. Budge replied that he had been sent to Egypt at public expense, that the collection he was to have acquired from Sir Francis Grenfell had vanished unaccountably, and he therefore felt it his duty to supply in its place other objects from other sources. A stalemate followed: Baring ordered Budge again to desist from making purchases and to return all he had bought; Budge maintained he was not a member of Baring's staff and therefore not subject to his orders. He added that he would continue to do his utmost to increase the collections in the British Museum, faced with the competition from the other great powers and, as he put it, 'many Little Powers' in Europe who had their agents in Egypt buying for their national collections. The interview, Budge wrote, 'ended abruptly'.

The Consul General then wrote officially to Budge to place on record the fact that the export of his purchases was forbidden by law, and alerted the Service of Antiquities in Alexandria to prevent their being trans-shipped. Budge, however, was in luck again: his friend de Montmorency had been transferred from

Aswan to Alexandria, and was able to override all opposition. As Budge recalled: 'General de Montmorency declined to be moved either by wishes or threats, and one day he and I stood on the quay and watched my twenty-four cases leave the harbour under the care of a friendly officer from Aswan.'

Two days later Budge followed them to England, and was gratified to receive the official congratulations of the British Museum trustees on his enterprise. On 2 April 1887 the Secretary wrote, 'the Trustees this morning passed a Minute expressing their warm approval of your intelligence and energy in carrying out the purpose of the Mission entrusted to you and undertaken by you at so short notice.'

So warmly did the trustees approve Budge's activities, that by December he was back in Egypt. He had heard that a large cache of papyri had been found in western Thebes, and had alerted his superiors to the need to purchase it before the other museums found out. In Alexandria Budge met the British Consul Charles Cookson, who said that he had been informed by dispatch from Cairo that an important discovery of papyri had been made in Upper Egypt, and that the British Museum had sent out an official to acquire it. If Budge were that same official, Cookson continued, then he could count on no official help in his illegal project to export antiquities, and he might better employ himself enjoying the sunshine and the hospitality of his good friend General de Montmorency. Should Budge attempt to carry out his mission to acquire the papyri, Cookson warned, the Consul would oppose with every means in his power the exportation of antiquities that ought to be preserved in Egypt 'to proclaim to the Modern Egyptians the past glory of their country'. General de Montmorency told Budge to get on with the job he was sent to do, and if he had any problems he knew where to come.

The most persistent and inescapable problem confronting Budge was the precise and pedantic Eugène Grebaut, Director of Antiquities, who had assumed office on the departure of Maspero. After the easy-going regime of Maspero, Grebaut had decided to reform the Service of Antiquities into an organisation that kept more carefully to the letter of the law that constituted it.

He called on Budge at the Royal Hotel in Cairo. At the initial meeting it seemed that Grebaut's desire for reputation had prevailed over his zeal for his job. He stressed his ambition to be seen as a worthy successor to Maspero, and reminded Budge that the British Museum had presented his predecessor with a complete set of their Egyptological publications as a public acknowledgement of his scholarly eminence. Could Budge possibly so arrange it that the trustees might honour him in the same way? Budge hinted this might depend on Grebaut's liberality towards their representative in Egypt, feeling for a moment that he might have the upper hand. But that night Grebaut set the police to watch Budge's hotel.

Budge's picaresque account of what followed is no doubt coloured by his lively imagination and desire to portray himself as a resourceful rogue, rescuing the treasures of the Nile from the blundering, bureaucratic Grebaut.

Budge evaded Grebaut's guards, and set out for Luxor, where he charmed the locals into showing him a large and important collection of papyri. On the following day he was placed under arrest by the local chief of police on the orders of Grebaut, who was following in a steamer. It so happened that the captain of the steamer had a daughter who was to be married that very day at one of the villages on the bank of the Nile. The steamer just chanced to run aground the previous evening, and be so embedded that it was impossible to move her until the wedding was over. Grebaut ordered a donkey so he could continue his pursuit of Budge, but the villagers, hearing the animal was for the hated Director of Antiquities, drove all the donkeys into the fields, pleading that they could not catch any.

While delighted to hear the news, brought by a runner, Budge had his own problems. Grebaut's delay meant Budge had an entire day in which to spirit away his finds. However, they were stored in a house that had been placed under guard, with policemen on the roof, and one at each corner. At first this did not seem to be an insurmountable problem; the dealers who were in league with Budge used a simple technique that had a long history of success – namely to get the guards drunk and offer them money. The guards, however, refused the cognac. The dealers, commending the guards on their fidelity and integrity, retired with a great show of disappointment.

In fact the dealers went next door to the manager of the Luxor Hotel, whose garden wall was positioned against the basement wall of the house. The manager immediately understood the problem and set his gardeners tunnelling through the wall. As the wall was made of unbaked mud bricks that could be removed with very little noise, it was only when it came to shoring up the sides of the tunnel with wooden planks that it seemed necessary to distract the guard. As a reward for their incorruptible public spirit, the manager sent a large brass tray heaped with rice and raisins, half a sheep sitting on top, and the whole soaked in boiling mutton fat to them. As the guards feasted, still watchful and at their posts, the gardeners quietly carried out all the antiquities along the tunnel and into the hotel. Because they could not manage to squeeze through a mummy and a coffin, Budge left them behind so Grebaut would have something to confiscate when he finally arrived.

If the story so far has a whiff of *opera buffa*, its conclusion is touched with unconvincing farce. According to Budge, he set off for Cairo with the boxes containing his illegal antiquities, accompanied at a distance by a group of policemen under orders from Grebaut. He travelled the last leg of the journey by rail, arriving at Cairo station in the middle of the night. Finding no porters to help with the boxes, he sat by them in the station, waiting for daylight when the porters came on duty. The group of policemen sat at a little distance and kept him under observation. At first light Budge saw two British officers out for their morning ride, and greeted them as social acquaintances. Seeing an English gentleman in difficulties, they ordered the watching policemen to pick up the crates of contraband and carry them into the town. Seeing a file of policemen carrying goods under the leadership of two mounted British officers, the customs officers stationed on the Kasr an Nil bridge saluted smartly and waved them on.

The final hurdle was overcome with the help of Major Hepper of the Royal Engineers who, hearing that the contents of the boxes had been purchased with British Museum funds supplied by the British Treasury, declared them public property which it was his duty to protect, and shipped them out with his personal baggage.

Budge had satisfied himself that the Service of Antiquities was grossly inefficient and its officers corrupt. That he should have so easily won the support of the British officers against the considerable influence of Sir Evelyn Baring is perhaps surprising. The Consul General, however, had, through his distant and imperious manner, affronted his fellow countrymen, and there was always sympathy in an army of occupation for the view that laws should not be put into effect that seriously inconvenienced the citizens of the occupying power.

Budge, too, was a persuasive exponent of the view that he was smuggling abroad the treasures of Egypt for their own good. As Egypt was the cradle of civilisation, so her antiquities were those of the civilised world. They could not be left to the whims of the local dealers, the erosion of wind and sand, or the ineffectual and destructive guardianship of the Service of Antiquities. The proper home of the memorials of Egypt was the British Museum. There they were safe even from the Egyptians:

> From time immemorial the Egyptians have plundered the tombs of their dead. The neolithic Egyptians stole flints, stone and earthenware jars . . . In dynastic times, when jewels, rings, ornaments, amulets, etc., were buried with the dead, thieves broke into the tombs and stole them . . . Whether a king built a pyramid to cover his body or hewed a tomb in the bowels of a mountain, the result was the same; the thief found his way into the sarcophagus chamber and robbed the dead . . .

In modern times the treasures were taken to rot in the Boulaq Museum, Budge wrote, where the waters of the Nile wash against the wall and the rising mist condenses on the glass cases of the mummies. How could the souls of the royal dead of Egypt rest when their mortal remains were treated so shabbily? Many 'psychical men' had visited the mummies in the British Museum, and confirmed they were visited nightly there by departed souls. The conditions at the Museum were such as to promote the 'free intercourse between their bodies and their free spirit souls'; it was not possible to communicate with the souls of the royal mummies in Cairo because their bodies had been treated with such careless disrespect by the Service of Antiquities. Budge in this way was able to enlist the support of the ancient Egyptians themselves:

> Whatever blame may be attached to individual archaeolo-

gists for removing mummies from Egypt, every unprejudiced person who knows anything of the subject must
admit that when once a mummy had passed into the care of
the Trustees and is lodged in the British Museum, it has a
far better chance of being preserved there than it could possibly have in any tomb, royal or otherwise, in Egypt.

Chapter Nine

The Archaeology of Unconsidered Trifles

THE FIRST LEAFLET TO BE DISTRIBUTED by the Egypt Exploration Fund declared a commitment to 'sentimental archaeology'. This immediately aligned it with the policies of Sir Evelyn Baring rather than the practices of Wallis Budge:

> A Society has been formed for the purpose of cooperating with Professor Maspero, Director of Museums and Excavations in Egypt, in his work of exploration. The Society undertakes to conduct excavations especially on sites of Biblical and classical interest, without infringing the Egyptian law, by which objects found are claimed by the Boolak Museum. M. Maspero, on his part, agrees to the publication of results by the Society.

It may seem unwise for a new society seeking to attract subscribers to declare its intention to abstain from bringing home the results of its excavations; the founders of the Fund, however, correctly judged that they could count on support so long as they contributed to the public debate on the Scriptures. By the 1880s, orthodox Bible scholars in England were still able to look forward to the triumph of traditional views. When Professor William Robertson Smith spread some of the more liberal notions in his popular lectures and books, he was called to trial before the Free Church Presbytery of Aberdeen and dismissed in 1881 from his chair. The trial caused a public scandal. At issue was the reliability of the Old Testament as a record of historical events.

Almost a century had passed since the Institute of Egypt had opened the country to the investigation of its past; sites had been excavated from the Delta to the second cataract; weighty volumes had been published recording in detail the finds and expounding the ancient history of the Nile Valley. But there were gaps: even Birch's Society for Biblical Archaeology had failed to lay before the public any archaeological proof of the events recorded in the Old Testament. The Egypt Exploration Fund therefore needed to launch itself with an investigation that would catch and hold public interest in the controversy, and to employ as its first excavator a man qualified to make a contribution.

Edouard Naville was a Swiss Egyptologist and biblical scholar. He had a comprehensive formal education uncommon in his field, having studied at the University of Geneva, King's College London, and the Universities of Bonn, Paris, and Berlin. He had been a student and literary executor of Lepsius, helping with the publication of the great *Denkmaeler*. Naville's interests were mainly philological and his religious orientation conservative. He came to the Fund with a proposal for an investigation that suited it perfectly.

In the first chapter of Exodus, it is recorded that the children of Israel multiplied in Egypt and became so numerous and strong, that when a new king, who knew nothing about Joseph, came to power, he saw them as a threat. This king set up taskmasters over the people, reduced them to slavery, and forced them to build two cities as supply centres that were called Pithom and Rameses. Lepsius had identified Rameses, but Reginald Stuart Poole had challenged its identification in Smith's *Dictionary of the Bible*. When Naville approached the Fund with a proposal to excavate an alternative site for the cities, it seemed an ideal scheme to excite the public imagination. If the great store cities had indeed been built, they would have been so substantial that traces would remain. If these could be unearthed and the king responsible for them identified, there would at last be independent scientific evidence for the Exodus.

The classical writers gave hints that helped with the cities' location: Herodotus had described the canal that connected the

Red Sea with the Nile as passing 'Patumos, a city in the Arabian nome'. Patumos had been identified as the city of Pa-Tum or Pi-Tum, meaning the 'house of Tum'; Tum was the ancient Egyptian sun god of Heliopolis. The French scholar Chabas had pointed out in 1864 that Pi-Tum of the Egyptians must be the Pithom of the Old Testament, and suggested it was probably sited at either Abu-Keshed or at Tell el-Maskhuta, about ten miles south-west of Ismailya, a suggestion he afterwards withdrew. Naville, however, having consulted geographical texts and noting that the monuments of Ismailya were dedicated by Ramesses II to Tum, decided to revive the idea, and to investigate the site of Tell el-Maskhuta. He first had to wait until the wars of 1882 ended, and then for the Nile to subside sufficiently to allow for excavation in the Delta. In January 1883 he set out, funded by a donation of 500 pounds from Sir Erasmus Wilson, who had promised a further 100 pounds if it should be needed.

Naville's main aim, and that of his backers, was to discover a tangible, archaeological link with the Bible, and in this he was completely successful. He uncovered the remains of a city, a military camp with fortifications, and a number of other structures that could have been store houses. There was evidence that the city had been constructed by Ramesses II, but no signs that would link it with the Israelites. Nevertheless, the *Illustrated London News* headlined its report of the discoveries 'A Buried City of The Exodus', and concluded:

> The first definite geographical fact in connection with the sojourn in the Land of Egypt has been established by the excavations at Pithom. The historical identification of Rameses II with Pharaoh the Oppressor also results from the monumental evidence. One short exploration has upset a hundred theories and furnished a wonderful illustration of the historical character of the Book of Exodus.

The 'wonderful illustration' did not convince all interested parties. Not for the first time interpretation of the evidence depended on the religious allegiance of the interpreters: those most anxious for confirmation of the historicity of the Old Testament were most willing to find it in Naville's excavations at Tell el-Maskhuta. Others were sceptical, and the resulting controversy generated excellent publicity for the Fund and increased its membership. There was another minor triumph at Tell el-Maskhuta. Maspero persuaded the Khedive to present two of the best sculptures found there – a granite falcon and the squatting figure of a scribe – to Sir Erasmus Wilson, who passed them on to the British Museum.

The launch of the Fund's work in Egypt had been a great success: the very walls built by the Israelites in bondage had been discovered; the pharaoh of the Exodus was at last identified; a gratifyingly heated scholarly debate had received wide publicity; and, as a reward for its bold and unprecedented decision to abide by the law that forbade the export of antiquities, the Fund had carried off the finest treasures it had unearthed.

The next target for Naville was the ancient royal seat of the pharaohs – the city of Zoan, which the scriptures suggest was the ancient capital of Egypt where, in the time of Moses, wonders occurred. There was general agreement about the city's location: a barren and fever-ridden spot in the eastern Delta called Tanis by the Greeks and San by the Arabs.

Amelia Edwards set to work drumming up funds with her customary zeal: she corresponded with a clergyman in America, the Rev. William Copley Winslow, who launched a campaign in the Press for 'Spades for Zoan'. The poet and hymn-writer John Greenleaf Whittier joined in, albeit hesitantly, writing to the Treasurer:

> I am glad to have my attention called to the excavation of Zoan. The enterprise commends itself to every reader of the Bible, and every student of the history and monumental wonders of Egypt. I would like to have a hand in it. I hesitate a little about disturbing the repose of some ancient mummy who, perchance, Hobnobbed with Pharaoh glass to glass or dropped his halfpenny into Homer's hat, or doffed his own to let Queen Dido pass but curiosity gets the better of sentiment and I follow the example of Dr Holmes [Oliver Wendell Holmes] by enclosing an order of Lieut. Governor Ames for one of his best shovels.

Sir Erasmus Wilson, who had been elected President of the

Fund, promised 1,000 pounds, and Mr W. Fowler, a member, promised 50 pounds for Tanis if nineteen others could be found to give the same amount.

Naville had already visited the place and was confident he would repeat his success at Tell el-Maskhuta of verifying the scriptures as well as enhancing the collection of the British Museum. Suddenly, however, Naville withdrew, claiming that pressure of work prevented him from going to Egypt at that time. His enemies suggested he was too fond of his home comforts; certainly the description of Tanis by Wilkinson as 'the habitation of fishermen, the resort of wild beasts and infested with reptiles and malignant fevers' cannot have appealed to the middle-aged scholar. In any case, Naville returned to his edition of the *Book of the Dead*, leaving the Egypt Exploration Fund with a vacancy.

The man who was chosen to fill it became the most famous and influential Egyptian archaeologist of modern times, the pioneer of modern archaeological method, and the first Professor of Egyptology in England. 'He found archaeology in Egypt a treasure hunt,' wrote his biographer, 'and left it a science.'

A formal education was not possible for William Flinders Petrie because his parents were committed to the Brethren Movement of Fundamentalist Christians, who believe in separating themselves from the 'profanities' of secular society. His father – a strict Sabbatarian who once wrote to his next-door neighbour 'on keeping their Parrot quiet on Sundays' – gave William lessons on the literal interpretation of the Scriptures, but left him to his own devices in the matter of secular education. As a boy he nourished passions for chemistry, geology and coin-collecting, the last bringing him into contact with the British Museum where he developed a sharp eye for a forgery.

In 1866 father and son read *Our Inheritance in the Great Pyramid* and were seized by a new enthusiasm. The author, Charles Piazzi Smythe, an eminent astronomer and Fellow of the Royal Society, happened to be a family friend. This, together with his extreme piety, may have recommended the book's bizarre theories to the Petries. These were based on John Taylor's *The Great Pyramid – Why was it built and Who built it?*, which had been published in 1859. Taylor insisted that the Great Pyramid could not have been built by man: it was too perfect in its dimensions, too precisely orientated to the points of the compass, too nearly placed on latitude 30°. Mankind could not have reached the stage of technological progress necessary to construct the Pyramid unaided in the short time since the creation of the world in 4,004 BC. It therefore followed that it must have been built under Divine guidance; once correctly interpreted, its orientation and dimensions would convey God's message to mankind.

Using Vyse's and Perring's measurements, Taylor observed that the height of the Pyramid bore the same relationship to its perimeter as the diameter of a circle does to its circumference. So the ancient Egyptians, through Divine guidance, had squared the circle. Based on this theory, Taylor postulated a 'pyramid inch' consisting of 1.001 of an imperial inch, of which twenty-five made up a 'sacred cubit'.

Piazzi Smythe based his theories on Taylor's measure. The Great Pyramid's dimensions were, Smythe confirmed, based on this measure. Furthermore, the entire progress of civilisation from earliest biblical times was symbolised by the passages, steps, and changes of slope that led to the Pyramid's Grand Gallery.

The Petries, father and son, were enthused by these notions, which seemed to wed scientific method and biblical record. William wrote to Smythe, expressing his enthusiasm and pointing out that the distance of the sun from the earth was exactly '10 to the 9 times the vertical height of the Great Pyramid' – a further confirmation of its Divine origin. In 1870, at the age of seventeen, William wrote to the *English Mechanic and World of Science*, defending the pyramid theory against its critics. *Researches on the Great Pyramid*, his first book, appeared four years later in 1879. It sought to confirm 'those distinctive principles of its design and construction first announced by the sagacity of John Taylor and Professor Piazzi Smythe'.

William Petrie got his first chance to visit Egypt in 1880, intending to carry out a survey of the Great Pyramid in search of further evidence to support his theories. Although his work was confined to the Pyramid, he noticed with distaste the destructive results of excavations being carried out in nearby tombs by the Department of Antiquities:

The savage indifference of the Arabs, who have even stripped the alabaster off the granite temple since Mariette uncovered it, and who are not at all watched here is only surpassed by a most barbaric sort of regard for the monuments by those in power. Nothing seems to be done with any uniform or regular plan; work is begun and left unfinished . . . It is sickening to see the rate at which everything is being destroyed, and the little regard paid to its preservation; If allotments all over the hill were made to the different European Government museums, with free leave to take all they liked, and power to preserve it here, something more satisfactory might be done. Anything would be better than leaving things to be destroyed wholesale; better spoil half in preserving the other half than leave the whole to be smashed.

Petrie collected a number of smaller items. As the tourist season drew to a close, the dealers who traded around the pyramids were ready to sell off their wares cheaply, and Petrie knew enough about forgeries to be able to purchase with confidence. He bought bronzes, coins, and scarabs, and also small, unregarded pieces of pottery that he had been asked to collect by Dr Birch at the British Museum. He seems to have been surprised and mildly shocked that Maspero, Director of Antiquities, advised him not to declare the items at customs, but to carry them off in his pockets.

Reviews of Petrie's book were generally favourable, *The Times* and the *Saturday Review* being particularly enthusiastic. Amelia Edwards wrote at length, concluding:

There can be no second opinion as to the special importance both of the work that Mr Flinders Petrie has done and of the book he has written; yet the latter is so unostentatious that readers may well fail to realise the importance of the services he has rendered to history and to science.

Petrie showed the book to Poole at the British Museum, who did not hesitate to recommend the young man to the Egypt Exploration Fund to replace Naville, and Amelia Edwards gave the recommendation her warm support.

Petrie was engaged at a salary of 250 pounds a month, which was to cover the cost of the excavation as well as his personal expenses. In one important particular Petrie insisted that his terms of employment be different from those of Naville: he insisted on being allowed to buy small antiquities that might be found by his workmen or brought to the dig by dealers, which Petrie saw as the basic materials from which ancient history could be deduced. True, there was the problem of the law, which held that all antiquities, however small, were the property of the Boulaq Museum, but Petrie had worked out a solution: he would present himself to Maspero and ask to work in Egypt as an agent of the Museum, authorised to purchase antiquities on its behalf. At the end he would present the entire collection to Maspero, and ask only to be allowed to take home the objects that Maspero did not want. These would then be available to the Fund for distribution to the British and American museums, together with 'a hint that donations are very acceptable'. This seemed an excellent scheme, so long as Maspero approved. Petrie was told to travel to Egypt via Paris, where he called on the Director of Antiquities to seek his consent. Maspero readily gave it, on the condition that the arrangement be kept a secret until he returned to Cairo.

Petrie went on from Paris to establish himself at Tanis. When Naville had visited the place he had described it as hideous, which Petrie confirmed by his own experience:

The flat expanse, as level as the sea, covered with slowly drying salt pools, may be crossed for miles, with only the dreary changes of dust, black mud, water, and black mud again . . . the only objects which break the flatness of the barren horizon are the low mounds of the cities of the dead; these alone remain to show that this region was once a living land whose people prospered on the earth . . . The miserable Arab huts of San first meet the eye . . . with on the one side a muddy stream into which they throw their dead buffalo, and from which they drink, and on the other a swamp full of rotting graves and filth. But the high mounds which rise behind this sickening mass of dead fish and live babies, bowls and flies are the remains of Roman and Greek Tanis, a city well built and ordered.

Petrie built himself a small wooden hut, and engaged about seventy men, women, and boys to clean the area. He insisted on paying them himself to make sure the money went into hands he had seen at work. He would start the work himself, seeing the diggers in position at 5.30 each morning, and blowing a whistle to set them off. He would retire to his hut between 8 and 9 for breakfast, but keep an eye on the workers through a telescope from his front door. He was a strict employer, always on the watch for slackness and unforgiving where he came across it. He dosed himself daily with quinine and strychnine to keep away the marsh fevers, and lived on tinned food from Cairo. He kept a journal, which he sent home for his close family and friends. Hearing of it, Amelia Edwards saw an opportunity and used it as the basis of a series of articles in *The Times*. She credited Petrie with half the fees, and wrote to him at the end of his first season in the ardent tones of a devotee.

At Tanis in 1884, Petrie uncovered two of the largest structures the ancient Egyptians had ever created: the temple and the giant colossus of Ramesses II, which he thought must have been the largest statue ever carved. It was made of red granite from Aswan, and originally may have stood almost 100 feet tall. It was positioned in the hieratic attitude, with arms at the sides and the left foot forward – a majestic, lonely figure visible for many miles across the low, dark swamps. Only fragments remained.

It was not, however, the most immense, but the smallest of antiquities that caught Petrie's interest. Strewn over the ground of the temple site were hundreds of beads, glazed amulets, fragments of pottery and ornaments of terracotta and glass, bronze and ivory furnishings from the houses of the Ptolemaic period, as well as coins from the wealthy villas of the Romans. None of these things had aroused the interest of Petrie's predecessors – they were neither impressive, aesthetically pleasing, nor made of precious metals – but Petrie was beginning to work out a way of interpreting the clues they offered to Egypt's past. He built wooden cases to house these unconsidered trifles in, and packed them with his own hands.

The items first had to be taken to the Boulaq Museum, where Petrie was saddened to find that Maspero kept so many for the Museum. This was part of the agreement, but Petrie had a sneaking suspicion that they were intended only for the Museum shop, where they would be sold to tourists. Even those that found their way into the permanent collections would be swamped by all the unidentified and unlabelled contents of the exhibition cases. However, Petrie was allowed to take home a sufficient collection to be exhibited at the Royal Archaeological Institute in London before being divided between the British Museum and the Museum of Fine Arts in Boston.

Petrie was anxious to get back to Egypt the following winter to follow up a discovery he had made in the west part of the Delta. By chance, one day he had bought from the dealers at Giza a small alabaster figure of a finely carved warrior, which he identified as being Greek rather than Egyptian. He asked where it had been found, and was told of a location called Nerib, near Kafr Dowar in the Delta. Petrie found there was no such place, but luckily met two of the dealers from Giza. They took him to Nebeira, where, they said, the statue had come from. He recorded in his journal:

Oh what a feast of pottery! The whole ground is thick with early Greek pottery . . . and it seemed almost sacrilege to walk over the heaps with the fine black lustrous ware crunching under one's boots . . . it seemed as if I was wandering in the smashings of the Museum's vase rooms. Such a half hour I never had before.

It was obviously the site of a wealthy Greek settlement, and Petrie kept its discovery a secret until he had the opportunity to excavate. The Fund gave him the chance in the winter of 1884, and by November he was back in Cairo buying stores and making plans. Near the site Petrie rented an old stone farmhouse, and began the work of sifting through and recording the pottery. Then he noticed a piece of broken stone that served as part of the gatepost in the gateway of his house. It was inscribed in Greek. The inscription began, 'This city of Naukratis . . .' Petrie had discovered the most important Greek trading centre of ancient times.

Herodotus mentions that Naucratis was the only early Greek foundation in Egypt. It had been granted a monopoly of trading in the 6th century BC, and had grown to become the most important Greek centre in Egypt before the foundation of Alexandria. Its location had been a matter of dispute among Egyptologists for a generation.

Petrie immediately telegraphed Poole with the news and set about looking for a workforce. He had to wait until the end of the maize harvest, when the local villagers came to the site looking for work. Petrie was once again paymaster and foreman, starting the day with his whistle and observing the work through his telescope.

One local irritation was in the shape of the Gizawiya, dealers from Giza who were curious about the new discovery and hung about the edges of the work trying to buy antiquities. Occasionally Petrie would limber up for a day's digging by chasing them across the fields, leaping canals and dodging between bushes. Less engaging were the irritations from London. Both Poole and Amelia Edwards wrote regularly to Petrie enquiring about progress, frequently communicating contradictory instructions from the Fund. On receiving the telegraphic news of the discovery Poole had refused to give it any publicity, pending further confirmation. Amelia, however, was always keen to drum up new support for the Fund, and conceived a publicity gimmick that involved selling bricks made without straw, such as those the cruel Pharaoh had forced the Israelite slaves to make. Would Petrie be so good as to send her 1,000 such bricks from Pithom? Petrie pointed out that the trade in relics was of dubious morality; that the cost would be enormous; and that it would be dishonest to claim that the bricks had been made by Israelite slaves, since ancient Egyptian bricks were often made without straw. The scheme was abandoned.

The discovery of Naucratis was sensational news, particularly at the growing American Branch of the Egypt Exploration Fund. Amelia Edwards, whose energetic correspondences had brought the Branch into being, reported that it had 171 subscribers, of whom 'three are heads of colleges, twenty-seven dignitaries of the church, nineteen distinguished university professors and thirty two members of Congress.'

Scholarship, however, breeds controversy; and archaeology, it has been said, is not a science but a vendetta. The Fund's enemies at home were sharpening their knives. The reports of Naville's discoveries at Tell el-Maskhuta had already stirred up animosities, and the publication of his *Pithom* was made the occasion for an attack on the Fund, which had supported him. Both Poole and Naville suspected the influence of what Amelia Edwards had come to call 'the Bs': Birch and Budge at the British Museum remained hostile to the Fund, even though they were the main beneficiaries of the antiquities brought home legally by its excavators. Birch had declared his opposition to the Fund since its inception, although he had asked Petrie to bring back some samples of pottery; the priorities that Wallis Budge had come to accept in evaluating antiquities had far more in common with the dealers of Cairo and Bloomsbury than with Flinders Petrie.

It was Budge who drafted a letter to the Fund from the Museum complaining that the antiquities that had been donated were without value. The trustees, it said, could not be recommended to accept 'a vast quantity of pottery and small objects which from our point of view are worthless'. Although the assertion was later withdrawn, Petrie was furious. 'The false statements of that letter', he wrote to Amelia, 'and the gross ignorance it showed of genuine and scientific archaeology bar me from having anything to do with that quarter again.' The estrangement was to last for the rest of his life.

The event happened at a bad time. A month earlier Petrie had resigned from the Egypt Exploration Fund, annoyed by the waste and inefficiency he saw in the management, and disappointed that Naville had been chosen to carry out the Fund's excavations for the following year. Petrie temporarily was cast adrift on his own resources; then, Amelia Edwards, with whom he kept up good relations, wrote to him with the news that a considerable sum had been placed at his disposal by 'a very wealthy and intelligent man (merchant class) who has travelled in Egypt and is enthusiastically fond of Egyptian antiquities'. She had only recently met the man, but already felt he might well become 'a sort of Sir Erasmus Wilson'. She would spring into action only if Petrie gave his consent: 'if you like the matter, I will begin tunnelling my mines and laying my gunpowder'.

Amelia laid siege to Jesse Haworth, a wealthy Manchester businessman. Soon Haworth placed sums of money at Petrie's disposal without preconditions: 'He is a religious man,' Amelia wrote, 'and if you could throw any light on the Bible . . . he would be gratified. But he does not want plunder and he wishes

to keep quite out of sight, and not to be mentioned in any way.'
Petrie was launched on his freelance career in the company of the
most effective publicist and accommodating sponsor in the
history of archaeology.

Relieved of financial anxieties, Petrie's main obstacle was the
Department of Antiquities. He clashed with Grebaut, as did
Budge, but for wholly different reasons. Petrie was anxious to
excavate and record, not to plunder; he was concerned that the
Museum's staff were augmenting the destruction they were commissioned to prevent: 'The deeds of the Bulak Museum in
Egypt', he wrote, 'remind me of that blackbird in our garden
who used to pick off all the finest bunches of currants, eat one,
and leave the rest to rot on the ground.' Petrie had to approach
Grebaut for permission to dig as an independent agent. Grebaut
pointed out that the English already had been granted permission to dig in the Delta and in Aswan; he wanted to keep the rest
of Egypt for the French. 'The money is here,' complained
Petrie, 'the worker is here, but the dog is in the manger and has a
nice warm bed in the hay, and does not want it disturbed.'

Ironically, rumours were spread that Petrie had been smuggling out cases of antiquities. He had been careful to clear everything with Maspero, and a letter from the retired Director
cleared things up, but Petrie was incensed that he should be
associated with Budge's methods, which he found offensive. He
wrote to Amelia Edwards:

When Grebaut knows how the Bugbear [their nickname for
Budge] has acted, he will be riled. That sweet'un took six
cases and passed them at Bulak, but left 17 others to be dealt
with as military baggage, to the confoundment of his military friends. After he left, those 17 came down the Nile and
had to be sent out; one was a block of ¾ of a ton, and, as no
packing could be found for it, they had, at Assuan, boxed it
in railway sleepers, spiked together with six inch nails! This
was a tough morsel for military baggage; but Major Bagnold
(who told me) had it cased in canvas, painted all over, and a
fine formal direction painted on it, and so it went.

So opposed was Petrie to the removal of treasures from Egypt
that he helped to organise a committee in London that blos-

somed into a Society for the Preservation of the Monuments of Ancient Egypt. The first members were from the artistic and intellectual circles of the capital: Amelia Edwards, of course; the painters Holman Hunt, Burne-Jones, and G. F. Watts; the Oxford Professor of Assyriology, Professor Archibald Sayce, and Sir Henry Layard, who became British Ambassador to Constantinople. The group persuaded the authorities of the Antiquities Service to raise a tax of 100 piastres on every tourist. This, together with admission charges to the Bulaq Museum, and the sale of antiquities in the Museum shop, was to be applied to the repair and maintenance of some of the Theban temples, and doors for the Tombs of the Kings. They pressed for the appointment of an English inspector to survey damage and make recommendations; Lord Salisbury, the Minister of State for Foreign Affairs, was persuaded to write to Sir Evelyn Baring, asking him to put the proposals to the government of Egypt.

Baring, although sympathetic to the Society's aims, was still sensitive to resentment from the French. He had abandoned his earlier hopes to arrange for an early withdrawal of the British garrison in Egypt, and by the mid-1880s had decided it would be unwise to fix a date for the British departure if the land was not to slide back into 'the tranquil Oriental barbarism' of former days. Another ever-present possibility was that the French would move in as the British moved out. The extent and nature of British interference in Egyptian affairs was a matter for Baring's day-to-day judgement – nowhere had it been spelled out in official communications – but he was aware that every decision he made was scrutinised and criticised by the French, who he categorised as anglophobes to a man. By February 1888 he wrote to Lord Salisbury, 'They are so unreasonable and have so much incurable hatred of England that I should dread any very glaring exhibition of our sovereignty in Egypt at this moment.'

Baring was also uncomfortably aware that the French had been the first to take an interest in the ancient monuments of Egypt; they alone had created the Museum and the Antiquities Service at a time when Britain preferred to leave such things to the enterprise of private individuals. The Service was almost the last stronghold of French influence in Egypt, and Baring was reluctant to interfere with it, particularly when it sought to restrain the acquisitiveness of his fellow countrymen. His desire to underplay the urgency of the Society's proposals led him to be less than insistent in supporting its requests, and the scheme, opposed by Grebaut, came to nothing. Baring did manage to set up a committee to make recommendations on the allocation of excavation permits, but for the most part seems to have allowed Grebaut to have his own way in the discussions. On one occasion Petrie called on Baring to complain about the procrastinations and inefficiencies of the Antiquities Service to find him sympathetic but impotent. Baring, he reported, 'was quite open and pleasant on the subject, but is evidently not free to take a strong course. "The whole difficulty is that one man Grebaut", said he again and again, with a fist on the table.'

In 1892 Grebaut was removed back to France and there were hopes of an easier future. Before leaving, however, he managed to steer new regulations through the Council of Ministers. The regulations, issued on 17 November 1891 by Khedival decree, provided that no excavations in Egypt would be permitted without the express authority of the Director of Museums and Excavations, after examination by the Permanent Committee on Egyptology. All objects found belonged by law to the state, and should be deposited in the Museum. In consideration of the excavator's expenses, the government proposed an ingenious method of recompense: the objects would be divided into two portions of equal worth, for which the Administration and the excavator would draw lots. The Administration reserved the right to buy from the excavator any piece included in the portion that fell to him. The Administration would make an offer, which the excavator was at liberty to refuse and suggest a higher price. The Administration then had the choice of either buying the piece at that price, or selling it to the excavator at the price of its original offer.

While these regulations seem reasonable, Petrie realised they applied much more to the treasure-hunting archaeologists than to himself, since, not knowing what he would be allowed to keep, he would be forced to record every object on the site, and then lose half to the Museum. He saw the imposition of the regulations as the failure of British diplomacy to protect British interests, and told his friends he was considering applying for French or German citizenship so he could get the support he needed. His friends dissuaded him. It was fortunate for British

Egyptology that he stayed; Petrie not only enlarged the scope of the subject, but revolutionised its methodology.

Three days after the imposition of the new regulations, on 20 November 1891, Petrie began digging at Tell el-Amarna, built by the heretic King Akhenaten when he abandoned Thebes and moved the capital of Egypt to this site. Here he and his wife Nefertiti, surrounded by chosen and devoted officials, worshipped the sun god Aton. Tell el-Amarna is a wide open amphitheatre in the cliffs, almost equidistant from the rejected cities of Thebes and Memphis. Petrie found it a daunting prospect: 'It is an overwhelming site to deal with', he wrote. 'Imagine setting about exploring the ruins of Brighton, for that is about the size of the town.'

Petrie soon found, in the area of the palace, what he described as 'the most important discovery artistically that there has been since the Old Kingdom statues of Mariette'. It was the painted pavement of the palace, 250 feet square, with a formal border of bunches of lotus flowers alternating with dishes of food. A pathway crossed the pavement with a painted lake on each side containing fish and plants: around each lake a rural scene had been depicted of calves playing in the bushes, and pintail duck rising from clumps of reed and papyrus.

Petrie designed and built a walkway nine inches above the pavement so visitors could pass over without damaging it, and covered the entire surface with a thin coat of tapioca water, applied gently with his forefinger, which dried to a thin protective film. The pavement became a major tourist attraction, and for some years Cook's steamers included it in their Nile tour itinerary. Unfortunately, although the Society for the Preservation of the Monuments of Egypt provided a shed to protect the pavement, no provision was made for a path from the landing stage, and the tourists trampled down the cultivated fields on their way to the site. One night, the villager who owned the fields hacked the pavement to pieces as it was the only way to save his crops.

The year after Petrie's discovery, in 1892, Amelia Edwards died, leaving an endowment in her will to found a Professorship of Egyptian Archaeology at University College, London. The will specified that no one holding office in the British Museum could be eligible for the post, which ruled out Budge, and that the appointee must not be more than forty years of age, which eliminated most of the other candidates thought to have sufficient distinction to be eligible. In fact Amelia had a specific candidate in mind, and had let her executors know her wishes.

Petrie was duly appointed. His terms recognised the continuing need for him to be involved in 'research work of active exploration', and allowed him the winter months free to continue his work in Egypt, which took the direction of investigations into the pre-Dynastic cultures of the Nile.

Because earlier excavations had concentrated on valuable and saleable works of art, there was little evidence of the origins of Egyptian civilisation. Egyptologists swapped theories, the most popular being that the rulers of Egypt had brought their culture with them from Mesopotamia, and imposed it on the conquered people. At Quft, a small town north of Luxor, Petrie discovered crude limestone statues of the patron god Min that were clearly more primitive than any statues previously found. Then, at Naqada a little further south, he uncovered a great cemetery containing thousands of primitive fragments: flint knives, stone palettes and mace heads, as well as pottery that was not made with a wheel, and there was not a trace of writing anywhere. Petrie knew he was in contact with a culture more ancient than any previously identified. At first he thought it must be a new race of invaders, probably from Libya, however careful classification of the styles of pottery showed that the culture had evolved over a long period of time. It became clear that Egyptian prehistory could be studied in the Nile Valley without the need to call on 'migration' theories.

The turn of the century brought a change in the fortunes of English Egyptology. In 1899 Maspero was persuaded to return to Cairo as Director of Antiquities. He tightened procedures against illegal excavation, and arranged for the Public Works Department to appoint two inspectors, both English, one for Middle Egypt as far as Abydos, and the other for the south. Maspero also advanced the progress of Egyptology by granting the Abydos concession to Petrie.

Abydos is famous as the burial ground of Thinis, the earliest dynastic capital of Egypt, and the location of the grave of Osiris, where the annual ritual mysteries of the death and resurrection of the god were enacted. In ancient times it was a place of pilgrimage, and most Egyptians wished either to be buried there or to have their mummy taken for a time to pay homage to the god before final burial. Both Mariette and Maspero had dug over the site and carried off statues for the Bulaq Museum. Petrie had tried many times to get permission to dig, but had always been refused in favour of the French. Emile Amélineau had been granted the concession in 1895, and had employed a large work-force to search for marketable antiques. He claimed they had carried off everything of value, and had smashed to smithereens what they did not take away. Petrie found the smithereens of value: by identifying the names of kings from fragments of stone vessels and jar sealings, and by collating them by stylistic affin-ities and differences, he was able to arrange an historical sequence. When his finds were exhibited in London, Petrie noticed that the unconsidered trifles were educating public taste: 'A new public feeling appeared: instead of only caring for things of beauty or remarkable appearance, people hang over the tables, fascinated by the fragments of the 1st Dynasty. Some workmen would spend their whole dinner hour in the room.'

Petrie continued his annual excavations in Egypt for forty years. No one man ever worked at so many sites or made so many significant finds. He also founded a new and more re-sponsible school of archaeologists which, by concentrating on the minute and obscure objects, was able to uncover a long period of prehistoric development.

By using the method of sequence dating, cultures of increas-ing sophistication could then be identified with some accuracy. Sequence dating works on the principle that when articles are discarded, the one that is thrown away today will land on top of the one thrown away yesterday. It is therefore reasonable to sup-pose that objects found near to the surface of the ground are more historically recent than those lower down. Applying this principle to different styles of pottery found at different levels, Petrie was able to identify seven successive stages of pre-Dynas-tic pottery, each linked to the one before and after by at least one common feature. Objects found in association with these styles of pottery could be assumed to share their ages. Petrie explained his approach to the subscribers of the Egypt Exploration Fund by using a simple analogy:

If in some old country mansion one room after another had been locked up untouched at the death of each successive owner, then, on comparing all the contents, it would easily be seen which rooms were of consecutive dates and no-one could suppose a Regency room to come between Mary and Ann, or an Elizabethan room to come between others of George III. The order of rooms could be settled to a certainty by comparing all the furniture and objects. Each would have some links of style in common with those next to it, and much less in common with others which were farther from its period . . . The principle applies to graves as well as rooms, to pottery as well as furniture.

Petrie's methods were time-consuming and tedious, as it was necessary to record carefully the exact position of each object. There were those who preferred to dig rapidly and make off with the richer prizes. Naville, with the dash and impatience of the old school, would have none of it: 'You might as well', he wrote, 'make a plan of the position of raisins in a plum pudding.' Petrie's method, however, was the one that survived and came to dominate in the practice of field archaeology. His insistence on the importance of observing and recording every object found, no matter how humble, replaced the slapdash treasure-hunting of his predecessors.

Petrie also made significant discoveries: the city of Naucratis was followed by that of Kahun, a compact, walled town of the Middle Kingdom; the great pre-Dynastic cemeteries at Naqada; treasures from Tell el-Amarna; and fine archaic material from the royal tombs of Abydos, where through his findings he was able to arrange the earliest kings of Egypt in sequence. No one in the entire history of Egyptology made as many major archaeological discoveries.

As his techniques became more widely known, and began to be adopted in archaeological circles, Petrie was persuaded to write a manual. In *Methods and Aims in Archaeology* (1904) there are indications of why, perhaps, Petrie was slow in becoming fashionable. Enumerating the qualities necessary for a good archaeologist, he includes: a strong historical sense; a good education in arts and sciences; acute powers of observation and an accurate visual memory; the ability to draw accurately; an understanding of the languages of the ancient civilisation one is investigating, and ability to speak that of the modern inhabitants of the land in which one digs; the archaeologist also should be physically robust, ready to work long hours with the pick and shovel, physical condition evidenced by 'the shortness of his fingernails and the toughness of his skin . . . Nothing can be a substitute for fingerwork in extracting objects, and clearing ground delicately; and one might as well try to play a violin in a pair of gloves as profess to excavate with clean fingers and a pretty skin.' The dedicated archaeologist must also dress the part: 'the man who cannot enjoy his work without regard to appearances, who will not strip and go into water, or slither on slimy mud through unknown passages, had better not profess to excavate.'

In his manual Petrie gave detailed advice on choosing workmen, the best age being between fifteen and twenty years, after which 'many turn stupid'; and on the correct way to treat them: 'The better class of these workers are one's personal friends, and are regarded much as old servants are in a good household.' It is far better to do without, than to trust, an overseer. The archaeologist should rely on his own supervision. A system of 'vigilant surprises' upon workers is a good idea, approaching the workings ideally along sunken ground. The telescope is invaluable, as witnessed by the anecdote Petrie recalls in which at Tanis he watched a line of women busily walking out of a deep pit and tipping their baskets at the top – the telescope revealing that the baskets were all empty.

Petrie's life-style became legendary. Any money he was given had to be shared between his own needs and those of the dig, and so he cut his own to the minimum. He had one table at which he would work and eat:

> . . . lighted by a very few small apertures in the wall just below the ceiling. In a trough down the centre of the table stood a double row of tins, containing the various kinds of food, and, nearby, a can opener. His idea of satisfying the pangs of hunger, when they became intense, was to eat from several tins at random, until they were empty. He took for granted that his staff would do the same.

So wrote an American observer of the Petrie camp, who added

that two of Petrie's colleagues had become engaged whilst nursing each other through ptomaine poisoning. Another American visitor wrote, 'He must have lost many of the niceties of feeling by so continuously "roughing it". I was sitting talking to him when off came his shoe, right before me, while he shook out the stones. He wore no stockings and his dusty foot was exposed.'

The best summing up of Petrie at work is in the biography of James Breasted, the first American Professor of Egyptology who rose to distinction in the subject. Breasted was on his honeymoon and on his first visit to Egypt when he first met Petrie, and was cordially received at the Petrie camp:

> His clothes confirmed his universal reputation for being not merely careless but deliberately slovenly and dirty. He was thoroughly unkempt, clad in ragged, dirty shirt and trousers, worn out sandals and no socks. It was one of his numerous idiosyncrasies to prefer that his assistants should emulate his own carelessness . . . He served a table so excruciatingly bad that only persons of iron constitution could survive it, and even they assuage their hunger by sharing the comparatively luxurious beans and unleavened bread of the local fellahin . . . The fact remains that he not only miraculously survived the consistent practice of what he preached, but with all his eccentricities . . . established in the end a record of maximum results for minimum expenditure which is not likely to be surpassed.

Chapter Ten

Interlude and Grand Finale

T HE PAINTINGS OF THE AMERICAN ARTIST Joseph Lindon Smith were so realistic that they were very nearly
trompe-l'oeil. The artist would be photographed,
brushes in hand, standing for example in an Egyptian temple, in
front of what appeared to be two identical images; so real was
Smith's rendition that the viewer had to be told which was
reality and which the painting. Joseph Smith (1863-1950) spent
many years in Egypt making these astonishing replications,
during which time his imagination was caught by the tale of the
'Curse of Aton'.

When King Akhenaten (1353-35 BC) deserted the religion of
his ancestors, he obliterated all the images of their god Amon-Ra
from the capital city of Thebes and persecuted the priests of
Amon. After the King's death, the former religion was restored.
Joseph Smith had heard the tale that the priests had pronounced
a curse on Akhenaten. The effect of the curse was that
Akhenaten's soul and body were doomed to wander separately in
space and never to be reunited for all eternity.

Joseph Smith decided to arrange the enactment of a ritual in
which Queen Tiyi, the mother of Akhenaten, would appeal to
the gods of the underworld, represented by the hawk-headed
Horus, for the pardon of her son. The ritual was to be performed
before an audience in the Valley of the Queens. Smith's wife
would play the part of Queen Tiyi; Hortense Weigall, who was
married to the Inspector of Antiquities at Luxor, would play

Akhenaten; and Smith himself – although unthreatening in demeanour, being small and mild, with balding head, spectacles, and a walrus moustache – would play Horus, the hawk-headed sun god. This was to be more than a mere bout of amateur dramatics. By their brief essay into histrionics, the trio hoped to effect the reunion of Akhenaten's wandering soul and body.

The script was carefully prepared with the assistance of the Inspector from Luxor and, Joseph Smith records, 'based upon the archaeological data'; the approval of the Director of Antiquities, Maspero, was sought and obtained. Attendance was to be by invitation only, and this took the form, Joseph Smith records, of a 'long and learned document, beginning with a quotation from a demotic inscription' that told the tragic story of the curse.

Invitations were accepted by all the most distinguished in the field of Egyptology: the Masperos, the Petries, Lord and Lady Carnarvon, the Navilles, Legrain, G. Elliot Smith, John Garstang, Howard Carter, and Ernesto Schiaparelli among others. The famous actor-manager Herbert Beerbohm Tree was in Luxor at the time, and, having admired the script, begged an invitation for himself.

The cast were in a state of excitement at the first and only rehearsal, held three days before the performance was due. Things got off to a fine start as Smith made his first entrance as the god Horus. Then Hortense made her entrance. She seemed to be less than fully engaged in the part, and Smith recalled that 'the lack of dramatic in her acting made me, as stage director, intervene to coach her'. He swept onstage, declaiming her lines with gusto to an unexpected response: 'without warning a terrific peal of thunder, flashes of lightning and a sudden gale' drowned his voice. As he stopped speaking, the storm just as suddenly ceased. Smith carried on. Reverting to his own part, he intoned sacred words and, in a burst of red fire, Corinne appeared. As she began to sing Akhenaten's hymn to the rising sun, a sharp squall of rain and large hailstones blew up and her fellow actors rushed for shelter.

Joseph Smith took courage from the maxim of the theatre that a bad dress rehearsal means a good first night. That night, the two leading ladies had an identical dream: they were each standing alone in the Ramasseum when the great stone statue dedicated to Amon-Ra slowly came to life, unfolded his arms, and struck them with his flail – Hortense on the stomach and Corinne across the eyes. The next morning Corinne was carried off to Cairo hospital with a violent attack of trachoma, her 'sight was despaired of', and Hortense, in the adjoining room, after an abdominal operation that 'proved almost fatal'. Smith records that 'forty-eight hours after the rehearsal every actor and member of the rehearsal audience had been removed from Luxor by a severe attack of illness'.

Arthur Weigall, Inspector of Antiquities, whose published account of the episode is substantially the same as that of Smith, remained unconvinced that it demonstrated the malevolence of the ancient dead: 'I do not think that the possibilities of that much under-rated factor in life's events, coincidence, have been exhausted in the search for an explanation of our tragedy . . . but, at the same time, I try to keep an open mind on the subject.'

The grand finale of Egyptian discovery is an archaeological drama on the epic scale. It 'starts like Aladdin's miraculous lamp and ends like a Greek saga of Nemesis'. So wrote the sister of the principal actor, George Edward Stanhope Molyneux Herbert, sportsman, art collector, and fifth Earl of Carnarvon.

After a serious motor-car accident that left him with breathing difficulties, Lord Carnarvon was advised by his doctors to spend his winters abroad. 'He decided', writes his son, 'in 1902 to go to Egypt about the middle of January when the pheasant shooting had ended.' There he met Lord Cromer, who recommended the country but said he would be bored to tears without a hobby, and suggested archaeology. Lord Carnarvon discovered he could satisfy his taste both for gambling and for collecting antiques by investing his money and energies into excavation. The field was highly unpredictable: in the bran tub of the Nile Valley the amateur enthusiast was as likely to stumble on buried treasure as the expert. The odds could be shortened by selecting the areas most likely to yield results, and Lord Carnarvon realised he needed an agent who knew the local situation. He chose a man who at the time was earning his living in Egypt as a water-colour painter – Howard Carter.

Carter had arrived in Egypt in 1891 at the age of seventeen, having been engaged to help with the drawings of an archaeological survey. He worked with Petrie at Amarna, but the great man was not impressed: 'Mr Carter is a good natured lad', he wrote, 'whose interest is entirely in painting and natural history . . . it is of no use to me to work him up as an excavator.' Carter, however, had gone on to work with Naville, Griffith and Maspero before being appointed in 1899 to the Antiquities Service as Inspector General of Monuments of Upper Egypt. A dispute with some French tourists led to his resignation from the Service in 1905, and so, at the time he met Carnarvon, he was again earning his living from painting.

Over the next five years Carter and Carnarvon excavated in fifteen different locations in the area of Thebes, gradually amassing a collection of antiquities and carefully recording the location of their finds. In 1912, with Carter's collaboration, Carnarvon published *Five Years' Explorations at Thebes*, a sumptuous record of their work together.

Carter's ambitions lay across the river, in the Valley of the Kings. Here, where the burial places of the greatest of Egypt's monarchs had been discovered, lay the best hope of fulfilling the dream of all excavators: to find an undisturbed royal tomb.

Since Belzoni had made his first discoveries, the Valley had been investigated by dozens of energetic explorers during the 19th century. Belzoni had left the place confident there was nothing left to find, and his opinion was confirmed by Henry Salt, who 'resided there for four months, and laboured in a like manner to find another tomb, but in vain'. Lepsius had measured the whole area with Prussian thoroughness, and declared that all had been revealed. Then, however, the French Egyptologist Victor Loret, then Director of Antiquities, had discovered at the turn of the century a cache of nine mummies of pharaohs in the tomb of Amenophis II.

From 1903 the concession to dig in the Valley of the Kings had been held by the wealthy American businessman Theodore M. Davis, whose early excavations had been supervised by Carter. Davis had succeeded in unearthing more tombs, and had published his findings in six opulent volumes. Since he was digging for the Antiquities Service, the finest of the objects he discovered went to the Cairo Museum. By 1912 it seemed that the Valley and Davis had exhausted each other, but he was reluctant to surrender the concession. Carter and Carnarvon had to wait until 1914 to take over the area from him. Their permit to excavate provided that 'the work of excavation shall be carried out at the expense, risk and peril of the Earl of Carnarvon by Mr Howard Carter', and stipulated that Carter should always be present at the dig. The permit was renewable annually until 16 November 1923.

The First World War delayed the start of work. Carnarvon rushed back to England, and Carter was assigned to a department of the civil service for organising labour battalions. Following Gallipoli the Turks invaded Egypt in 1916, but were promptly driven out and the war receded. By 1917 Carter was able to open his campaign in the Valley.

'The difficulty was', he wrote, 'to know where to begin, for mountains of rubbish thrown out by previous excavators encumbered the ground in all directions.' Most of these excavators had been single-minded in their search for buried treasures, and had not left records of the areas they had examined exhaustively. The only comprehensive way for Carter to search was to dig lines down to bedrock across the entire Valley.

The 1917 season produced nothing. The following year Carnarvon came out to Egypt and the two men dug for seven months without a find. In 1919 they came on a cache of thirteen alabaster jars bearing the signs of Ramesses II. 'As this was the nearest approach to a real find that we had yet made in the Valley,' Carter wrote, 'we were naturally somewhat excited.' The excitement had to carry them through two further barren seasons in 1920 and 1921, when digging in the terrible heat of the enclosed Valley throughout the season produced nothing at all.

In the summer of 1922 while visiting Lord Carnarvon at Highclere, Howard Carter was told that the search in the Valley was to be called off. Carnarvon had spent around 50,000 pounds on the excavations; he was fifty-six years old and in poor health; his fortunes were feeling the squeeze of post-war inflation; he had lost confidence that there were other tombs to be found in the Valley, and even if another royal mausoleum was unearthed, like all the rest it probably would have been robbed.

Carter refused to give up. He wanted just one more season to investigate the only spot in the entire Valley that had not yet been dug. He was prepared to pay for the work himself, he said, if Carnarvon would give him permission to dig under the concession. If he should be successful, the discovery would be credited to Carnarvon. Faced with such generosity of spirit, Lord Carnarvon agreed to finance one final season before withdrawing from Egypt.

The small area of land on which Carter was pinning his hopes was below and just to the side of the entrance to the tomb of Ramesses VI, a popular tourist attraction. He had discovered here a collection of 20th Dynasty workers' huts, but had not tried to excavate beneath them because the work would get in the way of the tourists visiting the tomb. All other possible sites in the area however had been exhausted, and the tourists would have to take second place. Carter assembled the workmen on 3 November 1922, and told them to dig a trench straight through the middle of the huts.

The next morning Carter arrived at the site shortly after dawn. The workmen stood in a silent group, looking into the bottom of the trench. Carter peered down – there, cut directly into the limestone bedrock, was a clean white step. It led to another, and then to a third, and on down into the soil. On reaching the twelfth step, the upper part of a plastered and sealed door was revealed. Carter bored a hole in the top and peered through to see a passage filled with rubble. It could be the entrance hall of a royal tomb, or just a cache of objects. The workmen cleared the doorway, revealing four more steps. On the door itself was the seal of the high priests of the necropolis: a recumbent jackal over nine prostrate captives. It was the entrance to a tomb; the seal of the necropolis made it likely to be a royal one, and it had not been entered since the same date as the workmen's huts. Since the huts had been built for the construction of the tomb of Ramesses VI in the 20th Dynasty, whatever lay beyond the door had been undisturbed for over 3,000 years. Carter ordered the stairwell to be filled with rubble, posted a guard, and sent a telegram to Carnarvon: 'AT LAST HAVE MADE WONDERFUL DISCOVERY IN VALLEY. A MAGNIFICENT TOMB WITH SEALS INTACT. RE-COVERED SAME FOR YOUR ARRIVAL. CONGRATULATIONS.'

Carter had to wait eighteen days for his benefactor to arrive. During this time he reflected on the possibilities that lay beyond the sixteen steps. Because of certain clues that had been picked up in the area, he had in mind the as yet undiscovered tomb of King Tutankhamun.

In 1907 Theodore M. Davis had discovered a small underground chamber in which were an uninscribed alabaster figure and a broken wooden box containing pieces of gold-leaf, embossed with the names of Tutankhamun and his queen. Nearby Davis found a faience vessel also inscribed with Tutankhamun's name. He thought that the underground chamber must be the empty, despoiled tomb of the king. But he had also found nearby about one-dozen white pottery jars containing linen marked with the name of Tutankhamun, some bags of chaff and of natron, and the bones of birds and animals. Davis sent these to the Metropolitan Museum in New York, where the curator of the Egyptian Department identified them as the materials used by the embalmers when preserving the body of Tutankhamun, and the remains of the feast they had after the work was completed. It seemed obvious that Tutankhamun was indeed buried in the Valley, and probably not far from the place where Davis had made his finds.

It did seem unlikely that a royal tomb would be sited in such an insignificant place and so close to the threshold of another, but the more obvious possibilities had been exhausted and Carter was optimistic. On the site of his discovery he erected a stone tablet, on which he painted the coat of arms of Lord Carnarvon.

On 23 November Carter had the stairwell cleared in anticipation of the arrival of Lord Carnarvon. The seals of Tutankhamun appeared without any ambiguity on the lower part of the door. The following afternoon Lord Carnarvon descended the sixteen steps and waited for Carter to break the seals. The first disappointment then struck them: the seals of Tutankhamun were on the original plaster, but those of the necropolis authorities were on restored blocking. The tomb had been broken into and resealed in ancient times, which explained the objects found by Davis that must have been removed by the thieves. It was a setback, but the fact that the tomb had been resealed indicated that the authorities thought it still contained something of value. Carnarvon and Carter pressed on with guarded optimism.

On 25 November, clearing out the rubble from the inclined corridor behind the door, they found broken potsherds, alabaster jars and fragments of small articles, all pointing to the fact that the tomb had been plundered. By the afternoon of the next day, thirty feet from the entrance, they discovered a second sealed door, almost an exact replica of the first. It bore the seal of Tutankhamun and of the royal necropolis. Again there were signs that the door had been opened and resealed. The group waited for Carter to make the next move:

> The decisive moment had arrived. With trembling hands I made a tiny breach in the upper left hand corner. Darkness and blank space, as far as the iron testing-rod could reach, showed that whatever lay beyond was empty, and not filled like the passage we had just cleared. Candle tests were applied as a precaution against possible foul gases, and then, widening the hole a little, I inserted the candle and peered in, Lord Carnarvon, Lady Evelyn and Callender standing anxiously beside me to hear the verdict. At first I could see nothing, the hot air escaping from the chamber causing the candle flame to flicker, but presently, as my eyes grew accustomed to the light, details of the room within emerged from the mist, strange animals, statues, and gold – everywhere the glint of gold. For a moment – an eternity it must have seemed to the others standing by – I was struck dumb with amazement, and when Lord Carnarvon, unable to stand the suspense any longer, enquired anxiously, 'Can you see anything?' it was all I could do to get out the words, 'Yes, wonderful things'.

Inside were gold-plated chariots, and two life-sized statues of the king in black bitumenised wood with golden kilts and head-dresses facing each other; there were three gilt couches with carved sides, beds, chairs, inlaid caskets, and alabaster vessels; there was a golden throne inlaid with semiprecious stones and surrounded by faience vases, statuettes, bows, walking sticks, and a heap of valuable objects, any one of which would have made the excavation worthwhile. Carter enlarged the hole, and his companions one by one gazed on the wonders beyond the door. 'Surely never before in the whole history of excavation', Carter wrote, 'had such an amazing sight been seen as the light of our torch revealed to us.' The 26 November 1922, was 'the day of days, the most wonderful that I have ever lived through, and certainly one whose like I can never hope to see again'.

The next day they returned, and with the help of electric lights were able to make a careful examination of the room. It was obvious that someone had broken through the door and that the objects in the room had been disordered, though it was un-imaginable that thieves would have left so many valuable things behind; perhaps they had been disturbed. The function of the chamber was not clear. It seemed to be a storehouse of treasures, but not a tomb: there was no sarcophagus and no mummy. In the north wall, between the two statues of the king, they saw a sealed door with a small breach in the bottom which had been re-paired, large enough to admit a boy or a small man. Underneath one of the couches they found a small irregular hole in the west wall which had not been repaired. The thieves had penetrated beyond, and when Carter peered through he saw a confusion of funeral objects in complete disorder, as if ransacked by someone in a hurry. The thief, wrote Carter, had 'done his work just about as thoroughly as an earthquake'. They realised they were in an antechamber, and that possibly a series of rooms lay beyond. 'Visions of chamber after chamber, each crowded with objects like the ones we had seen', wrote Carter, 'passed through our minds and left us gasping for breath.'

On discovering that the second chamber, which Carter called the annex, was also filled with objects, it became obvious that help was needed to record and catalogue them. Many would need a specialist's skills to preserve them from deterioration on coming into contact with the air. Carter requested the assistance of the Metropolitan Museum of Art in New York, and was granted the services of two draughtsmen, Harry Burton, photo-grapher, and A. C. Mace, archaeologist. Alfred Lucas, Director of the Chemical Department of the Egyptian government, who was about to leave on a three-month holiday, postponed it to be available. Dr Alan Gardiner, and Professor James H. Breasted of the University of Chicago lent their services for the interpre-tation of inscriptions. The most magnificent find in the history of Egyptology had succeeded in bringing together two inter-national figures in a co-operative project.

Carter arranged for an official opening of the tomb on 29 November, when a small party of distinguished guests, includ-ing Lady Allenby, wife of the British High Commissioner, the governor of the province, a number of other Egyptian notables, and a reporter from the London *Times*. The following day, Pierre Lacau, Director General of the Service of Antiquities, arrived and was shown round the antechamber. On 3 December it was sealed again with heavy timbers across the doorway, and the stairway was filled to surface level.

In London, *The Times* of 30 November 1922 announced the discovery as 'what promises to be the most sensational Egyptological discovery of the century', and the following day an article by Wallis Budge assessed its importance to archaeology. In view of the discoveries that were to come there is a certain irony in his words of consolation:

> It is, of course, disappointing that the thieves in ancient days succeeded in carrying off all the jewellery which was undoubtedly buried with the king; but, after all, there is a great deal of jewellery in Cairo Museum and many students will rejoice more in the discovery of these funerary appliances than they would do over ornaments of gold and precious stone.

Carter went to Cairo to order a steel gate that would make the tomb secure without the need to re-bury it each time they paused from work. He also bought chemical and photographic material, a motor car, packing cases of all sizes and packing materials for delicate objects, including thirty-two bales of calico and more than a mile of wadding and surgical bandages. On 17 December the steel gate was fitted, and on the 18th the work of clearing out the antechamber and annex began.

The work was executed meticulously. Carter had absorbed well the example of Petrie from his early years in excavation, and insisted that every object be taken out by hand so that its relationship to the objects near it could be noted. He wrote:

> It was slow work, painfully slow, and nerve-wracking at that, for one felt all the time a heavy weight of responsibility. Every excavator must, if he have any archaeological conscience at all. The things he finds are not his own property, to treat as he pleases . . . They are a direct legacy from the past to the present age, he is the privileged inter-

mediary through whose hands they come . . .

Every object was photographed and carefully identified and recorded before being moved, protected by the wadding and surgical bandages. One of the most beautiful items, a refined painted wooden casket which, Carter judged, 'far surpasses anything of the kind that Egypt has yet produced', contained a number of objects. So painstaking was Carter's approach to the task of preserving and recording every detail that it took him three weeks to empty the casket. Each object was carefully recorded and treated with chemical preservative before being carried out of the antechamber to the nearby tomb of Sethos II, which served as a workshop. Here they were secured behind a many-padlocked steel gate weighing one-and-a-half tons. Arthur Weigall, Inspector of Antiquities, was in official attendance:

> Day after day the crowd which assembled to watch the removal of different objects increased in size. Now it was a glistening chariot that was taken to the workshop; now a gilded chest or casket, and now a tray bearing bouquets of flowers or a collection of odds and ends. As each of these loads was carried along the valley, soldiers armed with rifles marched behind it, and pressmen and visitors ran by the side, clicking their cameras and scribbling their notes.

Archaeology under the limelight', wrote Carter, 'is a new and rather bewildering experience for most of us.' Within weeks of the announcement of his discovery, telegrams poured in from all over the world. Letters followed, and even advice on how to preserve the antiquities and to ward off evil spirits. There were religious tracts and denunciations, as well as lucrative offers of moving-picture rights and copyrights for the fashion world. *The Times* reported on 15 January 1923:

> All roads lead to 'Tutankhamun' these days, and whenever one rides out along the picturesque canal bank, past the native cemetery leading to the Valley of the Kings, there is a never-ending string of people on donkeys, or in sandcarts, along the road or over the hill, all moving in the direction of, or from, the newly discovered tomb. Urchins at every

turn offer you effigies in plaster of Tutankhamun, which, by the way, might just as well represent any other king . . .

The Christmas season brought a great increase in tourists, drawing pilgrims away from Bethlehem. The Egyptian State Railway opened a new train service between Cairo and Luxor called the 'Tutankhamun Special'.

The objects were carefully repaired, crated, and sent to Cairo. There were few indications that the intruders of ancient times had escaped with much, but Carter did find a gilded pedestal without its statuette, almost certainly golden, and a cloth in which were wrapped a handful of solid gold rings, as if the thieves had been disturbed and left in a hurry. He was even able to deduce that the tomb had been broken into twice. On the first occasion, the passage between the outer doors must have been cleared because Carter found objects from the tomb buried under the rubble. The first thieves mainly had been interested in gold and silver, but the second were after the costly oils and fats stored in the alabaster vessels, and had emptied them into water skins for easier transportation. The finger-marks of one of them could still be seen on a vessel that had been emptied of ointment.

The most exciting find of all was the sealed door in the north wall of the antechamber that screened off the secrets of the tomb. Behind this door, Carter prophesied with confidence, lay the sarcophagus and the mummy of Tutankhamun. If he were right, the young king who had succeeded Akhenaten at the age of nine and died at the age of eighteen, buried in the least imposing of the royal tombs in the Valley of the Kings, was the only one to lie undisturbed until the 20th century. For the first time in over a century of exploration in the Nile Valley, the excavators knew with certainty that what lay behind the sealed door was what was left on the day of a king's burial.

Carter and Carnarvon issued a joint public statement on 3 December 1922 stating their confidence that 'from the seals on the doorway still unopened there is every indication that we shall find Pharaoh Tutankhamun.' Although the tomb had been robbed, that the seals of the necropolis had been replaced meant that 'whatever may have happened to the metal objects of value, the King himself will be found intact'. Carter knew what lay behind the sealed door from his study of papyri, in particular a plan for the tomb of Ramesses IV held at Turin: the body of the king would be found, according to ancient custom, enclosed in the innermost of a nest of three coffins, protected by a series of funeral canopies. 'We shall be confronted', went on the forecast, 'with an unimaginably rich and archaeologically valuable result.'

On 16 February 1923, a group of twenty privileged persons, including the Carnarvons; the Egyptian Minister of Public Works; Pierre Lacau, Director of the Antiquities Service; Albert M. Lythgoe, Curator of the Egyptian Department of the Metropolitan Museum; assorted archaeologists; Egyptian officials; and a representative of the London *Times* took their seats on chairs placed in the cleared antechamber, facing the tomb's north wall and the great sealed door. A small platform had been raised against the door. The men in the audience removed their jackets in anticipation of the heat of the early afternoon, augmented by the electric lamps. Carter – pale, drawn, and expectant – mounted the platform and stated briefly that all that had been done, and anything that was about to be revealed, was entirely due to Lord Carnarvon. Then, hammer in hand, he turned to the sealed door. Arthur Weigall recalled that the time was exactly 1:50 PM:

> . . . as the first blows reverberated through the room, a thrill shot through me like something that burnt in my veins, and I seemed to see the Pharaoh, in the darkness on the other side of the doorway suddenly wake from his long slumber and listen. It was the ancient Egyptian belief that the sleep of death lasted three thousand years, and thus the time was up, and it might well have seemed to him that the day of resurrection was come . . .

After ten minutes Carter had hammered out a hole large enough to allow his hand holding an electric torch through. The torch light reflected against a gleaming surface against the other side of the wall. Wherever he played the light, on each side, up and down, he could not see beyond the reflection. There, he wrote, 'blocking the entrance to the chamber, stood what to all appearance was a wall of solid gold'. As Carter removed more stones from the door, the audience behind could see the gold wall; 'we could, as though by electric current', he wrote, 'feel the tingle of excitement which thrilled the spectators behind the barrier'.

By 3:30 PM the hole was big enough to crawl through. By the light of the arc lamps turned on it, they could see a huge golden shrine standing three feet below the antechamber. It was seventeen feet high and eleven feet wide, almost filling the room, and overlaid from top to bottom with gold. In the sides of the shrine were panels of brilliant blue faience with designs of magic symbols to ensure its strength and safety. It was only when Carnarvon and Carter squeezed past the shrine that they saw two golden doors at the far end with heavy bronze hinges, closed and bolted but not sealed. This was the crucial moment: had the thieves broken into the shrine? Carter drew the bolts and folded back the doors. There he saw within a second shrine with similar bolted doors. This time, however, the bolts bore a seal, and it was intact. They need penetrate no further.

'I think', wrote Carter, 'at the moment we did not even want to break the seal, for a feeling of intrusion had descended heavily upon us . . . We felt that we were in the presence of the dead King and must do him reverence.' The king could be left for a time until the treasures that lay in the outer chambers had been safely stowed. Carter and Carnarvon closed the doors of the shrine and left the inner chamber to allow the guests to see it. 'It was curious,' wrote Carter, 'as we stood in the Antechamber to watch their faces as, one by one, they emerged from the door. Each had a dazed, bewildered look in his eyes and each, in turn, as he came out, threw up his hands before him, an unconscious gesture of impotence to describe the wonders that he had seen.'

It seems astonishing that Carter and Carnarvon were content to wait for three months to find out what lay behind the door. Carter had the strength of character to resist the temptation to clear the tomb in a hurry; he was able to attend to the necessary preliminary work of preserving and recording his finds without needing hastily to settle the question of the undiscovered mummy.

There is another explanation of Carter's sang-froid: he knew perfectly well what lay beyond the sealed door because he had already broken through it. The supposition – which would also explain the accuracy of Carter's forecast of what would be found – is that he broke through the doors on the first occasion in November 1922 when he entered the antechamber with Lord

Carnarvon and Lady Evelyn; that the three examined all the inner chambers and then re-sealed the doors; and that the subsequent well-publicised 'discoveries' were staged to have maximum impact on the world's Press. There is nothing improbable or even improper about this suggestion. Carter and Carnarvon were perfectly entitled, under the terms of their concession, to enter and search the tomb they had discovered. They might well have wanted to be discreet about what lay beyond the wall in order to keep control over access, and this could best be effected by a gradual disclosure in stages of the chambers and their treasures.

Then Carter and Carnarvon decided to call a halt. It had become traditional to close the digging season in February and wait for the cool of the autumn. So, on 26 February the doors were shut and barred by a heavy iron gate, reinforced with baulks of timber. A force of eighty workmen then carried hundreds of baskets of sand and limestone chips, and poured a total of 1,700 tons of them into the shaft of the tomb. Carter retired to the workrooms to busy himself with cataloguing and crating the objects for removal to the Cairo Museum.

The Press, however, had rapidly become a major problem. Lord Carnarvon had been persuaded to give exclusive coverage of the find to *The Times*, on the grounds that this would avoid having to deal with the competing claims of the world's newspapers. The rest of the Press were of course opposed to the arrangement. 'By handing over what may be called journalistic rights in the Valley of the Tombs to the sole control of the *Times*', thundered the *Daily Express*, 'they treated the find in advance as their own private property'. The paper went on: 'The Egyptian government, with its newly awakened sense of nationality, has forwarded the contrary view that King Tutankhamun and his belongings are the national treasure of Egypt.' This was touching on a tender area of concern. Carnarvon and *The Times* seemed to be congratulating Egypt on having the good fortune to be explored by Englishmen possessed of the national virtues of probity, integrity, and incorruptibility. But not all Egyptians were content to perform merely a service role in the discovery. Egyptian newspapers did not take kindly to having to rely on a foreign journal for details of what was happening in their own country. The Egyptian Minister of Public

Works complained: 'It is an unheard of thing that we Egyptians should have to go to a London newspaper for all information regarding a tomb of one of our own kings', and the *Egyptian Gazette* complained that 'Egyptians in London who have read Lord Carnarvon's article feel indignant because Egyptians are thanked only for guarding and serving'. Local feeling in Egypt about the discovery was assessed by *The Times*:

> Among Egyptians, however, interest in the find is mainly concentrated on its intrinsic value and on the fear that many of the objects should get into British hands . . . No amount of argument and explanation appears to satisfy the average Egyptian's mind on this point, and today the mass of Egyptians are firmly convinced that Lord Carnarvon has stolen the most valuable pieces in the chambers.

Egyptian nationalists began to insist publicly that the treasures be sold to pay off Egypt's national debt. Carter and Carnarvon differed on the question of the disposal of the treasures. Carter wanted the contents of the tomb to be kept intact in a special wing of the Cairo Museum. He insisted that if Carnarvon renounced all his rights, the Egyptian government would be generous in its compensation. The disagreement between the two became public knowledge and the Press rejoiced: 'Where the carcase is, there are the eagles gathered together' quoted the *London Star*. The days had gone when, as Carter recalled, a difference with a rival excavator was settled by 'laying for him with a gun'. But the differences between the two men persisted, they had to be settled in the glare of worldwide publicity and involved national policies. Carter's quarrel with Carnarvon was never wholly resolved.

In the spring of 1923, according to the memoirs of the present Lord Carnarvon, 'my poor old parent was bitten by a mosquito when sleeping. The following morning, as he always shaved with a cut-throat razor, he cut the top of the mosquito bite, but considered it unnecessary to do anything other than place a bit of cotton wool dabbed in iodine on to the wound'. Blood poisoning set in and, on 5 April 1923, at the age of fifty-seven, Lord Carnarvon died. Petrie described his death as a calamity, since he had financed the whole expedition and there seemed no one to

carry it on. Percy Newberry, who had brought the two men together, said: 'In the history of archaeological research, no such
tragic event has taken place as the death of Lord Carnarvon.'
The real tragedy seemed to be that Carnarvon had died without
knowing whether the ambition of his expedition had been
achieved: did the mummy of Tutankhamun lie in the inner
chamber or not?

In the autumn of 1923 Carter began work to settle the matter
once and for all, Carnarvon's widow having agreed to his continuing the work on the same terms as before. The clearing of
the 1,700 tons of rubble from the stairway began on 23 October
and was completed on 20 November, when electric lights were
installed and Carter set his men to work in the tomb. They
began by tearing down the plaster wall that separated the antechamber from the burial vault, and installing lifting equipment
to remove the shrines.

Dismantling the shrines took eighty-four days. Each shrine
was surrounded by a cord carrying seals, with an intact knot; the
tomb was whole. The doors of each shrine were closed by ebony
bolts. As each successive shell was removed, the gold shone
brighter. Finally they reached the fourth and last shrine. The
cord was cut, Carter drew back the ebony bolts and, as he swung
back the doors, he saw 'an immense yellow sarcophagus, intact
with the lid still firmly fixed in its place, just as the pious hands
had left it'.

The final ceremony would be the opening of the sarcophagus
when, for the first time in 3,000 years, the body of Tutankhamun would be revealed. The day was fixed for 12 February
1924, and Carter invited nineteen guests: two Egyptians, the
local governor and an official of the Ministry of Public Works;
three Frenchmen – including of course Pierre Lacau, the Director of Antiquities – and a number of English and American
archaeologists, including representatives of the Metropolitan
Museum, the University of Chicago, Liverpool University, and
the Cairo Museum.

The lid of the sarcophagus, which was made of rose granite,
was discovered to have a crack in it, which made the lifting difficult. Angle irons were passed along each side of the lid so the two
parts could be raised together. The guests (less the women, who
were forbidden to enter) descended to witness the raising of the

sarcophagus lid. Carter described the moment:

> Amid intense silence the huge slab, broken in two, weighing
> over a ton and a quarter, rose from its bed. The light shone
> into the sarcophagus. A sight met our eyes that at first
> puzzled us. It was a little disappointing. The contents were
> completely covered by fine linen shrouds. The lid being
> suspended in mid-air, we rolled back those covering
> shrouds one by one and as the last was removed a gasp of
> wonderment escaped our lips, so gorgeous was the sight
> that met our eyes: a golden effigy of the young boy king, of
> most magnificent workmanship filled the whole of the in-
> terior of the sarcophagus.

The party left the tomb, dazed by the splendour of what they
saw, the lid of the sarcophagus still suspended above. *The Times*
reported the discovery the following day, rejoicing in an editorial
that Carter and his colleagues had 'looked upon that which no
eye had seen for thirty-two centuries – the coffin and carved face
of a monarch who was buried five hundred years before
HOMER sang, and while the people of Israel were still bond
slaves in Egypt . . . A splendid service has been done to Art and
History. A great undertaking has been faithfully and wisely carried out with consummate skill.'

At the tomb itself, however, celebrations were marred. Carter
planned to take the wives of his collaborators down the next day
only to discover that police had been posted at the site with instructions to bar the women if they tried to enter. Carter's colleagues refused to work further unless their wives were allowed
to see the fruits of their labours. In a fury of frustration, Carter
went to the tomb, cut off the power, locked the steel door and
pocketed the keys. Lacau, the Director of Antiquities, ordered
Carter to hand over the keys. He refused. In the British Parliament, the Secretary for Foreign Affairs was asked if he would
approach the United States government with a view to a joint
protest, but Ramsay MacDonald replied that the suggestion did
not commend itself at the time.

Hanging over the mummy of Tutankhamun was over a ton-
and-a-quarter of solid granite, suspended by equipment that was
designed to raise, and not to support for long periods, heavy

weights. The world's Press took note. In Paris, the *Journal des Débats* demanded that Carter hand over the keys to Lacau; *The Times* was not slow to spot the influence of France in the affair: 'The friction which has led to the closing of the tomb and to abrupt suspension of the work is unfortunately . . . due largely . . . to the influence of unnecessary mischief-making from outside.'

On 20 February, the Egyptian Cabinet authorised Lacau to 'reopen the tomb and resume work at the earliest possible moment'. A proposal was put to the Egyptologists of the New York Metropolitan Museum of Art to take over the work; it was refused. Lacau announced that Carter was at liberty to continue at the expense, and under the control of, the Egyptian government. He too refused, declaring that he would never set foot in the tomb again. On 22 February, Lacau, with a body of armed police led by the Chief of Police, conducted a party of workmen equipped with crowbars, axes and hacksaws to the tomb. They filed through the chains holding the padlocks, smashed through the bolts of the inner gate, and passed through the antechamber to the burial chamber. The granite lid of the sarcophagus was still hanging over the body of Tutankhamun. They placed baulks of timber across the open top of the sarcophagus and lowered it on to them.

Although the Egyptian government had taken over the tomb by force, there remained the question of the ownership of the treasures of Tutankhamun. The terms of the original concession granted to Carnarvon provided that tombs that 'are discovered intact shall be handed over to the [Egyptian] Museum whole and without division'; it was not anticipated that such tombs would be found. In the case of 'tombs which have already been searched', which was the case of all tombs previously discovered, the Museum reserved the right to all mummies, coffins, and sarcophagi and to 'all objects of major importance from the point of view of history and archaeology'. The ownership of the rest of the objects was not clearly defined, but the concession provided that 'the permittee's share will sufficiently recompense him for the pains and labour of the undertaking'.

There was clear evidence that the tomb of Tutankhamun had been 'searched', and the Carnarvons had some expectation of recompense for the expenses of fifteen years' work in the Valley.

However, the legal provisions governing excavation in Egypt since 1835 had not seriously affected the activities of those involved, and the Carnarvons had no great hopes of enforcing what they saw as their legal rights. The heir to the estate remembers contacting distinguished counsel, Sir Edward Marshall Hall, KC, for advice, to be told that the case would be heard by a court of five judges: one English, one French, one Italian, and two Egyptians; 'The Egyptians would be instructed as to the verdict they should return and, to make quite certain of the outcome, the Italian would be bought. So I forgot the distasteful affair.'

A case was brought against the Egyptian government by Carter and Lady Carnarvon, and on 12 March 1924 a mixed court in Cairo ruled in their favour. The court, however, was unable to enforce its judgement against the opposition of the Egyptian government, and was overruled by a court of appeal in Alexandria, which declared on 2 April that 'Mixed courts were not empowered to interfere with the administrative decisions of Government.' The Egyptian government reasserted its sovereignty by barring Carter and members of the Carnarvon family from ever again entering the tomb of Tutankhamun.

The case received wide publicity in England. Questions were asked in Parliament, but ministers, aware of the growing nationalism in Egypt, were anxious to avoid getting involved. Ramsay MacDonald, Labour Prime Minister, saw no reason to interfere. On 12 February 1924 he told the House: 'Howard Carter, in his excavation work in Egypt is a private individual and subject to the provisions of the Egyptian law of antiquities.'

That might well have ended the matter, and Carter could have ended his days patrolling the lucrative lecture circuit in America, to which he then directed his energies, had not Sir Lee Stack, British Commander-in-Chief in Egypt and Governor General of the Sudan, been assassinated on 19 November in Cairo. British war-ships took up their positions off Alexandria, British troops paraded in Cairo, and reparations were demanded of the Egyptian government. Zaghlul Pasha resigned and was replaced by a Ziwar Pasha, a politician more amenable to British interests. Carter was recalled to Cairo where he met with the new Prime Minister and Cabinet to discuss terms for recommencing work. On 13 January 1925, there was an interchange of letters between

Carter and the Minister of Public Works in which the Countess of Carnarvon renounced her claims to the tomb of Tutankhamun. The Minister promised in return that she would be allowed her choice of duplicates from the objects found there. On 25 January the tomb was re-opened, with Carter once more in charge.

By the following autumn the tomb had been cleared and the necessary lifting equipment and electric lights installed to allow the sarcophagus lid to be raised again. Inside were three coffins, each set inside the other. The innermost coffin, six feet long, was of solid gold and contained the mummified body of the young king. The head was hidden by a gold mask covering the face, neck and chest. On the king's feet were gold sandals, and the toes were wrapped individually in gold leaf. The mummy itself bore a royal diadem of gold on the head, four gold collars, amulets and sacred symbols, thirteen bracelets studded with semi-precious stones, and five pectorals of gold and jewels. In the wrappings of the body, Carter found a total of 143 precious objects of gold and jewellery. As usual, he was methodical and meticulous in recording and preserving every object. He was not, however, unmoved by the experience:

At such moments the emotions evade verbal expression, complex and stirring as they are. Three thousand years and more had elapsed since men's eyes had gazed into the golden coffin. Time, measured by the brevity of human life, seemed to lose its common perspectives before a spectacle so vividly recalling the solemn religious rites of a vanished civilisation. But it is useless to dwell on such sentiments . . . The emotional side is no part of archaeological research.

Beyond the burial chamber was a small store-room whose door had not been bricked up. Carter called this the inner treasury. Having glanced over its contents, he had it closed up so he would not be distracted while emptying the burial chamber. It is another sign of Carter's super-human patience that the room remained closed for four years.

In the doorway of the store-room was the figure of the jackal-like god Anubis, guarding the treasures within, and on the ground behind a small reed torch with a clay pedestal bearing the incantation 'to repel the enemy of Osiris [the deceased] in what-ever form he may come'. Along the south wall were many black, sealed chests, and on the wall opposite a row of treasure caskets ornamented with ivory, ebony, and gesso gilt.

It took two years to unpack the contents of these chests and to send them – a bewilderingly opulent collection of objects – to the Cairo Museum. Over 2,000 objects were put on show there for the astonishment of the world. Their ownership was finally accepted as belonging to the Egyptian government. The agree-ment Carter had made with Prime Minister Ziwar Pasha and his Cabinet in 1925 failed to survive the five successive changes of government that took place in the succeeding five years, and in 1930 the government of Nahas Pasha announced it would not allow any of the antiquities to leave the country, promising monetary recompense to the Carnarvon estate.

The disposal of Tutankhamun's mummy caused as much international friction as the treasures surrounding it. Just before he died Carnarvon had expressed the wish that the body of Tutankhamun, if discovered in his tomb, should be allowed to remain there. The matter became one of international debate: in England and America letters were written to the Press for and against the removal of the body; should it be taken for safe-keeping to the security of the Museum, or left in peace in its final resting place? *The Times* opened its correspondence columns to the debate. Rider Haggard expressed his distaste at the notion that the final fate of Tutankhamun might be 'to be laid half naked to rot in a glass case in the museum at Cairo'. The British Parliament could not ignore a matter of international scandal, and questions were asked repeatedly in the House of Commons, evaded by the reply that the matter was one for the Egyptian government. William Leech, MP, delighted the House by asking the Prime Minister:

> . . . if he has received any request from Egyptian citizens for permission to ransack the tombs of British kings and queens in Westminster Abbey and elsewhere, if the British Museum has stipulated that relics, coffins, bodies, etc., shall be handed to them, and if requests have been received, what reply did he propose to make to them?

It was even reported from Cairo that King George had written to the Egyptian authorities expressing the hope that the mummy of Tutankhamun would not be placed on exhibition in Cairo – a message that had been received locally as yet another example of British imperialism invading Egyptian affairs.

It was finally decided that the mummy should remain in its tomb. It was in poor condition, and Carter feared that the long journey to Cairo might damage it further; the climate of Upper Egypt was far more likely to preserve it than the humidity of the Delta, and Luxor was of course keen to keep its major tourist attraction. On 31 October 1926 Carter re-wrapped the mummy and placed it in the outer wooden coffin, which was then lowered into the sarcophagus and allowed to remain where it had been discovered.

The discovery of the tomb of Tutankhamun changed irrevocably the course of archaeology in Egypt. Firstly, because it created a new public interest in the subject. In Europe and America hundreds of thousands of people were caught up in the continuing saga of the clearing of the tomb, as the Press kept the story alive. Museums discovered a new popularity for their Egyptian holdings, and scoured their basements for any objects that could claim a connection with Tutankhamun. The Metropolitan Museum in New York placed on view the objects Theodore Davis had unearthed from the Valley of the Kings that led him to suppose he had found the tomb; the public flocked to see them. The New York Historical Society discovered among the Abbott Collection of antiquities a blue faience seal with the sign of Tutankhamun and put it on show; people queued around the building to see it. Thousands of applications flooded the United States Patent Office for trademarks incorporating the name 'Tutankhamun'. There were Tutankhamun hats, bathing-suits, umbrellas and walking sticks. In Paris, London, and New York the fashion houses were caught up in an Egyptian vogue of turbans, pencil-slim dresses, and embroidered designs from the tomb paintings.

The Tutankhamun discovery was not only the most opulent, spectacular, and widely publicised event in the whole history of excavation along the Nile Valley; it bridged the different worlds of 19th and 20th century excavating. When Carnarvon began his search in Egypt, it was still possible for an English aristocrat to be advised to take up archaeology to ward off boredom. Lord Cromer, who gave the advice, was the most powerful individual in the land, and Egypt was deemed to be grateful for the services rendered by the energies of foreign excavators. The climate changed, however, during the period that Carter and Carnarvon worked in the Valley of the Kings. By the time the great discovery was announced, Egypt was an independent sovereign state, jealous of its right to control the activities of foreigners and to challenge their assumptions of superiority. Before Tutankhamun, it was accepted that the excavator was the rightful owner, if not of the treasures, at least of the secrets he unearthed, to be revealed as and when he chose. Carnarvon's exclusive contract with *The Times*, entered into in all innocence, called into question his right to sell information about Egypt's past, and, consequently, the propriety of his being there at all. The outcome of the challenges thrown up by the Egyptian government in the glare of publicity surrounding the Tutankhamun expedition was that excavation in Egypt became recognised as a favour conferred by the host government on visiting experts – rather than the other way round.

There had been no doubt in the minds of Bonaparte and his savants that they were on a civilising mission in Egypt, saving the natives from the Mamelukes and revealing to the world the key role her ancient culture had played in its development. Those who followed them excavating her ancient monuments did so to enrich private collections or the museums of the world; when Egyptians came to realise the high value set on their antiquities, they reacted by stirring up a brisk trade in them. The museums of Europe and America presented themselves as secure havens where the ancient treasures of Egypt were safe from the depredations of modern Egyptians, and these attitudes were still in vogue when Carnarvon began his search. However, in the end the treasures of Tutankhamun were kept in Egypt and the body of the king left secure in its tomb by an independent government of Egypt determined to assert at last its ownership over the ancient monuments within its boundaries, and to take into its own hands the preservation of its ancient heritage.

Bibliography

About, Edmond, *The Fellah* (London, 1870).

Athanasi, Giovanni d', *A brief account of the Researches and Discoveries in Upper Egypt, made under the Direction of Henry Salt Esq.* (London, 1836).

Baikie, James, *A Century of Excavation in the Land of the Pharaohs* (London, 1923).

– *Egyptian Antiquities in the Nile Valley* (London, 1932).

Baines, John and Jaromír Málek, *Atlas of Ancient Egypt* (Time Life Books, 1984).

Belzoni, G. *Narrative of the Operations and Recent Discoveries within pyramids, temples, tombs and excavations in Egypt and Nubia . . .*, 2 vols (London, 1822).

Bevan, Samuel, *Sand and Canvas* (London, 1849).

Biblical Archaeology, Transactions of the Society of (1878 to 1913) (London).

Birch, Samuel, *Ancient History from the Monuments of Egypt* (London, 1875).

– (ed.), *Records of the Past*, 12 vols (London 1874-81).

– 'Description of an Egyptian Tomb New Preserved in the British Museum', *Archaeologia*, Vol XXIX, 11, 1842.

Blunt, Wilfred S., *Secret History of the British Occupation of Egypt* (London, 1922).

Bonwick, J., *Pyramid Facts and Fancies* (London, 1877).

Bratton, F. G., *A History of Egyptian Archaeology* (London, 1967).

Breasted, Charles, *Pioneer to the Past, the story of James Henry Breasted, archaeologist* (New York, 1943).

– *A History of Egypt* (New York, 1909).

– *The Dawn of Conscience* (New York, 1933).

Brugsch, H. F. K., *A History of Egypt under the Pharaohs*, 2 vols (London, 1879).

Budge, Sir E. A. Wallis, *By Nile and Tigris*, 2 Vols (London, 1920).

– *The Rise and Progress of Assyriology* (London, 1925).

"Bunsen's Egypt", *British Quarterly Review*, Vol XXIII, 61, April 1856.

Bunsen, C. C. J., *Egypt's Place in Universal History*, 5 vols (London, 1844-57).

Caillaud, Frédéric, *Travels in the Oasis of Thebes* . . . (London, 1822).
Capart, Jean, *The Tomb of Tutankhamun* (London, 1923).
Carnarvon, The Earl of, *Ermine Tales* (London, 1980).
Carrott, Richard G., *The Egyptian Revival. Its Sources, Monuments and Meaning* (Berkeley, 1978).
Carter, Howard and A. C. Mace, *The Tomb of Tutankhamun discovered by the late Earl of Carnarvon and Howard Carter* (London, 1923).
Ceram, C. W., *Gods, Graves and Scholars* (London, 1952).
– *The March of Archaeology* (New York, 1958).
Champollion (le jeune), *L'Egypt sous les Pharaohs* (Paris, 1814).
Charles-Roux, F., *Bonaparte: Governor of Egypt* (Methuen, London, 1977).
Charmes, Gabriel, *Five Months at Cairo* (London, 1883).
Clair, Colin, *Strong Man Egyptologist* (London, 1957).
Clayton, Peter A. (ed.), *The Rediscovery of Ancient Egypt* (London, 1982).
Clot-Bey, A. B., *Aperçu General sur l'Egypte* (Brussels, 1840).
Combes, Edmond, *Voyage en Egypte* (Paris, 1846).
Conder, Josiah, *The Modern Traveller* (London, 1830).
Connor, Patrick, (ed.), *The Inspiration of Egypt: its influence on British Artists, Travellers and Designers 1700-1900* (Brighton Borough Council, 1983).
Cottrell, Leonard, *The Mountains of Pharaoh* (New York, 1956).
– *The Anvil of Civilisation* (New York, 1957).
Cromer, Lord, *Modern Egypt* (London 1908).
Crook, J. Mordaunt, *The British Museum: a case study in architectural politics* (London, 1973).
Crow, W. B., *A History of Magic, Witchcraft and Occultism* (London, 1972).
Curl, James, *The Egyptian Revival*, (London 1978).

Daniel, Glyn, *A Hundred and Fifty Years of Archaeology*, 2nd edn (London, 1973).
David, Rosalie, *The Egyptian Kingdoms* (London, 1975).
Dawson, Warren R. and Eric P. Uphill, *Who Was Who in Egyptology* (London, 1972).
Denon, D. V., *Voyage dans la Basse et la Haute Egypte* (Paris, 1802).
Disher, M. W., *Pharaoh's Fool* (London, 1957).
Driault, Edouard, (ed.) *Mohamed Aly et Napoléon (1807-1814): correspondance des consuls de France en Egypte* (Paris, 1925).
Drower, Margaret S., *Flinders Petrie, a life in archaeology* (London, 1985).
Drummond, Sir William, *Memoir on the Zodiacs of Esmen and Dendera* (London, 1821).
Duff Gordon, L., *Letters from Egypt* (London, 1865).

Ebers, George, *Richard Lepsius: a biography*, translated by Zoe Dana Underhill (New York, 1887).
Edmonstone, Sir Archibald, *A Journey to two of the Oases of Upper Egypt* (London, 1822).
Edwards, Amelia B., *A Thousand Miles up the Nile* (London, 1877).
– *Pharaohs, Fellahs and Explorers* (London, 1891).
Edwards, I. E. S., *The Pyramids of Egypt* (Harmondsworth, 1961).
Erman, Adolph, *The Ancient Egyptians* (New York, 1965).
Evans, Joan, *A History of the Society of Antiquaries* (Oxford, 1956).

Fagan, Brian M., *The Rape of the Nile* (London, 1977).

Flower, Raymond, *Napoleon to Nasser: the story of modern Egypt* (London, 1972).

Gardiner, Sir A. H., *Egypt of the Pharaohs* (Oxford, 1961).
– *Egyptian Grammar*, 3rd edn (Oxford, 1969).
Glanville, S. R. K., *The Growth and Nature of Egyptology* (Cambridge, 1947).
Gliddon, George R., *Ancient Egypt: monuments, hieroglyphics, history, archaeology, and other subjects* ... (Augusta, Georgia, 1847).
Greener, Herbert, L. S., *The Discovery of Egypt* (London, 1966).

Halls, J. J., *The Life and Correspondence of Henry Salt Esq., F.R.S. etc., His Britannic Majesty's Late Consul General in Egypt*, 2nd edition (London, 1834).
Herold, J. Christopher, *Bonaparte in Egypt* (1962).
Hoskins, G. A., *Visit to the Great Oasis of the Libyan Desert* (London, 1837).
– *Winter in Upper and Lower Egypt* (London 1863).
Hoving, Thomas, *Tutankhamun: the untold story* (New York, 1978).

Iversen, E., *The Myth of Egypt* (Copenhagen, 1961).
– *Obelisks in Exile* (Copenhagen, 1968).

James, T. G. H., *The Archaeology of Ancient Egypt* (London, 1972).
– (ed), *An Introduction to Ancient Egypt* (London, 1979).
– *The British Museum and Ancient Egypt* (London, 1981).
– *Excavating in Egypt* (London, 1984).
Jollois, Prosper, *Journal d'un Ingenieur Attaché a l'Expedition d'Egypte (1798-1802)* (Paris, 1904).

Kenrick, John, *Ancient Egypt under the Pharaohs* (London, 1850).
Khater, A., *La Régime Juridique des Fouilles et des Antiquités en Egypte*, Institute francaise d'archéologie orientale du Caire, Recherches, Tome XII (Cairo, 1960).

Lane, E. W., *The Manners and Customs of the Modern Egyptians* (London, 1836).
Legh, Thomas, *Narrative of a Journey in Egypt* (London, 1816).
Lepsius, C. R., *Letters from Egypt* (1853).
– *Discoveries in Egypt* (1853).
Linant de Bellefonds, L. M. A., *Journal d'un Voyage* (Khartoum 1958).

Mariette, Auguste, *Voyage dans la Haute Egypte*, 2 vols (Paris, 1878-80).
– *Outlines of Ancient Egyptian History* (London, 1892).
Mariette, Edouard, *Mariette Pacha* (Paris, 1904).
Maspero, Gaston, *Manual of Egyptian Archaeology* (London, 1895).
– *Auguste Mariette, notice biographique et oeuvres diverses* (Paris, 1904).
Maspero, Sir Gaston, *Egypt: Ancient Sites and Modern Scenes* (London, 1910).
Mayes, S. H., *The Great Belzoni* (London, 1959).
Mertz, Barbara, *Temples Tombs and Hieroglyphs: the story of Egyptology* (New York, 1964).
Michaelis, A. T. F., *A Century of Archaeological Discoveries* (London, 1908).

Osburn, William, *Israel in Egypt: or the books of Genesis and Exodus illustrated by existing monuments* (London, 1854).

Palmer, William, *Egyptian Chronicles, with a harmony of Sacred and Egyptian Chronology* (London, 1861).
Petrie, W. M. Flinders, *Ten Years digging in Egypt, 1881-1891*, The Religious Tract Society (London, 1892).
– *Methods and Aims in Archaeology* (London 1904).
– *Seventy Years in Archaeology* (London, 1931).
Pratt, Ida A., *Ancient Egypt, sources of information in the New York Public Library* (New York, 1925).

Rawlinson, George, *History of Ancient Egypt*, 2 vols (London, 1880).
Rhind, A. Henry, *Thebes, Its Tombs and their Tenants* (London, 1862).
Richardson, Robert, *Travels along the Mediterranean and parts adjacent; in company with the Earl of Belmore, during the years 1816-17-18*, 2 vols (London, 1822).
Richmond, Sir J. C. B., *Egypt 1798-1952; her advance towards a modern identity* (London, 1977).
Roberts, David, *The Holy Land*, 6 vols (London, 1855).
Ruffle, John, *Heritage of the Pharaohs: an introduction to Egyptian archaeology* (Oxford, 1977).

Sayce, Rev. A. H., *The Egypt of the Hebrews and Herodotus*, London, 1895.
– *Reminiscences* (London, 1923).
Sharpe, Samuel, *History of Egypt*, 2 vols (London, 1846).
Smith, Grafton Eliot, *Tutankhamun and the discovery of his tomb by the late Earl of Carnarvon and Howard Carter* (London, 1923).
Smith, Joseph Lindon, *Tombs, Temples, and Ancient Art* (University of Oklahoma Press, 1956).
Spineto, Marquis, *Lectures on the elements of hieroglyphics and Egyptian Antiquities* (London, 1829).
[UPHAM, E.] *Memoranda illustrative of the tombs and sepulchral decorations of the Egyptians; with a key to the Egyptian tomb now exhibiting in Piccadilly. Also remarks on Mummies and observations on the process of embalming* (London, 1822).

Vyse, Richard Howard, *Operations Carried on at the Pyramids of Gizeh in 1837*, 2 vols (London, 1840).

Wakeling, T. G., *Forged Egyptian Antiquities* (London, 1912).
Weigall, A. E. P., *Guide to the Antiquities of Upper Egypt from Abydos to the Sudan Frontier* (London, 1910).
– *Tutankhamun and other essays* (London, 1923).
White, Andrew D., *A History of the Warfare of Science with Theology in Christendom* (London, 1955).
Wilkinson, J. G., *Manners and Customs of the Ancient Egyptians*, 3 vols. (London, 1837).
– *Modern Egypt* (London, 1843).
Wilson, John A., *Signs and Wonders upon Pharaoh: a history of American Egyptology* (University of Chicago Press, 1964).

Winslow, William Copley, *The Queen of Egyptology; Amelia B. Edwards* (Chicago, 1892).

Wood, Alexander and Frank Oldham, *Thomas Young: Natural Philosopher* (Cambridge, 1954).

Wortham, John D., *British Egyptology (1549-1906)* (Newton Abbot, 1972).

Index